Local Community in the Era of Social Media Technologies

CHANDOS PUBLISHING
SOCIAL MEDIA SERIES

Series Editors: Geoff Walton and Woody Evans
(emails: g.l.walton@staffs.ac.uk and kdevans@gmail.com)

This series of books is aimed at practitioners and academics involved in using social media in all its forms and in any context. This includes information professionals, academics, librarians and managers, and leaders in business. Social media can enhance services, build communication channels, and create competitive advantage. The impact of these new media and decisions that surround their use in business can no longer be ignored. The delivery of education, privacy issues, logistics, political activism and research rounds out the series' coverage. As a resource to complement the understanding of issues relating to other areas of information science, teaching and related areas, books in this series respond with practical applications. If you would like a full listing of current and forthcoming titles, please visit our website www.chandospublishing.com or email wp@woodheadpublishing.com or telephone +44 (0) 1223 499140.

New authors: we are always pleased to receive ideas for new titles; if you would like to write a book for Chandos in the area of social media, please contact Jonathan Davis, Commissioning Editor, on jonathan.davis@chandospublishing.com or telephone +44 (0) 1993 848726.

Bulk orders: some organisations buy a number of copies of our books. If you are interested in doing this, we would be pleased to discuss a discount. Please email wp@woodheadpublishing.com or telephone +44 (0) 1223 499140.

Local Community in the Era of Social Media Technologies

A global approach

Hui-Lan H. Titangos

CP

CHANDOS
PUBLISHING

Oxford Cambridge New Delhi

Chandos Publishing
Hexagon House
Avenue 4
Station Lane
Witney
Oxford OX28 4BN
UK
Tel: +44 (0) 1993 848726
Email: info@chandospublishing.com
www.chandospublishing.com
www.chandospublishingonline.com

Chandos Publishing is an imprint of Woodhead Publishing Limited

Woodhead Publishing Limited
80 High Street
Sawston
Cambridge CB22 3HJ
UK
Tel: +44 (0) 1223 499140
Fax: +44 (0) 1223 832819
www.woodheadpublishing.com

First published in 2013

ISBN: 978-1-84334-696-8 (print)
ISBN: 978-1-78063-361-9 (online)

Chandos Social Media Series ISSN: 2050-6813 (print) and ISSN: 2050-6821 (online)

Library of Congress Control Number: 2013946175

Typeset by Domex e-Data Pvt. Ltd., India.

Contents

List of figures and tables   *xi*

List of abbreviations   *xv*

About the author   *xvii*

Acknowledgements   *xix*

Preface   *xxi*

Part 1   History: Never A Dull Moment   **1**

1   Local community: a long view   **3**

   A long process   3

   In the era of social media technologies   5

   Notes   8

2   Santa Cruz Public Library, California: a brief review   **9**

   Monterey Library Association: the first public library in California   9

   Santa Cruz Library Association: the predecessor of SCPL   14

   First head librarian: Minerva Waterman   19

   Preserving Pacific West heritage: Hubert Howe Bancroft   20

   Preserving Pacific West natural resources: John Muir   27

   Notes   31

3   The rise of local authors and content   **33**

   Santa Cruz County history and Margaret Koch   35

   Chinese Gold and Sandy Lydon   35

   Hihn-Younger Archive and Stanley D. Stevens   35

   Pathways to the Past   36

   Notes   37

4   Putting Davenport on the map   **39**

Librarian historian: Alverda Orlando   39

Davenport Cement Centennial   41

Lime Kiln Legacies   43

Urgency in history preservation   46

Notes   47

Part 2   The Era of Library 1.0   **49**

5   Santa Cruz Public Library: community on the web   **51**

Full-text Local History Articles   51

SCPL Local History Gallery   57

Local online databases   74

Notes   78

6   Shanghai Library: windows to the world   **81**

The opening of Shanghai   81

The Xujiahui Library: the first library in Shanghai   83

The Shanghai Library   85

Shanghai International Library Forum (SILF)   90

The Window of Shanghai (WoS)   91

Notes   93

7   Oslo Public Library: digital efforts   **95**

History   95

The Deichman Digital Workshop (Deichmans Digitale Verksted)   96

Kinoteket (Cinematheque)   97

Traditional library services in digital form   98

Notes   100

Part 3   Present: Library 2.0   **101**

8   Santa Cruz Public Library: learning and using Library 2.0   **105**

Introducing a local community   105

Learning Library 2.0: 23 Things @SCPL		109
Notes		117
9	**Bibliotheca Alexandrina: carry forward capital of memory**	**119**
	Goals	120
	Mission and vision statements	121
	Digital projects	122
	Open Knowledge	125
	Science and Technology	125
	Webcast	127
	Digital Assets Repository (DAR)	127
	Notes	128
10	**Oslo Public Library: rejuvenated OPAC**	**129**
	The Pode Project	129
	Two phases	130
	Experimentation with FRBR	131
	Note	133
Part 4	**Social Media for Local Community**	**135**
11	**Using social tools: Staff Picks in blogs**	**137**
	SCPL Staff Picks: publishing opportunity for librarians	137
	Ideal Web 2.0 participatory environment	141
	Second chance for non-bestsellers	143
	Future means more improvement	143
	Notes	144
12	**YouTube: the power of crowdsourcing**	**147**
	History	147
	Reaching out to local communities	148
	BAchannel	149
	SCPL on YouTube	149
	Note	150

13 Using social tools: RSS feeds   **151**

What is RSS?   151

RSS at BA, Shanghai Library, and SCPL   152

More extensive usage of RSS at Canton Public Library   153

Notes   154

14 Using social networks: Pinterest   **155**

What is Pinterest?   155

People connecting   156

Content sharing   156

Simple designing   156

Real-life problem solving   157

Notes   158

15 Using social sites: Twitter and Weibo   **159**

What is Twitter?   159

Twitter at SCPL and BA   160

Weibo at Shanghai Library   160

Notes   161

16 Using social sites: Facebook and Renren   **163**

Facebook usage   163

A brief history   165

Technical features   166

The concept of gift economy   166

Personal account vs. Facebook Page   167

Notes   173

Part 5   Future: Library 3.0 and Beyond   **175**

17 Local needs vs. global resources   **177**

Implications of Web/Library 3.0 for libraries   177

The machine as human assistant: from Watson to Siri   180

More flexible and scalable resource usage in meeting
increasing demand for library services   183

Stretching local resources through efficient usage of social
media tools   183

Better integration with other online information sources: the
Semantic Web   184

Better information evaluation, organization, and access   185

Crowdsourcing projects – the power of volunteering   186

Notes   194

18 The librarian's role as information manager   197

Findability: a priority in designing and managing well-linked
information   198

Accuracy: a priority in evaluating information   200

User protection: a dilemma and an opportunity for information
managers   200

Demystifying computer programming: let's tweak some codes
as needed   201

Notes   201

19 The librarian's role as teacher   203

Systematic and continuous training of staff members   203

Ongoing adult classes and other tutorials for the public as
technologies advance   204

Notes   206

20 The librarian's role as leader   207

Provision of active links to new and future magazine articles
with local content   208

Links to e-documents   210

Links to historical e-directories   214

Links to e-newspaper clippings   215

Links to e-directories for more local organizations   216

Links to promote local authors and publications   217

Leadership in local history, local value, and involvement 218

Notes 220

21 The librarian's role as innovator in transforming the OPAC 223

What is the OPAC? 223

Development of the OPAC 224

Bookstore approach 224

BISAC approach 225

Pode approach: making OPAC "of the web" 228

Notes 232

22 Technology, staff, and community 233

Technology 233

Staff 236

Community 237

Notes 238

Appendices

1 Sample titles on Santa Cruz available in the SCPL and LC catalogs 241

2 Staff Picks on the Readers Link page 247

3 Historical documents at SCPL 249

Bibliography 261

Index 273

List of figures and tables

Figures

1	El Cuartel, ca. 1887	10
2	El Cuartel, ca. 1880	11
3	Monterey Public Library, funded by Andrew Carnegie	12
4	The new Monterey Public Library, June 1952	13
5	New Monterey Branch Library, ca. 1930s	13
6	Dr. C. L. Anderson, first chairman of the Santa Cruz Library Association	15
7	The Santa Cruz Public Library in the Hotaling building	17
8	The Santa Cruz Carnegie (Main) Library, 1904	18
9	Enrique Cerruti interviewing General Mariano Vallejo, March 1875	22
10	"Our Gallery of Cranks. No. 3. – The Boss Historian"	24
11	The Bancroft Library, University of California, Berkeley, 1911, First Floor	26
12	John Muir at Merced River, 1908	29
13	John Muir and Roosevelt at Glacier Point, 1903	30
14	A panoramic view of Davenport, ca. 1910	40
15	The cornerstone of Davenport Cement Plant, 2012	41
16	Davenport Cement Plant was permanently shut down in 2010	42
17	An oil-burning "patent" kiln on the former Cowell Ranch, ca. late 1950s	45

18 The original front elevation of the historic Salz
   Leathers building remains unchanged in 2012   54

19 The historic Salz Leathers has been renovated as the
   Tannery Arts Center   55

20 The living quarters for artists, musicians, and performers
   within the Tannery Arts Center   56

21 Laurel bull donkey, an engine used to hoist logs onto
   flatcars bound for the mill   62

22 Ox team pulling wagonload of lumber in the
   Santa Cruz Mountains   63

23 The Loma Prieta Lumber Company's motorcar #3
   pushing a flatcar loaded with supplies   64

24 Grovers Mill   65

25 Quarrying rocks on the Cowell Ranch   66

26 Wright's Station was used to ship fruit to canneries
   in San Jose   66

27 The lighthousekeeper's house at the Pigeon Point
   Lighthouse   67

28 Neptune Casino, built by Fred Swanton in 1904, burned
   to the ground 22 June 1906   68

29 The Santa Cruz Aerie 460 band playing for a crowd
   in front of the Santa Cruz Post Office   69

30 The Grand Arch of the Native Sons of the Golden West
   on Pacific Avenue, 9 September 1891   70

31 The Capitola Hotel in Capitola, California   71

32 The Cooper House, located in downtown Santa Cruz,
   was the Court House at the turn of the century   71

33 A lively place for young children – inside Scotts Valley
   Library, 2012   73

34 Scotts Valley Branch Library, 2012 – the former
   Scotts Valley Roller Rink   73

35 The pyramid-shaped structure of Shanghai Library, 2006   86

36 Approaching the entrance of Shanghai Library, 2006   87

37   An interior courtyard of Shanghai Library, 2006   88

38   Another interior view of Shanghai Library, 2006   89

Tables

8.1   All non-book media circulation   107

8.2   Language resources circulation   107

16.1   Facebook subscriber growth 2011–12   164

21.1   WordThink Grid call numbers based on BISAC categories   228

List of abbreviations

ALA	American Library Association
Alex Med	Alexandria and Mediterranean Research Center
API	Application Program Interface
BA	Bibliotheca Alexandrina
BISAC	Book Industry Standards and Communications
CID	Community Information Database
CLS	Customized Library Services
CPW	California Powder Works
DIY	do it yourself
DRA	Data Research Associates, Inc.
EIR	environmental impact report
FRBR	Functional Requirements for Bibliographic Records
GeneSoc	Genealogical Society of Santa Cruz County
HTML	Hypertext Markup Language
HTTP	Hypertext Transfer Protocol
IBM	International Business Machines Corp.
ILS	Integrated Library System
ISIS	International School of Information Science
LC	Library of Congress
LHPP	Local History Photograph Project
MAH	Santa Cruz Museum of Art and History

MARC	MAchine-Readable Cataloging
MCLD	Maricopa County Library District
NAS	Network Access Services
OCLC	Online Computer Library Center
OCR	Optical Character Recognition
OPAC	Online Public Access Catalog
OPL	Oslo Public Library
PCC	Program for Cooperative Cataloging
RDA	Resource Description and Access
RDF	Resource Description Framework
RSS	Really Simple Syndication
SCPL	Santa Cruz Public Library
SDO	Staff Development Office
SILF	Shanghai International Library Forum
SMC	Sheet Music Catalog
SMS	short message service
SPARQL	Simple Protocol and RDF Query Language
SRU	Search and Retrieve URL
UCSC	University of California Santa Cruz
UNESCO	United Nations Educational, Scientific and Cultural Organization
URL	Uniform Resource Locator
WoS	Window of Shanghai
XML	Extensible Markup Language

About the author

Hui-Lan H. Titangos is Collection Management Services Librarian at Santa Cruz Public Libraries. She holds a Graduate Certificate in Information Management and an MLIS from the University of California at Berkeley. Her previous experience includes working for the DIALOG Corporation, Pacific Neighbourhood Consortium, and Shanghai Filmmakers' Association. She came to Santa Cruz in 1989 and fell in love with its landscape and, most of all, with its people. She is the author of six working papers about Santa Cruz published in journals such as *Library Management*, *Chinese Librarianship* and the *Journal of Educational Media and Library Sciences*.

The author can be contacted via the publisher.

Acknowledgements

While I was contemplating the topic of effective information storage and retrieval in the digital age, I was contacted by Chandos Publishing for a possible book proposal. Publisher Dr. Glyn Jones and Commissioning Editor Jonathan Davis helped me tremendously to define my idea and expand my horizon. My other editors, George Knott and Ed Gibbons, worked tirelessly with me to smooth out all obstacles in the publicity and pre-production stages. My copy-editor, Judith Oppenheimer, has impressed me with her razor-sharp analytical mind and observations.

During the writing process I received valuable support and cooperation from many libraries both near and far, most notably from my director, Teresa Landers, manager, Janis O'Driscoll, and colleagues such as Jeanne Czarnecki, Sarah Harbison, Heidi Jaeger-Smith, Eric Stricker, Donna Swedberg and Ann Young at Santa Cruz Public Libraries; Dennis Copeland, Historian and Museums, Arts and Archives Manager of the City of Monterey at Monterey Public Library; Susan Snyder, Lee Anne Kolker and Lorna Kirwan at the Bancroft Library; Dody Anderson at Watsonville Public Library; Gail Mason at Santa Clara County Library; and Ann Kunish at Oslo Public Library.

Meanwhile, I want to express my gratitude to my professional mentors: Dr. Michael K. Buckland, who encourages me to write about local communities and library and information services; Alverda Orlando, who has inspired me with her narratives of colorful characters in Santa Cruz County; and Gary Decker, who has launched not only digital projects but also my intellectual curiosity about the unique history of Santa Cruz County.

Last but not least, I should thank my academic, professional and supportive family for the completion of the project, particularly my brother, Dr. Ying Huang, who has helped me to crystalize my thinking on trends in technology; my sister, Hui Huang, who has enabled me to write by taking care of our elderly mother; and my husband, Paul, who has taken new photographs and managed the historical photographs for this book.

Preface

As a library user and professional, I was both excited and concerned at the news that George R. Lawrence's six panoramic aerial photographs of Santa Cruz in 1906 had at last been made available through the Library of Congress (LC) (*http://lcweb2.loc.gov/ammem/collections/panoramic_photo/pnphtgs.html*).[1] My excitement was due to the fact that they would be a valuable addition to Peter Nurkes' "Notes on the 1906 Aerial Panorama of Santa Cruz by George Lawrence," an existing page on the website of Santa Cruz Public Libraries (SCPL) (*http://www.santacruzpl.org/history/articles/182/*). With his high-quality and multi-angled camera work, Lawrence would surely provide a unique view of what it had been like in 1906, for anyone interested in the history of Santa Cruz County, California.

My concern, on the other hand, was based on the probability that interested users could easily have missed that particularly critical piece of news, especially if they did not subscribe to *Santa Cruz Sentinel*'s mobile app or RSS feed. Furthermore, there is no live hyperlink from SCPL to LC's source for Peter Nurkes' article. Of course, with the aid of Google, people can eventually gather all the relevant sources by using search terms like "George Lawrence Santa Cruz." The real challenge comes if they know neither the name of the photographer nor the time period. With a search on "Santa Cruz aerial photography" they will inevitably be faced with about 331,000 results.

With this concern in mind, I have found it necessary to revisit the familiar topic of information storage and retrieval in the digital age. The advent of social media technologies has dramatically changed the scene in the information world: it shortens the distance between library users and the rest of the world through tools and sites such as YouTube, Facebook, Twitter, and Pinterest. Information is at last available at the users' fingertips through increasingly sophisticated technology like IBM's Watson, Apple's Siri personal assistant, and numerous apps (application software) for mobile and computing devices. As it promised, the Semantic Web seems to have given us an even more ideal solution to the old dilemma of the natural language approach and linkage to resources.

New technologies have helped greatly to connect local communities to the wider world. This book aims to capture this experience, starting with the model of Santa Cruz County, in order to develop a truly global approach to libraries both within and outside the United States. The first two parts of the book cover the early efforts to record the history of the local Santa Cruz area, and Library 1.0. Parts 3 and 4 examine the present situation with Library 2.0, and its benefits. Part 5 is a discussion of future directions and the implications of Library 3.0.

In his *Library Services in Theory and Context*, Dr. Michael Buckland has written:

> Specifically, new technology improves the physical storage and handling of records. However, the fact that a record has been stored in some place does not mean that you know that it exists, that you could find it if you wanted it, that you could understand what it signified, that you could believe it, that it is not contradicted by some other record, or that just those who should have access to it do have access to it.[2]

Social media technologies are no exception to these six challenges, raised in the late 1980s. In our success or failure in searching for and evaluating the requested information, we library professionals often ask ourselves the same six basic questions in a quest for whether technology can be the sole and ultimate solution for the constant workload of storage and retrieval in a library world without any human intervention. Past experience has told us that technology is always changing, to be replaced by a better successor. However, our role as library professionals remains surprisingly the same: to store and organize the world's information, and to help users to find and evaluate the information that they need but that is hard to get. Our role will not diminish; on the contrary, ours is to be entrusted with a new set of responsibilities and a new scope of work in the era of social media technologies and beyond.

Notes

1. Griggs, Gary. "Our Ocean Backyard: A 1906 View of the Santa Cruz Waterfront." *santacruzsentinel.com. Santa Cruz Sentinel*, 17 December 2011. Web. 30 July 2012.
2. Buckland, Michael K. *Library Services in Theory and Context*. 2nd ed. Oxford: Pergamon Press, c1988. 214. Print.

Part 1
History: Never a Dull Moment

1

Local community: a long view

Abstract: This chapter discusses the meaning of community as defined by the philosopher Josiah Royce. It defines social media and looks briefly at the efforts of libraries, since the advent of social media, to develop new services for their users, to use social media to develop their local user communities, and to bring the world to their communities. It introduces the four libraries that are the focus of the book.

Key words: Josiah Royce, provincialism, social media, traditional media, instant messaging, local community, *Library Journal* Movers and Shakers, Open Cover Letters, social media campaigns.

A long process

To bring the world to our local community, or to take our community to the world, is by no means a novel concept belonging exclusively to the twenty-first century. On the contrary, it is the continuation of a long process initiated by American philosophers such as Josiah Royce more than a century ago, when he proposed a wholesome *provincialism*, and its vital function as an essential basis of true civilization. The vital difference, however, lies in the fact that it is only in the age of social media that we are able to realize both concepts at once. The term "provincialism" was first used in 1770 to define (1) a dialectal or local word, phrase, or idiom; and (2) the quality or state of being provincial.[1] In *Race, Questions, Provincialism, and Other American Problems*, Royce raises the term to a new level:

> For me, then, a province shall mean any one part of a national domain, which is, geographically and socially, sufficiently unified to have a true consciousness of its own unity, to feel a pride in its own ideals and customs, and to possess a sense of its distinction

from other parts of the country. And by the term "provincialism" I shall mean, first, the tendency of such a province to possess its own customs and ideals; secondly, the totality of these customs and ideals themselves; and thirdly, the love and pride which leads the inhabitants of a province to cherish as their own these traditions, beliefs and aspirations.

Why should we extol provincialism so highly? Royce was one of the first scholars to recognize the vital relationship between a province/community and the world:

> My thesis is that, in the present state of the world's civilization, and of the life of our own country, the time has come to emphasize, with a new meaning and intensity, the positive value, the necessity for our welfare, of a wholesome provincialism, as a saving power to which the world in the near future will need more and more to appeal.[2]

Royce cautions us, in our pursuit of provincialism, against three major evils or obstacles, namely, a refusal to be assimilated into a new community, a leveling tendency to crush individuality, and a mob mentality that appeals to the emotions. Why do we need to concern ourselves with these three obstacles today, in the age of social media technologies? First of all, in order to feel and foster a local pride in their own traditions, the members of a community, the locals, need to be ready to teach the stranger, or to transplant their wisdom, and the latter needs to be willing to learn. Second, Royce, as a philosopher, was acutely aware of the leveling tendencies of his time and beyond, namely, the danger of losing local spirit, pride, independence, and individuality in the face both of man's imitative tendencies and of the ease of modern communication, through which everyone can learn and read the same daily news. With the passage of time, Royce's concern has become increasingly relevant to our constant efforts to keep local while at the same time we are being constantly flooded with information in the age of television and the internet.

Finally, Royce's mob/crowd spirit deals with emotional excitability. It is in fact a form of leveling tendency on a national level when millions of people fall under the influence of a few charismatic, national leaders and their words. Looking back in history, we can find numerous instances of this in various places around the world, such as Adolf Hitler in Germany from 1934 to 1945, Benito Mussolini in Italy from 1925 to 1943, Joseph

Stalin in the former Soviet Union from 1922 to 1952, and Mao Zedong in China from 1945 to 1976. A remedy that Royce prescribes is to keep the province awake so as to save the nation:

> there are social groups that are not subject to the mob-spirit. And now if you ask how such social groups are nowadays to be fostered, to be trained, to be kept alive for the service of the nation, I answer that the place for fostering such groups is the province, for such groups flourish under conditions that arouse local pride, the loyalty to one's own community, the willingness to remember one's own ways and ideals, even at the moment when the nation is carried away by some leveling emotion.[3]

In the era of social media technologies

A characteristic of our present efforts to bring the local community and the world together is the simple fact that, for the first time in history, the availability of social media enables us to effectively overcome Royce's three obstacles. We are able to connect and share our local community with the world through social sites such as Facebook and YouTube, reaching a bigger global community and so fostering individuality. We are also able to bring the world and its relevant resources to our community via social tools such as RSS (Really Simple Syndication) and tagging, so as to discourage an uninformed emotional and political mob/crowd spirit. These two important factors not only differentiate our present efforts from those of earlier times, but also underscore what that difference means for the provision of library services to members of the community, for "Advocacy and messaging in the social networking sphere is not so much about broadcasting to a billion people with the hope that a few care about the information they're receiving, as it is about targeting a smaller, more vested number of individuals and letting them share the information they're concerned about with their own networks."[4]

What is social media? According to a definition provided by University College, London,[5] the term "social media" refers to methods of allowing any user to publish content online. Unlike traditional media such as television and print technology, it consists of web-based and mobile technologies, including blogs, music/image/video sharing, internet posting, instant messaging, crowdsourcing and Voice over Internet

Protocol. There are four main types of social media: writing one's own blogs or commenting on other people's blogs (blogging, for example, Weibo – a Chinese microblog), publishing images or audio/video (Flickr, YouTube), posting on social networking sites (Facebook, Renren – a Chinese Facebook – Twitter, Pinterest), and collaborating on shared online collective projects (for example, Wikipedia articles).

The major difference between the traditional and social media lies in how messages are delivered and consumed, or, rather, in the passive consumption of the content delivered by the one, versus a participatory manner of consumption of the other. Content consumers now have almost infinite choices and want to select and comment on what they consume, rather than being passive consumers only.

The goal of social media is to share information with interested individuals who may or may not be within reach, and to create online communities through collaboration and trust. "One of the things social networks excel at is collaboration; they provide an excellent opportunity for family and friends to gather stories, and everyone can add their own thoughts. Entire communities can do this: It can be a shared heritage."[6]

The theme of *Library Journal*'s "Movers and Shakers 2012" concentrates on community builders, and predominant in the coverage is their innovative use of social media. In 2004, Lisa Bunker, social media librarian at Pima County Public Library (Arizona), created the site Harry Potter Fandom (*http://www.facebook.com/pimacountylibrary*) for a 27-branch library system. With thousands of Twitter followers and Facebook friends of Potter, she has developed a social media brand for her library and turned social media into a new customer service desk, a virtual library, and a news channel for the library and the community. Another distinctive characteristic of 2012 movers and shakers is their deep roots in their communities. During his search for library jobs, Stephen X. Flynn, Emerging Technologies Librarian at College of Wooster Libraries (Ohio), realized that he and other job candidates were in dire need of inspiring cover letters. This motivated him to create Open Cover Letters (*http://opencoverletters.com/*), a website showcasing anonymized cover letters that had helped candidates to land their jobs. With the aid of effective posts from Facebook and Twitter, he has transformed his site into a valuable community resource with contributions from successful jobholders.[7]

Since 2008, a great majority of libraries in the United States have been experiencing budget cuts as a result of persistent economic downturns. To resolve budget woes, some libraries reacted by resorting to passive money-saving measures such as enforcing furloughs, shortening library hours, cutting materials budgets, and laying off staff. More libraries, however, bravely ventured to initiate ballot measures (referenda) for stable funding. Beth Dempsey reports in her *Voters Keep the Doors Open* that 88 percent of libraries that asked their communities to fund them were rewarded with a "yes." Communities responded positively to campaign messages such as that created by Whitehall Township Public Library (Pennsylvania; *http://whitehall.lib.pa.us/*): "good libraries make attractive communities, and attractive communities command higher home prices." The libraries in question launched extensive social media campaigns, although there is no conclusive evidence as to the effectiveness of their contribution to the success of the ballot measures. These campaigns did suggest, however, that libraries could become natural centers for the utilization of social media within local communities. Thus, changing attitudes and expectations among local residents, as a result of the rise of social media both as a technology and as a social movement, might lead to change in the functions of a library.

Facebook and Twitter have proven to be two of the most effective social media sites for reaching communities:

> With or without hard evidence of its ability to drive a win, social media has the undeniable allure of reaching large groups simultaneously and repeatedly. For example, with Michigan's Genesee District Library's reported Facebook participant base of 5000, its messages can be crafted and distributed to this significant population within minutes. Twitter is an ideal tool for reminding supporters to vote.[8]

To examine Royce's viewpoint on the local community and apply it to the age of social media, this book will select four libraries to show the communities that they serve and the local pride and spirit that they foster through the provision of appropriate library services and programs. As social media is about sharing information with interested individuals, and about creating online communities through collaboration and trust, there is no one set of social media tools to fit all purposes. To demonstrate how libraries have been using a variety of social media tools to serve the specific needs of their communities, the four libraries have been selected as a focus group, namely, Santa Cruz Public Library (SCPL), Shanghai Library, Oslo Public Library (OPL) and Bibliotheca Alexandrina (BA). Owing to the breadth and depth of social media penetration in the local community, several other libraries have already been mentioned in this chapter, and there will be other libraries mentioned in the course of this book, such as the Bancroft Library, the Bodleian Library, Canton Public Library (Michigan), Darien Library, Monterey Public Library, the New York Public Library, Perry Branch Library of Maricopa County Library District (MCLD), Rangeview Library, San Jose Public Library, the University College London Libraries, and the University of California Santa Cruz Library.

Notes

1. "provincialism." *webster.com*. Merriam-Webster, Incorporated, 2012. Web. Accessed 30 July 2012.
2. Royce, Josiah. *Race, Provincialism and Other American Problems*. New York: Macmillan, 1908. 61–2. Print.
3. Royce, Josiah. *Race, Provincialism and Other American Problems*. New York: Macmillan, 1908. 95–6. Print.
4. Zandt, Deanna. *Share This! How You Will Change the World with Social Networking*. San Francisco: BK, c2010. 12. Print.
5. "What is social media?" *ucl.ac.uk*. University College London, 1999–2012. Web. Accessed 30 July 2012.
6. Kelsey, Todd. *Social Networking Spaces: from Facebook to Twitter and Everything in Between*. New York: Apress, c2010. 13. Print.
7. Fialkoff, F. "Movers and Shakers 2012." (cover story). *Library Journal* [serial online]. 15 March 2012; 137(5): 23. Available from: MasterFILE Premier, Ipswich, MA. Accessed 26 July 2012.
8. Dempsey B. "Voters Keep the Doors Open." *Library Journal* [serial online]. 15 March 2012; 137(5): 64–8. Available from: MasterFILE Premier, Ipswich, MA. Accessed 26 July 2012.

2

Santa Cruz Public Library, California:
a brief review

Abstract: This chapter provides historical background on the birth and growth of public libraries in California, after the formation of the new state. It examines three critical time periods: 1849, when the Monterey Library Association was formed as the first public library in California; 1868, when the Santa Cruz Library Association was founded; and 1878, when the subscription library became a tax-based institution after the passage of the Rogers Act for maintaining free library services. Also mentioned are Hubert Howe Bancroft and John Muir, two historical figures who made tremendous contributions to the preservation of the historical heritage and natural resources in California.

Key words: Santa Cruz County, El Cuartel, Monterey Library Association, Santa Cruz Library Association, Minerva Waterman, subscription library, Rogers Act, Santa Cruz Carnegie Library, Andrew Carnegie, H. H. Bancroft, Bancroft Library, John Muir.

Monterey Library Association: the first public library in California

The Monterey Library Association was established when, on the initiative of the Reverend Dr. Samuel H. Willey, Monterey civic leaders successfully raised funds by persuading citizens to purchase $40 shares in a public library. With $1500 raised from the sale of shares, the Association purchased its opening-day collections from New York. Housed in El Cuartel, a Mexican government building built in 1840, the library was equipped with a reading room that was stocked with books, newspapers, magazines, maps, and government documents. There were two kinds of arrangements for using the library: shareholders were

Figure 1 El Cuartel, ca. 1887. Location of the first public library and first newspaper in California, former Mexican-era government and military barracks building, later US Army headquarters. C.W.J. Johnson, photographer

Source: 274.v3.jpg. Courtesy of Monterey Public Library–California History Room.

allowed to borrow books, and non-shareholders were expected to pay a monthly subscription of one dollar. Users who wanted to borrow a book were required to leave a cash deposit of twice the value of the book being borrowed.

The Monterey Library Association can be regarded as the first public library in California, not only because of its pioneering endeavors to establish a public library in California but also, more importantly, because of its record of library administration. Unlike many early library associations, it had a constitution, regulations, and a book catalog, namely, the *Constitution and Rules of the Monterey Library Association, Together with a Catalogue of Books, Organized 1849*, published by O'Meara & Painter, Printers, in 1854. There were two sets of rules applicable to the library and reading room, and the Association's printed catalog listed 871 titles, one quarter of which were in Spanish. The collection was classified into two broad areas: serious (theological, legal, medical, scientific, and reference works such as the *Encyclopedia Americana* and Webster's Dictionary) and popular (history, biography, travels, and fiction). There were about 250 works of fiction, featuring

Figure 2 El Cuartel, ca. 1880. C. W. J. Johnson, photographer

Source: [W. Morgan Collection] 61-#2.v3.jpg. Courtesy of Monterey Public Library–California History Room.

American classics by Herman Melville and James Fenimore Cooper, and eighteenth-century and nineteenth-century English novels by Sir Walter Scott and Charles Dickens. With such a select list of authors, the Monterey Library Association intended to achieve community betterment by introducing world literature into the community of Monterey. This can be further proven by its declared dual goals, namely, to serve as a "nucleus around which the friends of literary and social refinement, and elevation, may cordially unite" and as an institution "to afford amusement, entertainment, and profit to a large class who, without its aid, would waste their time in the frivolities and questionable pastimes so prevalent in our State."[1]

The decline of the Monterey Library Association was due largely to the 1849 Gold Rush and California's admission to statehood in 1850. The former attracted the population away from Monterey and into the gold-mining regions, whereas the latter removed the capital to Sacramento after California became the thirty-first state. In the following decades, before it finally turned over its assets to the City of Monterey in 1906, the Association suffered a spiraling downturn in its fortunes.

In 1911, the new, publicly funded Monterey Public Library was opened at 425 Van Buren Street, with a grant from Andrew Carnegie and

Figure 3   **Monterey Public Library, funded by Andrew Carnegie.**
It opened its doors in 1911 and remained in the building
until 1952

Source: 4046.v3.jpg. Courtesy of Monterey Public Library–California History Room.

a land donation from Mrs. A. M. Freitas. The building was designed by
California architect William Weeks in the Mission Revival style, and the
library was housed there until 1952, when the voters of Monterey passed
a $350,000 bond measure to construct a new home for the Monterey
Public Library. The new library at the corner of Madison and Pacific
Streets was designed by California architect William Wurster in the
Second Bay tradition, and today remains one of California's architectural
gems.[2]

To meet the needs of the local community, a new Monterey branch
library was built at 700 Laine Street in 1931. The branch library was in
operation for over 20 years until 1953, when the City Council proposed
to close it as a budget-saving measure. In spite of letters of protest,
petitions, and public meetings against the closure, the branch library was
permanently closed on 1 January 1954.

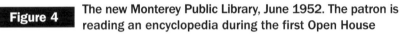

Figure 4 The new Monterey Public Library, June 1952. The patron is reading an encyclopedia during the first Open House

Source: 4125.v3.jpg. Courtesy of Monterey Public Library–California History Room.

Figure 5 New Monterey Branch Library, ca. 1930s (Note fisherman wood sculpture on corner of building.)

Source: 11.v3.jpg. Courtesy of Monterey Public Library–California History Room.

Santa Cruz Library Association: the predecessor of SCPL

SCPL is a medium-sized city–county library system with ten branches and one bookmobile. Lagging behind its Monterey counterpart by a few decades, the Santa Cruz Library Association, the predecessor of SCPL, was formed in 1868. As with other libraries in California at the time, the birth of Santa Cruz Library Association was driven by persistent effort from the community:

> The most important of the factors in the typical community was the moralistic or uplift drive. Other motives may have impelled certain people more, but nothing else was utilized so much to obtain public support and nothing else seems to have contributed so much to the library movement in so many communities. In California as a whole, it was the most obvious force behind the development of libraries prior to 1878.[3]

A provincial California rose after 1849, when good order was restored and the gold-mining era was replaced by the agricultural age. The provincial California, however, did not remain in a pure state for very long. Ever since the beginning of 1880s, California has been permanently infused with new immigration and a strong eastern influence, especially in Southern California. Kevin Starr, the former California State Librarian (1994–2004), concludes that

> If there is such a thing as DNA codes for states – and there may very well be! – then crucial to the sociogenetic heritage of California would be ethnic diversity. It began in the Native American era with its seventy to eighty language groups and its multitude of tribelets and kinship groups, and it continued through Spanish and Mexican eras.[4]

Indeed, the state's ethnic diversity has only intensified since the Gold Rush, when peoples of all colors and racial groups arrived in California. According to Starr, in the early 1900s, the city of San Francisco had a higher proportion of foreign-born residents than any other city in the United States. More than 80 languages were spoken in the Los Angeles Unified School District by the end of the twentieth century.

In as early as 1861, at a meeting in Temperance Hall, carpenter and builder Tom Beck proposed to form a library in Santa Cruz. Owing to the Civil War, which lasted from 1861 to 1865, Beck's proposal was not adopted until seven years later, in 1868, when the Santa Cruz Library Association was organized under a governing Library Board of Trustees composed of seven members, with Dr. C. L. Anderson as its first president. Through membership dues and donations of money and books, the library opened in March 1870, after Citizen John Brazer donated a room to the library and himself as a librarian.[5] Despite the fact that it was moved three times before the first library tax was levied in 1884, the Library Association not only managed to find space to house its collection of 3000 books and numerous pamphlets and unbound volumes, but also added a free reading room organized by the women of Santa Cruz, following a successful merger of two organizations. It was ranked as one of the foremost libraries in California.[6]

Figure 6 **Dr. C. L. Anderson, first chairman of the Santa Cruz Library Association and first president of the Library Board of Trustees, both established in 1868**

Source: Title_0587.v3.jpg. Courtesy of Santa Cruz Public Libraries.

In 1878, the Rogers Act was passed to establish and maintain free public libraries and reading rooms. Before the expiration of its effective duration of two years, the Act was superseded by a new law which became the fundamental statutory authority for the creation and maintenance of city libraries. The free library laws foreshadowed the decline of the privately owned subscription library associations and the rise and surge of the publicly financed public libraries in California. Public finance and control remains one of the winning factors in the survival and thriving of public libraries around the world, even in the age of social media, although there have been attempts at the privatization of public libraries as a social institution in the United States:

> Privatization of public services, including libraries, has been an issue for many years. In the 1980s, the federal government began to contract with private companies to manage and operate federal libraries. Other special libraries also have a history of privatization. However, only in the last 10 years have city and county governing bodies considered privatization of public libraries. For over 200 years, public libraries have earned the respect of the residents they serve ... With the development of a free education system in the US, many communities expanded the concept of public education by establishing public library services for their residents through tax support. Public libraries were viewed as a public good – a common resource available to all, funded by public dollars and governed by local residents.[7]

The expansion of public libraries in California was in direct response to national as well as state economic wealth:

> Then in its second generation as an American state, California was experiencing a tremendous exploitation of its natural wealth and climatic advantages, and this favorable economic growth provided the basis for support of educational and cultural institutions. The drive for community betterment was strong, as exemplified by the growth of active temperance and civic improvement organizations. In addition, the great increase in population set the stage for library growth.[8]

The same was true of Santa Cruz County, infused with a new life as a result of agricultural development and the availability of natural resources of land and water. The expansion of libraries also revealed the

Figure 7 The Santa Cruz Public Library in the Hotaling building (later called the St. George Hotel). Minerva Waterman, Librarian, is seated on the left. To the right is Mr. Cole

Source: Title_0672.v3.jpg. Courtesy of Santa Cruz Public Libraries.

inherent weakness in subscription-based library associations: "It is interesting to note that public library service began in the colonial United States through 'subscription libraries,' available only to those who could afford to pay the fee necessary to support their existence."[9] Restricted to fee-paying members only, they were thus unable to fulfill the mission of bettering the whole community, or to meet the needs of the community for permanent and free-to-all library services. Their limited access was also increasingly in conflict with the popular concept of treating the library as a community asset. Following national and state trends, and an act of legislature approved on 26 April 1880, Santa Cruz Library Association offered itself to the City of Santa Cruz in 1881, after the Library Board of Trustees had passed a transfer resolution to allow the City to manage, own, and support the library. The City accepted the offer in the following year, even though the library tax was not levied until 1884. Supported by the City library fund, the library significantly expanded its collection of more than 12,000 volumes, and about 4000 volumes circulated per month. To accommodate its expanding collections, the library was soon on the move again, moving first to the city hall in 1882, to the Hotaling building in 1894, and then to the Williamson and Garrett building, until the Carnegie Free Library building was completed in 1904.[10]

On 28 April 1904, the tax-supported Santa Cruz Free Public Library was formally dedicated in the Santa Cruz Carnegie Library building, with a collection of 14,000 volumes to serve a community of 10,000 residents.[11] The new library was made possible through a $20,000 grant

Figure 8   The Santa Cruz Carnegie (Main) Library, 1904

Source: Title_0681.v3.jpg. Courtesy of Santa Cruz Public Libraries.

from Andrew Carnegie, with additional funding for library furnishings from donations and fundraising events. In 1916, Santa Cruz County contracted with the Santa Cruz City Library and transformed it into a county library, following an agreement between the Library Trustees and the Santa Cruz County Supervisors. The realization of a county library was a proud milestone in the history of library development in California, as well as in Santa Cruz County, for, by 1917, "The efforts of a county library to extend its services to all parts of its area, even the most isolated and least populated, formed a saga of belief in the library and the right of every person to have access to a circulating book collection."[12] It officially opened a new chapter in the growth of a new library system: a public agency serving the general public.

First head librarian: Minerva Waterman

Minerva Waterman was elected as the first official head librarian in Santa Cruz, and one of the few female librarians in California at the time, for, prior to 1878, the position of librarian was usually taken by a man. Her 51-year tenure as head librarian lasted from 1890 to 1941. In 1899 she created the first library catalog, namely, a "finding list." It was searchable by author and title, with added brief but perceptive statements based on her own reading. Through her aggressive fundraising activities for the community, Waterman was able to expand branches into other areas of the county, such as Aptos, Seabright, Garfield Park, and East Side, the last three of which were built with awards from Carnegie. It is interesting to note fundraising events with a global interest, that is, "Among the Brahmins of India," a lecture by Dr. Emil Noble, Poster Exhibit, 27 November 1903, and an Art and Loan Exhibition, 14–16 April 1904.[13]

In the early stages of library development in California, a pronounced emphasis was placed on efforts to bring the world into the community through the creation of a book-centered organization, which is "a natural phase of community life," as R. E. Held writes in his *Public Libraries in California 1849–1878*. We find such efforts first in the Monterey Library Association's dual goals. Its selection of library materials is further evidence of such efforts. Similar efforts can be seen in Waterman's early policy of collection development, with its focus on classics and books with intellectual values:

There is a conclusion in the minds of some of the local library trustees that all valuable books, classics, or of intellectual stimulus, even though they may discuss things of questionable status, should be included in our library, and classed as "book of privilege," to be kept by the librarian under lock and key, and be loaned only to such persons as the librarian, in her judgment, might consider to be of mature mind.[14]

To conclude, the efforts of early libraries tended to focus on three areas: (1) inclusion of world classics to enlighten and better the community by cultivating and disseminating knowledge; (2) inclusion of popular titles and newspapers to entertain the community; and (3) provision of a meeting place for the welfare of the community. At this period, "The idea of preserving local records in libraries, if present to any extent, was not emphasized. The one notable library of historical materials that appeared during these years was the collection made by H. H. Bancroft, who created a large depository of materials for the history of the Pacific Coast."[15]

Preserving Pacific West heritage: Hubert Howe Bancroft

Hubert Howe Bancroft was born in Granville, Ohio in 1832. Before reaching the age of 19, he had already suffered the fate of dismissal as clerk at the bookstore of his brother-in-law, George H. Derby, in Buffalo, New York. He subsequently proved himself by convincing Derby to give him cases of books to sell back in his home state of Ohio. He completed his book consignments so well that he covered all his expenses and made a profit by peddling his stock of books all over his home state. On the strength of this success, not only was he invited back as a clerk, but he was also assigned to manage a new regional bookstore in San Francisco on Derby's behalf.

In 1852, Bancroft arrived in San Francisco. Even though the bookstore expansion plan never panned out as intended, due to a series of unfortunate events, including a change of heart regarding the store's location and the premature death of Derby, it was not long before the unemployed Bancroft found his feet again. He went to Crescent City, Oregon to do what he was best at: renting a space in a general store to sell books and stationery. While the general store went bankrupt,

Bancroft actually made a profit, which made it possible for him to return to California in April 1856. With a working capital of $5500 from his sister, Mrs. Derby, Bancroft bought $10,000 of books and stationery from New York on a special California credit.[16] In December 1856, he opened H. H. Bancroft and Company on Montgomery Street, San Francisco with his friend George L. Kenny. A year later, the business venture had proved to be a success and was ready for expansion. By April 1870, a new, five-storey building had been constructed at 721 Market Street to accommodate the expanded business, with Bancroft's growing personal library on the fifth floor. To devote himself to book collecting and writing, Bancroft decided on partial retirement and left his brother to take care of daily operations – hence the name change to A. L. Bancroft and Company, coinciding with the move to the new location.

Bancroft's interest in book collecting can be traced back to 1859 or 1860, as some sources indicate, when he was publishing a handbook on the Pacific Coast for editor William H. Knight.[17] To enable the editor to have convenient access to all books on California and the West, Bancroft discovered in himself an urge to collect works on the history of his adopted state, in addition to the 75 volumes pertinent to the subject on the shelves of his own bookstore. His collecting interest grew from early California imprints to items on the adjacent larger areas, and also deepened from California into Mexico, Central America, and the Rocky Mountain West. His book quest took him or his agents to bookstores and library auctions from New York, Boston, and Philadelphia to London, Paris, Germany, Spain, and Mexico. In the 1870s–1880s he managed to acquire important additions of Spanish manuscripts by sending his copyists and abstractors to the provincial California archives, to the land office, the mission archives and the archbishop's archives. If he could not secure original documents, he had transcriptions made of relevant portions, as in the case of the Archives of Spanish and Mexican California, then in the hands of the US Surveyor General. And when there were no documents at all, he created them – by seeking out and interviewing historical figures – in the form of the "Bancroft Dictations,"[18] which consisted of a collection of 188 biographical sketches, dictations, and notes relating to pioneers and settlers in the states of California, Arizona, Colorado, Idaho, Montana, Nevada, and Utah.

Seeing that so many influential pioneers and leading figures in California's history were still alive, Bancroft and his assistants recorded hundreds of pages of dictations or statements about their experiences.

With his able assistants such as Enrique Cerruti, an Italian who worked on Bancroft's western history project, H. H. Bancroft was presented with the entire collection of historical documents from General Mariano Guadalupe Vallejo. Cerruti's persuasion was such that the General called upon his countrymen to follow his example by contributing their valuable materials to Bancroft. From 1874 to 1875, the General willingly dictated to Cerruti his long statement of Californian remembrance, including affairs and events occurring from 1815 to 1845, a little-known period not covered by any literature. The dictation later became known as "Historia de California."

THIS PHOTOGRAPH

Represents the room in which General M. G. Vallejo, Commander General of the State of California during the year 1837, dictated the history of this country from 1770 to 1848. The lady to the left of Gen. Vallejo is Miss Rosana Leese, a highly intelligent and accomplished lady, who has rendered him valuable assistance in searching ancient documents. The venerable gentleman sitting at the right of Gen. Vallejo is Don Jose Abrego, in 1838 Treasurer General of the then Independent State of California. The gentleman sitting in front of General Vallejo is Henry Cerruti, the hero of Cobija, who in 1868 obtained from the Bolivian Congress the medal of "Well deserving of the cause of America." General Cerruti, next to General Vallejo, is the one who has contributed most toward the compilation of the great historical work. The gentleman sitting at the small table placed on the left hand side of Gen. Vallejo, is Don Vicente Gomez, who is busy making extracts from an inedited manuscript of father Junipero Serra, the founder of the Mission of San Carlos de Monterey.

| Figure 9 | Enrique Cerruti interviewing General Mariano Vallejo, along with the General's assistant and other figures of Mexican California, March 1875 |

Source: brk00003790_24a.v3.jpg. Courtesy of the Bancroft Library.

The Bancroft Library started with 10,000 volumes in 1868, but had grown to 133,779 titles by 1905, when it was sold to the University of California. The collection covered a variety of material types, such as books, manuscripts, periodicals, and newspapers. As for the size and scope of collection, Bancroft himself stated the following:

> There is no American collection with which this can fairly be compared. There are other large and costly private libraries; but the scope, plan, and purpose of the Bancroft Library place it beyond the possibility of comparison. It is made up exclusively of printed and manuscript matter pertaining to the Pacific States, from Alaska to Panamá ... And not only does this collection thus excel all others as a whole, but a like excellence is apparent for each of its parts. In it may be found, for instance, a better library of Mexican works, of Central American works, of Pacific United States works, than elsewhere exists. And to go further, it may be said to contain a more perfect collection on Alaska, on New Mexico, on Texas, on Colorado, on Utah, on Costa Rica, and the other individual states or governments than can be found outside its walls. Not only this, but in several cases, notably that of California, this library is regarded as incomparably superior to any state collection existing, or that could at this date be formed in all the United States or Europe.[19]

Bancroft was the embodiment of bookseller, book collector, printer, publisher, and historian. With the aid of his librarian, Henry Lebbeus Oak, and a staff of indexers, transcribers, and writers, Bancroft wrote and published a 39-volume set of the *Works of Hubert Howe Bancroft* during the period 1882–90. It is a collection on the Pacific Coast, including the Native Races, California, the Northwest Coast, Alaska, and the remainder of the American West. Within the set, the seven-volume *History of California* was his core focus. The reason was twofold: California was the reason why Bancroft had started to collect, write, and publish; and California had crowned itself with a succession of firsts in the nation during the 1870s–1880s, namely, in agriculture, tourism, motion pictures, and the aerospace industry. It was also a center of culture, commerce, and finance for the American West: "Current importance thus called for a more careful analysis of the local past. That past, furthermore, possessed so much of intrinsic appeal that it seemed a historian's grand opportunity. Therein is to be found the chief reason for giving it special attention."[20]

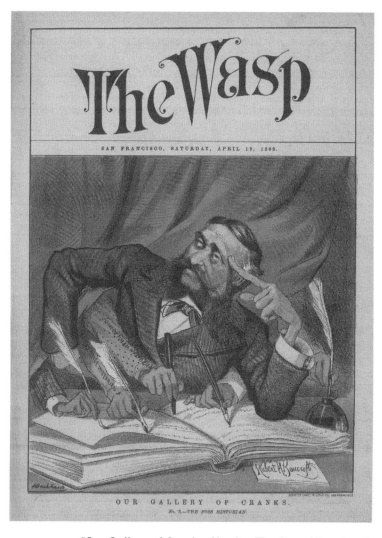

"Our Gallery of Cranks. No. 3.– The Boss Historian," cover of *The Wasp*, 18 April 1885, drawn by Henry Barkhaus. Bancroft's thirty-nine volumes were, admittedly, the work of many hands, although the "Boss Historian" did supervise and pass on the final product. The idea of production-line histories proved good material for *The Wasp*, an illustrated weekly magazine devoted to social and political satire, established in San Francisco in 1876

Figure 10

Source: brk00002560_24a.v3.jpg. Courtesy of the Bancroft Library.

It is also worth mentioning that the Bancroft index, on which more than 20 men had worked for years, at a total cost of $35,000, consisted of the following four components,

1. What (one of the abbreviated 40 to 50 main subject headings)
2. Where
3. If needed, a further breakdown of what or where
4. When.

During an era when library card cataloging was in its infancy and classification was too superficial for any specialized needs, the Bancroft index served as a key for tapping in to his vast collection. It also served as a guide to the literature that he and his writers needed to consult at every stage of the Pacific states history. Throughout the process of writing and publishing his works, Bancroft was keenly aware of these two key roles of the index:

> In further praise of his index Bancroft pointed out that the method could be adapted to any collection; he insisted that only through indexing could there be effective utilization of the contents of a large collection; and he reasoned that the larger the library, the greater the necessity for indexing. Pursuing this line of thought to its ultimate conclusion, he suggested that a universal index, covering the books of the world collectively, would be of incalculable advantage to civilization.[21]

Even though the Bancroft index was never adopted by any libraries, private or public, for any practical use, the concept has been somewhat adopted by Google to index the world's information and make it searchable.[22] The estimated timeframe of 300 years to index the world's information is again comparable to the undertaking of the Bancroft index. Furthermore, Bancroft is one of the forerunners of advocacy for the importance of a good index to a collection, especially a large one. His suggestion for a universal index is again echoed in the concept of web/Library 3.0 that we will examine in later chapters.

When Bancroft sold his library to the University of California in 1905 it was with the proviso that it be maintained as a separate library and that the core collection be added to over time. Before the collection could be transferred to Berkeley campus, San Francisco was visited by both earthquake and fire, on 18 April 1906. The original Bancroft library was, fortuitously, located just outside the fire zone, thus becoming the only major library in the city to escape unscathed by either severe damage or complete destruction – a fate suffered by almost all the libraries in San Francisco, such as the Mechanics' Institute Library, the former San Francisco Public Library, part of the Sutro Library, and a great part of the Library of the Society of California Pioneers, etc.[23]

Since the dedication of the Bancroft Library on Berkeley campus in 1906, the University of California has fulfilled its promise to H. H. Bancroft by deepening, widening, and expanding the original collection into a true national treasure on the history of California, the Southwest, and Mexico in the world. It has also observed the solid guidelines laid down by Bancroft: "Many of Bancroft's most significant acquisitions are built on the fact that there are two sides to every story – at least – and with a fine impartiality, befitting H. H. Bancroft himself, we attempt to collect the appropriate primary sources so that posterity, with a longer perspective, can be the judge."[24] As mentioned earlier, there were

Figure 11   The Bancroft Library, University of California, Berkeley, 1911, First Floor

Source: brk00002274_24a.v3.jpg. Courtesy of the Bancroft Library.

133,779 titles at the time of the acquisition. Just 108 years later, the total number of volumes has grown to nearly 800,000 in the new Bancroft Library, which in its turn has forever transformed the campus of Berkeley, just as Benjamin Ide Wheeler, President of the University of California from 1899 to 1919 stated on the occasion of the transfer of the original library:

> The purchase of The Bancroft Library marks a great day in the history of the university ... It means the inevitable establishment at Berkeley of the center for future research in the history of Western America; it means the creation of a school of historical study at the University of California; it means the emergence of the real university of study and research out of the midst of the colleges of elementary teaching and training.[25]

To conclude, there would be a gigantic hole in the early history of California and neighboring states were it not for Bancroft's foresight and his unique collection. There would be no intimate knowledge, either, of the local communities that settled, flourished, or disappeared in those states, especially in the state of California. California is where the strength of the Bancroft Library lies and where its resources are richest, and was H. H. Bancroft's very starting point as a collector and historian. He had the wisdom to recognize and believe in the continued preeminence of California, his adopted state. There have been many crises and natural disasters in the history of California. After the 1849 Gold Rush, and out of crises and disorders that followed, California emerged as the new, thirty-first state. Since the collapse of the dot.com bubble in 2000–1, more innovations and inventions have appeared in California, and in the San Francisco Bay Area in particular, the birthplace of many social media tools and networks.

Preserving Pacific West natural resources: John Muir

While H. H. Bancroft was engaged in recording and archiving pioneers, settlers, and the economic development of California in the areas of gold mining, logging, agriculture, building, etc., another notable newcomer arrived in San Francisco, on 29 March 1868, from Indianapolis. He was none other than John Muir, the naturalist and conservationist. Parallel to

Bancroft's interest in the Pacific Coast, Muir demonstrated his passion for the Yosemite Valley, California forests and mountains, and the formation of Alaska's glaciers. To thoroughly understand and appreciate wild Alaska, he joined three long and extended expeditions there between 1879 and 1881. Born in 1838 in Dunbar, a seaport in Scotland, 11-year-old John Muir immigrated to the Unites States in 1849 with his father, Daniel, who found kindred spirits in the gospel of Alexander and Thomas Campbell, due to his drift away from Scottish orthodoxy. In the previous year, Daniel had sold his prosperous feed and grain business and uprooted his family, in two batches, from Scotland to Marquette County, Wisconsin to start his ambitious 320-acre Fountain Hill Farm. It was not long before Daniel lost interest in farming and devoted himself full time to the work of the Lord. John Muir, the oldest of six children, not only had to help his father to establish the farm in the earlier days, but also worked as a farmhand continuously until he was 20. There were two major influences affecting John Muir's later life and outlook. In the family circle, his maternal grandfather, Gilrye, a butcher by trade, helped to shape John's feelings toward other creatures and his determination to explore wildness. From the culture of Scotland, he inherited his love for wildness, through the Romantic movement, especially its poets such as Robert Burns and William Wordsworth. In the second term of his university days he fell under the strong influence of Ezra Carr, a professor of chemistry and natural history at the University of Wisconsin at Madison.

It is something of a coincidence that Mark Twain and John Muir both came to California shortly after the Gold Rush and witnessed the aftermath of the gold mining. However, the two men took different stands, "One man's experience there made him a lifelong satirist who poked fun at moral improvers, while the other's made him a conservationist … Like the famous humorist, Muir no longer believed in the Westminster catechism of his ancestors, but unlike Twain, he still believed in the possibility of moral progress. After achieving a sufficiency of wealth, he wanted to spend the remainder of his days teaching Americans to take a new attitude toward nature."[26] Muir joined the conservation movement to advocate for the wise use of nature and natural resources, one of the reforms of the Gilded Age in California.

In June 1889, John Muir was invited to write about Yosemite by Robert Underwood Johnson, associate editor of *The Century*, a New York magazine with a clear focus on the history and conservation of the United States. John Muir's "The Treasures of the Yosemite and Features of the Proposed Yosemite National Park," published in the magazine in 1890, not only paved the way for conservation on a national scale but also

Figure 12   **John Muir at Merced River, 1908**

Source: brk00000899_24a.v3.jpg. Courtesy of the Bancroft Library.

resulted in the birth of Yosemite National Park, the third national park after Yellowstone and Sequoia. Before his death in 1914, John Muir left to the world his monumental conservation legacies. He was a co-founder of the Sierra Club in 1892 and served as its president until his death.

In addition, John Muir left us a vast literary legacy, such as *The Mountains of California* (Century, c1894). Two articles of his played a critical part in helping President McKinley back onto the path of forest conservation through the passage of a forest Bill in June 1897. These are "Forest Reservations and National Parks" (*Harper's Weekly*, June 1897) and "The American Forests" (*Atlantic Monthly*, August 1897). Instrumental in the passage of the National Park Bill in 1899, during the Roosevelt conservation era Muir was one of the great advocates for

Figure 13   John Muir and Roosevelt at Glacier Point, 1903

Source: brk00000900_24a.v3.jpg. Courtesy of the Bancroft Library.

Yosemite Valley to be granted national park status. The story of Stickeen is another most memorable bestseller of John Muir's. Originally published by the *Century* magazine in 1897 as "An Adventure with a Dog and a Glacier," it tells the ordeal of Muir hiking on a glacier with Stickeen, a friend's dog, during his 1880 expedition in Glacier Bay. On their way back, the dog became cut off on the far side of an ice bridge, scared by its abandonment and the dangerous crevasse. Even though Stickeen managed to cross the bridge and join Muir in safety, the guilt of having unnecessarily endangered another life haunted Muir for the rest of his life: "Stickeen's story revealed not only a richness of personality and character in the animal world but also shortsightedness bordering on incompetence in the outdoors."[27]

Notes

1. Held, Ray E. *Public Libraries in California, 1849–1878*. Berkeley: University of California Press, c1963. 9. Print.
2. "A History of the Monterey Public Library." *monterey.org*. Monterey Public Library, 2012. Web. Accessed 30 July 2012.
3. Held, Ray E. *The Rise of the Public Libraries in California*. Chicago: American Library Association, c1973. 131–5. Print.
4. Starr, Kevin. *California, a History*. New York: The Modern Library, c2005. [305]. Print.
5. Koch, Margaret. *Santa Cruz County: Parade of the Past*. Fresno: Valley Publishers, c1973. 206. Print.
6. Gillis, James Louis. "Descriptive List of the Libraries of California: Containing the Names of All Persons Who Are Engaged in Library Work in the State." Sacramento: California State Library, 1904. 74. Print.
7. "Keep Public Libraries Public, a Checklist for Communities Considering Privatization of Public Libraries." *ala.org*. American Library Association, June 2011. Web. Accessed 30 July 2012.
8. Held, Ray E. *The Rise of the Public Libraries in California*. Chicago: American Library Association, c1973. 31. Print.
9. "Keep Public Libraries Public, a Checklist for Communities Considering Privatization of Public Libraries." *ala.org*. American Library Association, June 2011. Web. Accessed 30 July 2012.
10. Souza, Margaret. "The History of the Santa Cruz Public Library System: Part 2 – 1881–1904." *santacruzpl.org*. Santa Cruz Public Libraries, n.d. Web. Accessed 30 July 2012.
11. Gillis, James Louis. "Descriptive List of the Libraries of California: Containing the Names of All Persons Who Are Engaged in Library Work in the State." Sacramento: California State Library, 1904. 74. Print.
12. Held, Ray E. *The Rise of the Public Libraries in California*. Chicago: American Library Association, c1973. 146. Print.

13. Souza, Margaret. "The History of the Santa Cruz Public Library System, a thesis presented to the Faculty of the Department of Librarianship," MA thesis, San Jose State College, 1970. 30. Print.
14. "What Books Are Unfit for Our Public Library Serious Problem before Local Trustees in Offering Questionable Literature for Public Perusal." *Santa Cruz Morning Sentinel*, 11 September 1910: 8. Print.
15. Held, Ray E. *Public Libraries in California, 1849–1878*. Berkeley: University of California Press, c1963. 129. Print.
16. Bancroft, H. H. *Literary Industries*. San Francisco: The History Co., 1890. 146. Print.
17. "Excerpt – Exploring the Bancroft Library." *signaturebooks.com*. Signature Books, 2012. Web. Accessed 30 July 2012.
18. "Brief History." *bancroft.berkeley.edu*, The Bancroft Library, 9 January 1999. Web. Accessed 30 July 2012.
19. Bancroft, H. H. *Literary Industries*. San Francisco: The History Co., 1890. 213–14. Print.
20. Caughey, J. W. *Hubert Howe Bancroft: Historian of the West*. Berkeley: University of California Press, 1946. 182. Print.
21. Caughey, J. W. *Hubert Howe Bancroft: Historian of the West*. Berkeley: University of California Press, 1946. 97–8. Print.
22. Mills, Elinor. "Google ETA? 300 Years to Index the World's Info." *news.cnet.com*. CBS Interactive, 8 October 2005. Web. Accessed 30 July 2012.
23. "Building the Bancroft." *bancroft.berkeley.edu*. The Bancroft Library, 18 July 2002. Web. Accessed 30 July 2012.
24. Faulhaber, Charles, and Stephen Vincent. *Exploring the Bancroft Library: The Centennial Guide to Its Extraordinary History, Spectacular Special Collections, Research Pleasures, Its Amazing Future and How It All Works*. Salt Lake City: Signature, 2006. 10. Print.
25. "Excerpt – Exploring the Bancroft Library." *signaturebooks.com*. Signature Books, 2012. Web. Accessed 30 July 2012.
26. Worster, Donald. *A Passion for Nature: the Life of John Muir*. Oxford: Oxford University Press, c2008. 305–6. Print.
27. Worster, Donald, *A Passion for Nature: the Life of John Muir*. Oxford: Oxford University Press, c2008. 260–1. Print.

3

The rise of local authors and content

Abstract: This chapter reviews the rise of local authors and content in California, looking at statewide endeavors by the California State Library under the leadership of James L. Gillis, and countywide endeavors by local authors/historians such as Margaret Koch, Sandy Lydon, and Stanley D. Stevens, who succeeded in bringing a local community to the world at different periods and levels.

Key words: California State Library, James L. Gillis, special collections, Margaret Koch, Sandy Lydon, Hihn-Younger Archive, Stanley D. Stevens, Santa Cruz Museum of Art and History, University of California Santa Cruz.

It was not until the beginning of the twentieth century that serious efforts to build special collections began at both the state and local levels. Located in Sacramento, the capital of California, the State Library set up the California Department under the leadership of James L. Gillis. During his tenure as California State Librarian (1899–1917), Gillis reorganized the State Library by extending the dictionary system of cataloging to all books in the collection, and by creating a separate Law Department and a California Historical Department. He also initiated the indexing of California newspapers so as to provide a reference service in the California Department, which thus had a book catalog and information cards on people who had made important contributions to the formation of California, such as pioneers, authors, musicians, and artists.

Gillis's great leadership reflected critical stages in the history of libraries and librarianship. He helped to create the first union catalog in the United States, and the Books for the Blind Department within the State Library. Through his organizational skills, he managed to extend the services of the State Library to all of residents of California. He helped to pass the 1909 County Free Library Law and the 1911 County Library Law. After the passage of these laws, Gillis was one of the first people to realize a need for trained librarians in the new system of county libraries, hence the first class of 15 students admitted in 1914 by the State Library's library school, which was merged in 1920 with that of Berkeley. On hearing that a library course had started at the University of California Berkeley campus in 1918, Gillis favored a merger, for he felt that two institutions should not be competing to give the same instruction and that the university was best suited to offer library education. Thus, the program at the State Library ended, having accomplished Gillis's goal of training librarians to work in the library systems that he had helped create. A total of 75 librarians graduated through the State Library.*

At the local level, public libraries began to develop special collections with local content. SCPL underwent such a transformation as well. Take the subject of Santa Cruz history, for instance. In the library catalog there are five titles on the city and twelve titles on the county – with one title overlapping – written and published between 1884 and the 1930s. The early local publications about the community of Santa Cruz have two notable characteristics: they tend to concentrate on the city of Santa Cruz and its neighboring cities and towns (Stephen Michael Payne's *A Howling Wilderness; a History of the Summit Road Area of the Santa Cruz Mountains, 1850–1906* (1978) is really a big step towards the wilderness of the Santa Cruz mountains); and they tend to be written by one-book authors.[1]

There has been a visible shift since the 1950s, when the community started to manifest its interest in tracing the history of the places where people lived. A list from scruzwiki.org (*https://scruzwiki.org/Local_Books*) is representative, but by no means exhaustive.[2] The phenomenon is a reflection of California's leading the whole nation in a series of scientific and technological breakthroughs. In such a promising and forward-thinking province, Californians, native or transplanted, both feel proud and regard the community as their own – hence the rise of local content. The following sections look at a number of notable writers and historians and their work on Santa Cruz County.

---

* See Appendix 1.

Santa Cruz County history and Margaret Koch

As a fourth-generation resident of Santa Cruz County, Margaret Koch was an exceptional local historian and writer. Born Margaret Rau in 1918 and married to Ed Koch in 1938, she spent most of her life on her grandparents' property in Santa Cruz. Between 1964 and 2001, while working as a staff writer for a local newspaper, the *Santa Cruz Sentinel* (1951–81), Margaret authored and co-authored nine titles on the city and county of Santa Cruz, most notably, *Santa Cruz County: Parade of the Past* (1973).

Chinese Gold and Sandy Lydon

Sandy Lydon is a professor of history at Cabrillo College. Besides teaching, he is also a local writer and historian. Since 1978, he has written and co-written more than a dozen titles. He is mostly known for his *Chinese Gold: the Chinese in the Monterey Bay Region* (1985) and an *Outline History of Agriculture in the Pajaro Valley* (1989).

Hihn-Younger Archive and Stanley D. Stevens

Stanley D. Stevens, a Librarian Emeritus at University of California Santa Cruz (UCSC), is another prolific local historian. He has created the Hihn-Younger Archive of the German-American Hihn and Younger families, one of the special collections at UCSC. Charles Bruce Younger Sr., together with the German immigrant and entrepreneur F. A. Hihn, is one of the main subjects of the archive. Younger was Hihn's principal attorney and dean of the legal community. Apart from their business associations, the Hihn and Younger families were united through the marriage of Agnes Hihn, F. A. Hihn's youngest daughter, and C. B. Younger Jr. The collections in the archive have been donated by the F. A. Hihn Company and related corporate enterprises, such as the Capitola-Hihn Company, the Santa Cruz Rail Road Company, the Santa Cruz Water Co., the Valencia-Hihn Co. They include maps, artifacts, correspondence, documents, memorabilia, and photographs of the Hihn and Younger families. Inventory, processing, acquisitions of new materials, and research are supported by two funds: the Hihn-Younger Archive Fund and income from the Louis Edwin Hihn Endowment, which supports the compilation, publication, and distribution of publications about F. A. Hihn and Charles Bruce Younger (Senior and Junior).[3] In addition to providing reference services and directing and coordinating daily operations and contributions, Stanley D. Stevens has compiled and edited a succession of publications since 1996.[*]

Pathways to the Past

In 2009, the Santa Cruz Museum of Art and History (MAH) published a special issue of the Santa Cruz County *History Journal* entitled *Pathways to the Past: Adventures in Santa Cruz County History*. This was the first book to cover the founding histories of major areas of the county, such as the North Coast, Santa Cruz Mountains, and the cities of Santa Cruz, Capitola, and Watsonville. Apart from its coverage of place origins, the book, through a rich mine of primary sources, puts great emphasis on people, either forgotten or never known by us today, most notably Michael Lodge, the overlooked pioneer, John Howard Watson, the elusive judge, and Lillian A. Howard, the mysterious artist.

Pathways to the Past is characterized by its comprehensiveness and wide subject coverage, from Steele Brothers' cheese to the Santa Cruz egg-laying contest (1918–31); from the Auto Tree to the Pogonip Polo Club; early artists, photographers, and architects; and from the introduction of spiritualism to government buildings (the Santa Cruz Post Office and its mural artist, Henrietta Shore). Another notable feature of the volume is that all the articles have been exhaustively researched by authorities on the subjects, such as Alverda Orlando on Davenport, Paul Tutwiler on Georgiana Bruce Kirby and organized spiritualism in Santa Cruz, and Carolyn Swift on the chronology of Capitola. Even though the book is a compilation of two dozen articles written by 22 contributors, readers will hardly detect a difference in style and tone. This is largely due to the expert and painstaking editing of Joan Gilbert Martin and two other editors. Each article was checked and edited at least three times.

---

[*] See Appendix 1.

Notes

1. "Profiles of State Librarians of California 1850–Present." *cslfdn.org*. California State Library Foundation, n.d. Web. Accessed 30 July 2012.
2. "Local Book." *scruzwiki.org*. Santa Cruz Wiki, June 2010. Web. Accessed 30 July 2012.
3. "About the Hihn Younger Archive." *library.ucsc.edu*. University of California Santa Cruz University Library, 2012. Web. Accessed 30 July 2012.

4

Putting Davenport on the map

Abstract: This chapter concentrates on the work of Alverda Orlando, a librarian/historian who has brought the obscure industrial town of Davenport to fame through decades of ceaseless researching and writing which reflects the rise and decline of several of the main industries of the Greater San Francisco Bay Area and of Santa Cruz County.

Key words: Davenport Cement Plant, Standard Portland Cement Company, Cemex, cement industry, lime industry, lime kilns, California, San Francisco Bay Area, Henry Cowell, 1906 earthquake.

Librarian historian: Alverda Orlando

Alverda Orlando is one of a number of local writers who have done remarkable work in bringing a local community to the attention of Santa Cruz County and wider areas. Situated about nine miles north of Santa Cruz City on Highway 1, the town of Davenport was founded in 1868. Before Orlando wrote "A Short History of Davenport, California" in 1961, a collection of stories that she compiled for a term paper towards her BA degree at San Jose State University, it was an obscure industrial community with a cement plant and a dedicated railway system. The town was so obscure that Orlando's professor rejected her term paper proposal on the grounds that there was no such place as Davenport in Santa Cruz County! Nevertheless, Orlando succeeded in convincing him through the real people of this coastal community and their stories.

After obtaining a Master's in Education and a Master's in Library Science from the same university in January 1962, Orlando started to work as a librarian for SCPL and kept up her interest in Davenport. She published a series of articles on Davenport, such as "Volunteers Develop Cliff Rescue Equipment" (*Fire Engineering* 127(12) 1974), "Four Communities Share Use, Purchase Cost of Ladder Truck" (*Fire*

Engineering 128(8) 1975), "From Steam to Electric: Standard to Narrow" (*Rail Classics* 4(2) March 1975), and "Walking Tour of Historic Davenport" (1985) for the Santa Cruz County Society for Historical Preservation.

It was not until her retirement as Branciforte Branch Library Manager in June 1992 that Orlando formally put Davenport on the map, through her involvement in the founding of the Davenport Resource Service Center and her publications in the *Santa Cruz County History Journal*. Notable articles written by her include "North Coast. Davenport and Its Cement Plant: the Early Years 1903–1910" (Issue 1, 1994), "Davenport: North Coast. The Wildest Ride in Town: Davenport's Cement Plant Railroad System" (Issue 2, 1995), and "The Deefense [*sic*] of Davenport / Hank and David Bradley, with commentary by Alverda Orlando" (Issue 6, 2009). In 1995, she also published two articles on SCPL's web page for the Santa Cruz County History: "Early History of Davenport" and "Whales along the Coast of Davenport."

Figure 14	A panoramic view of Davenport, with Hotel D'Italia in the foreground and Ocean Hotel, Meat Market, Baths, and the cement plant visible in the background, ca. 1910

Source: Title_0159.v3.jpg. Courtesy of Santa Cruz Public Libraries.

Davenport Cement Centennial

In 2006, Orlando collaborated with local historian Robert W. Piwarzyk and several plant personnel and area residents to compile a history of the Davenport Cement Plant, entitled *Davenport Cement Centennial: Honoring Our Past, Building the Future: the Story of the Davenport Cement Plant and the Important Part It Has Played and Continues to Play in California's History.* Unlike some books devoted to company history, *Davenport Cement Centennial* focuses not on larger-than-life founders or their insightful thinking and exemplary endeavors, but on a single and simple point: the unfolding of events in a continuing history. It narrates how the plant was conceived in 1903, when William Dingee, owner of the Standard Portland Cement Company, saw the potential of the significant limestone and shale deposits in the Ben Lomond Mountains. Together with his partner, Irving Bachman, he purchased property 12 miles northwest of the City of Santa Cruz and constructed the second-largest cement plant in the nation. A few months later San Francisco was hit by the devastating 1906 earthquake and subsequent fire.

Figure 15   The cornerstone of Davenport Cement Plant still remains distinctive, despite a couple of name changes, 2012

Source: DSC_1474.v3c.jpg. Courtesy of Titangos Photography Studio.

This historical background determined the future of the Davenport plant. To respond to the sudden, overwhelming demand for cement and concrete, the construction of the Davenport plant was completed one year ahead of schedule. In late 1906, the plant opened with limited operation. By 1910, its annual production had risen to 1.4 million barrels, an amount not exceeded until World War II. The importance of Davenport cement by no means diminished with the passage of time. On the contrary, its presence endures throughout the state of California to this day, in structures ranging from the San Francisco War Memorial Opera House (1932) to Golden Gate Bridge (1937); from the Bay Area Rapid Transit to the Oakland-Alameda Coliseum (1966); from the Stanford Medical Center to the expansion of San Francisco International Airport; not to mention countless private homes built in California's cities and suburbs, all of which used Davenport cement in their foundations.

Davenport Cement Centennial utilizes graphs and illustrations to trace the timeline over which the plant left its footprint on the history of California in general, and of the San Francisco Greater Bay Area in particular. A sidebar in the chapter "Building for Future Generations"

Figure 16   **Davenport Cement Plant was permanently shut down in 2010, four years after its centennial celebration**

Source: DSC_1451.v3.bw.jpg. Courtesy of Titangos Photography Studio.

uses clear and easy-to-understand language to explain what cement is and what types of cement Davenport produced. *Davenport Cement Centennial* is an interesting study that follows a century of innovative cement manufacturing. It shows how and from where the limestone was quarried; the mill processes involved in homogenizing the raw materials, calcinating them in the kilns, and further handling in the finishing mill. Transportation of the limestone to the plant and shipment of the finished product are also included. However, the book does not dwell exclusively on technology, but focuses also on the community behind the plant, the people who made natural resources and technologies work, and their small but whole society. The Davenport residents and cement plant workers built the one-room Pacific School in 1906, Crocker Hospital in 1910, a two-cell jail in 1914, and the St. Vincent de Paul church in 1915.

Lime Kiln Legacies

In 2007, Orlando and Piwarzyk, along with Frank A. Perry et al., published *Lime Kiln Legacies: the History of the Lime Industry in Santa Cruz County*. This is one of the very few published books devoted to the history of the lime industry of a specific area in the United States. The lime industry is a comparatively young industry in North America, although the history of the mining of lime rock to make lime can be traced back 7000 years to Turkey. Lime was not used for construction north of Mexico until European settlement, and lime manufacturing did not become a major industry in Santa Cruz County until the 1850s. So what is the significance of this book for today's readers?

Lime Kiln Legacies is the first complete history of the lime industry in Santa Cruz County. Making effective use of historical maps, photographs, census records, and newspaper clippings, the book systematically answers a series of critical questions: Of what is lime made? How was lime made? What companies were involved? Who were the lime workers? How did it get to the market? What was the impact of geology and geography? Despite the use of technical terms and concepts in the fields of geology, geography, and construction, the writers have done a first-class job, such as using the neutral word "limerock" so as to avoid confusing interchangeable terms like limestone and marble. The chapter on "Lime and Geology" not only clarifies three major kinds of rocks – igneous, sedimentary, and metamorphic – but analyzes the rocks quarried in Santa Cruz County, their geological descriptions, and principal outcrops near Davenport, Bonny Doon, Felton, Wilder Ranch State Park, and on the campus and in the environs of UCSC. The chapter "Tales Told by Kilns" successfully traces the two main types of kiln: pot and continuous kilns. There are 14 known kiln sites in Santa Cruz County. The chapter provides readers with thought-provoking suggestions as to the reasons for their particular styles of construction.

The rise and decline of the lime industry in Santa Cruz County coincided with the developing history of California. In the first half of the 1800s, only small amounts of lime began to be manufactured in Santa Cruz, primarily for missions that used lime in their construction. The surge in demand for lime production did not occur in Santa Cruz County until after the Gold Rush in 1848. A succession of wooden buildings burned down in San Francisco between 1849 and 1851, and the inadequacy of fire-extinguishing equipment ultimately convinced Californians of the benefits of masonry buildings. In 1884 alone, Santa Cruz County's lime production amounted to one third of the state of California's supply and three-fourths of the lime in the San Francisco market. After peaking in 1904, the lime industry in Santa Cruz County suffered a decline during the twentieth century and was finally replaced by a superior newcomer, the cement industry. As a construction material, cement not only makes a much stronger and harder mortar, but also produces concrete when mixed with water, sand, and gravel. To a great extent, *Lime Kiln Legacies* is a prequel to the *Davenport Cement Centennial*, mentioned above.

Lime Kiln Legacies is a history of the people involved in the lime industry in Santa Cruz County, by virtue of its frank and faithful recording of their lives and work, successes and failures, births and deaths. The chapter on "Lime Companies" is certainly significant, in the sense that it provides a comprehensive centennial history of 26 lime companies that were active between 1850 and 1950. But perhaps more importantly, it vividly retells the biographies, arranged chronologically, of the people who established, sold, merged, and fiercely competed in the lime businesses. Among its highlights are the mixed reviews of Henry Cowell, who all but succeeded in his goal of completely dominating the Pacific Coast lime businesses, and his children's legacies to the University of California, Santa Cruz High School, and the whole of today's county of Santa Cruz. There are few existing records of the innumerable people who quarried the rock, prepared the fuel, stoked the kiln fires, and shipped the lime to market. Unlike the owners of the lime works, who received extensive press coverage during their lifetimes, the lime workers

Figure 17 An oil-burning "patent" kiln on the former Cowell Ranch, ca. late 1950s

Source: Title_0578.v3.jpg. Courtesy of Santa Cruz Public Libraries.

remain nameless and faceless. To pay them due respect as a community, the book devotes a whole chapter to "People and Lime," reconstructing their lives and working conditions. This is done through the use of photographs, census records, local newspapers, and the special collections available at MAH, SCPL, and UCSC. The book sends a message to the community that limekiln legacies continue, even though the last lime kiln in Santa Cruz County was closed in 1946. The chapter "Lime and Place Names" alone adds a meaningful layer to life today in Santa Cruz County, as well as expanding on Donald Thomas Clark's *Santa Cruz County Place Names*.

Urgency in history preservation

Adopting the same urgency with which H. H. Bancroft recorded the experiences of early settlers and pioneers in California while they were still alive, Orlando initiated a preservation project to video-record interviews with the older generations in Davenport and nearby areas. Since 1997, she has demonstrated her long-standing commitment to the community by producing more than 56 video interviews with elderly local residents. The project to record the experiences of early Italian-American immigrants in Davenport and North Coast is sponsored by MAH and UCSC, and is hosted by the Davenport Resource Service Center. All the interviews were originally broadcast on Community Television of Santa Cruz County (*http://www.communitytv.org/*).

On 18 September 2011, North Coast Reunion 2011 held a ceremony to recognize and honor Alverda Orlando for her "many years of dedicated service and outstanding accomplishment to the North Coast Community" and for her lifelong achievements and efforts in preserving and extending Davenport–North Coast history.

In January 2012, MAH's History Forum honored two researchers/local historians for their commitment to the history of the Santa Cruz and Monterey Bay Area. At the ceremony, Orlando shared the 2011 James Dolkas Memorial Fund Award with Nicholas Barron, a researcher at UCSC.[1] Orlando was honored for her proposal for a two-stage research project: documenting the stories of North Coast farmers, and working with local videographer Peter McGettigan to video-interview the farmers. The Dolkas Award is a local history award that promotes understanding and awareness of the history of the Santa Cruz/Monterey Bay Area through publishing (writing/photographic, video, voice) or material structures (objects/buildings). The fund was set up in honor of James Dolkas, the founder and original president of the History Forum, a fundraising, membership support group. It typically selects one best research proposal each year. The 2012 Dolkas Award was significant in two ways: for the first time it was shared by two recipients; and for the first time the award was given to a member of UCSC.

At the age of 81, Orlando still has a clear focus: writing the history of Davenport, its history, cement plant, dairy and agricultural ranches along the North Coast, Santa Cruz County, following on from her recent research conducted on Italians from North Italy and Switzerland. A new website, "North Coast Faces" (*http://northcoastfaces.org/wp/*), has been set up to present a pictorial and oral history of Davenport, using portraits, interviews, and archival materials.

In 2009, Cemex Davenport Plant officials closed the plant temporarily, citing the weak economy. In January 2010, the plant was permanently shut down, due to the Mexico-based company's disappointing losses in the preceding year and the company's recent money problems,[2] thus ending one of the oldest businesses in the state of California and a monumental chapter in Santa Cruz County's economic history.

Since the shutdown of the plant, Orlando has been closely observing the fate of Davenport.[3] On 2 May 2012, more than 140 local residents showed up for a community meeting to voice their ideas and concerns about plans for the future of the former Cemex property. They put forward many popular suggestions, such as hiking, biking, camping, and horseback riding, and considered the redwood forest as part of their backyard. In order for the land to remain in a natural state, free from housing and other developments, in December 2011 an 8500-acre forest in the Santa Cruz Mountains above Davenport was purchased for $30 million by several conservation groups consisting of the Land Trust of Santa Cruz County, Save the Redwoods League, Peninsula Open Space Trust and Sempervirens Fund. The cement plant itself remains for sale.[4]

Notes

1. "Santa Cruz Museum of Art and History honoring two researchers, local historians." *Santa Cruz Sentinel*, 4 January 2012: B4. Print.
2. Alexander, Kurtis. "Cemex Announces It Is Shutting Its Davenport Plant." *santacruzsentinel.com. Santa Cruz Sentinel*, 22 January 2010. Web. Accessed 20 October 2012.
3. "Board Meetings: Times, Agendas, and Minutes." *pacific.santacruz.k12. ca.us*. Pacific School, 17 February 2011. Web. Accessed 30 July 2012. (*http:// www.pacific.santacruz.k12.ca.us/pdf/Board_Minutes_2-17-11.pdf*)
4. McCord, Shanna. "Community Offers Suggestions on Future of 8,500 Acres Surrounding Former Cemex Property." *santacruzsentinel.com. Santa Cruz Sentinel*, 2 May 2012. Web. Accessed 30 July 2012.

Part 2
The Era of Library 1.0

5

Santa Cruz Public Library: community on the web

Abstract: This chapter traces SCPL's efforts to bring a local community to the world since the early 1990s. It has launched a series of digital projects, such as Full-text Local History Articles, SCPL Local History Gallery, and Local Online Databases. Two notable team leaders are duly recognized: former reference coordinator Gary Decker, and Ann Young, the current webmaster.

Key words: Salz Tannery, Tannery Arts Center, California Powder Works, Scotts Valley Branch Library, Local History Photograph Project, Genealogical Society of Santa Cruz County, Postcard Project, Community Information Database, Local Ballot Measures, Sheet Music Catalog.

Full-text Local History Articles

In the mid-1990s, SCPL was among the first libraries in California to make full-text, illustrated articles on local history available on their websites. In addition to more than 400 contributed articles on the history of Santa Cruz County, SCPL included over 350 full-text local newspaper articles. All of the articles are searchable, either by author or by browsing a list of local history topics, covering the following subject areas:

- Architecture
- Arts
- Community Services
- Crime and Public Safety
- Cultural Diversity
- Disasters and Calamities

- Executive Order 9066 and the Residents of Santa Cruz County
- Films
- Government
- In the 19th Century
- In the 20th Century
- Libraries and Schools
- Making a Living
- People
- Places
- Recreation and Sports
- Religion and Spirituality
- Spanish Period and Earlier
- Tourism
- Transportation
- Unusual and Curious
- Weather and Population Statistics
- World War II

The selected writers are locally known historians specialized in their chosen fields. Take the category of Architecture, for instance. The topic has four sections: Bridges, Buildings, Landmarks, and Wharves. The writers have presented to the world a continuing and colorful local history, including the introduction of covered bridges in the County of Santa Cruz (which has more covered bridges than any other county in California), unique buildings such as the Flatiron building and the Octagon, and state historical landmarks like the center of Villa de Branciforte and the nearly century-old Santa Cruz Municipal Wharf.

California Powder Works

Among the local history topics, Making a Living – Other Industries is a section devoted to the industries that once flourished in Santa Cruz County. Not only does it provide an overview of the economic development of the city of Santa Cruz from 1850 to 1950, but it also presents a complete and detailed picture of major industries throughout the county, such as Agriculture, which includes growing berries, apples, grapes, beets, and potatoes, dairy farming, and winemaking; Mining of gold, lime, limestone, and stone; and Other Industries, such as whaling, fishing, lumbering, and tannery.

The California Powder Works and San Lorenzo Paper Mill was one of SCPL's early experiments in digitizing local publications. This publication traces the history of the two companies. Established in 1860, the San Lorenzo Paper Mill was the main supplier of brown wrapping paper for the San Francisco market. A year later, the California Powder Works (CPW) was founded to meet an urgent need for black gunpowder, used in the mining, railroad, and construction industries along the West Coast.

After the Civil War broke out, all shipments of black gunpowder from the East Coast were suspended, thus preventing Federal gunpowder from falling into the hands of Confederate raiders. After a careful survey by a number of businessmen in San Francisco, Santa Cruz was chosen as the best location for the manufacture of black gunpowder, for three main reasons: a consistent and plentiful water supply from the San Lorenzo River, an abundant supply of wood in the surrounding forests, and proximity to an ocean harbor. By 1864, CPW had become the first black powder producer on the West Coast, and eventually became the largest producer of explosives, including brown prismatic powder and guncotton (smokeless powder), west of the Mississippi River. In 1903, the DuPont Corporation bought a controlling interest in the CPW. In 1906, CPW was named the E. I. du Pont de Nemours Powder Company, and in 1912 it was renamed as the Hercules Powder Company. As the population grew, and, with it, concerns for public safety in the county, CPW had to shut down its operation in Santa Cruz and was eventually closed in 1914. During its 50 years of operation, CPW enjoyed technological progress: wooden barrels were replaced by metal cans to better preserve the quality of the powder; water power was replaced by steam power, and later by electricity; and shipment by sea was replaced by the railroad passing through the Santa Cruz Mountains from the Bay Area.[1]

Salz Tannery: friendship between Ansel Adams and Ansley Kullman Salz

Included in the section Making a Living – Other Industries is a story of the friendship between the photographer Ansel Adams and Ansley Kullman Salz, the owner of the Salz Tannery, a landmark Santa Cruz industry established from 1861 to 2001.[2] Now a gallery of Ansel Adams's photographs of the Tannery are available for viewing on the SCPL's website.

Figure 18 The original front elevation of the historic Salz Leathers building remains unchanged more than 151 years later, in 2012

Source: DSC_1517.v3c.jpg. Courtesy of Titangos Photography Studio.

In 1954, Salz asked Adams to photograph the leather-making process at his tannery. Adams's black and white photographs document a vanished industrial era. They show tannery founder Salz and his superintendent, Joe Bellas, holding the finished product (aa-001 and aa-0037), and the front of the historic Salz Leathers building, which remained unchanged for over 151 years (aa-018). They also meticulously record the tanning process, and skilled workers who manufactured leather at the tannery, such as Salz employees Mel Stubendorff and his co-worker tacking the hides onto large boards prior to drying (aa-006), Red McCafferty and his co-worker working with a machine called a "splitter" to separate the hide into two distinct layers (aa-009), an employee working on the glazing process that made the California Saddle Leather™ unique (aa-030), an employee illustrating a typical beamhouse outfit (aa-007), and a batch of vegetable-tanned – or tanoak – leather hanging until ready for shipping (aa-035).

Salz Tannery today: Tannery Arts Center

A year after the closure of the former Salz Tannery, in 2002, the City of Santa Cruz began working towards a new landmark project on the same site, namely, the Tannery Arts Center, a place to keep local talent from fleeing to other areas or states for more affordable living by subsidizing and supporting struggling artists. George Newell, the former executive director, stated the Center's vision and mission most eloquently: "We need an affordable place for artists to live, work, and show their work. That was the kernel of the vision for the Tannery Arts Center. We wanted to keep the creative talent here in Santa Cruz."[3]

Like many communities in the Greater San Francisco Bay Area, Santa Cruz County has a high concentration of artists, craftsmen, and musicians, both locally born and settled from all over the world. They are attracted by the region's mild climate, beautiful landscape, and liberal politics, which in turn have fostered and nurtured artistic creation and skillful craftsmanship. In Santa Cruz County, art events and festivals are held all year round by local organizations such as MAH, Santa Cruz Art League, the Downtown Association of Santa Cruz – which presents the First

Figure 19 The historic Salz Leathers has been renovated as the Tannery Arts Center, 2012

Source: DSC_1559.v3c.jpg. Courtesy of Titangos Photography Studio.

Friday Art Tour (*http://www.firstfridaysantacruz.com/*) each month – and the Cultural Council of Santa Cruz County (CCSCC), which hosts the Open Studios Art Tour (*http://openstudiosarttour.org/*) every October.

There is a large music community in the area. There are at least five major music festivals, for example, Cabrillo Festival of Contemporary Music (*http://cabrillomusic.org/*; 1961–), Capitola Twilight Concerts (*http://www.ci.capitola.ca.us/CAPCITY.NSF/AboutUpCmEvt.html*; June through August); Santa Cruz Baroque Festival (*http://www.scbaroque. org/*; 1974–); Santa Cruz Blues Festival (*http://www.santacruzbluesfestival. com/*; 1992–); and the Santa Cruz County Symphony (*http://www. santacruzsymphony.org/*; 1958–). In addition, the theater/performing arts have always had a strong presence in the area. To name a few, there are All About Theatre (*http://www.allabouttheatre.org/*), Mountain Community Theater (*http://www.mctshows.org/*), Santa Cruz Actors Theatre (*http://www.sccat.org/*), and Shakespeare Santa Cruz, a professional repertory theatre working in cooperation with the Theater Arts Department at UCSC and CCSCC.

Owing to a cost of living 87.9 percent higher than the US average,[4] and the expensive housing market in the county – with median home

Figure 20 The living quarters for artists, musicians, and performers within the Tannery Arts Center, 2012

Source: DSC_1552.v3c.jpg. Courtesy of Titangos Photography Studio.

prices hovering around the $479,600 mark even in a distressed property market[5] – few artists can afford a decent living space, let alone much-needed studios or workshops.

In partnership with Artspace of Minneapolis and other nonprofit organizations, the Redevelopment Agency (now defunct) initiated the renovation project by purchasing the Tannery site for $2 million and paying other expenses such as clearing the ground of toxic chemicals. A total of $40 million were spent on a three-phase project to create an arts center where artists could live, work, and create:

> Phase 1: In June 2009, a 100-unit apartment complex, Tannery Lofts, opened to the top applicants on the waiting list (which has an average two-year waiting period). The monthly rent is consistently below the market price.

> Phase 2: In June 2012, a 23,000 square foot art studio complex, renovated from two historic buildings, was officially opened for artists to rent as workshops for glassmaking, painting, printmaking, and sculpting, as studios for digital media and performing arts, or as galleries and classrooms for the arts community or the general public.

> Phase 3 and final: By 2014, the $5 million, 200-seat performing arts center will be ready for the first performance. "The final outcome will be integrated performing-creating-living space in Santa Cruz. That is unparalleled any place else in the country," states Rachel Anne Goodman, the present executive director.[6] The ultimate goal is to make the Tannery Center a truly vibrant arts campus or arts mecca, dreamed of by many generations of artists.

SCPL Local History Gallery

The SCPL Local History Gallery consists of two main parts: the early albums "Local History Postcards" and "Local History Photographs," and the later albums "Remembering the 1989 Loma Prieta Earthquake" and "New Scotts Valley Branch – From Roller Rink to Library." The former two albums contain 1500 images dating from the 1860s to the 1990s and donated from private and public, and personal or professional sources. The digitized photographs are all provided with notes written by library staff which describe the events, persons, buildings, dates, and places depicted, and have links to related articles on the SCPL website. To identify the persons, events, objects, and places in the photographs, library staff used a great variety of sources, such as local historians, notes written on the photographs, newspaper articles, and related books available in the SCPL system. SCPL Local History Gallery constitutes one of the first serious endeavors to bring a local community to the world since SCPL's founding in 1868.

Local History Photograph Project (LHPP)

The LHPP is the earliest effort to make available online more than 979 historical photographs in the SCPL's local history collection, and was made possible through generous loans by local agencies, nonprofit organizations, and individuals. The digital project was not realized until Gary Decker, the then reference system coordinator at SCPL, made a formal proposal to the library management to catalog, digitize, and store the local history photograph collection on the library's website.

In the late 1990s a survey of digital projects by public libraries in the United States indicated that 53.2 percent of projects obtained their grants from local government and private individuals and agencies, while 28.1 percent of projects received their funding from state and federal governments.[7] Decker secured funding to support his proposal through a gift from a private source earmarked for local history research in fiscal year 1998. The fund enabled the purchase of the Cumulus software for cataloging graphic materials, and also paid for the scanning and the hire of two temporary staff.

Headed by Decker and the internet librarian, the LHPP team was very lean and efficient. No money was spent on learning the software or cataloging system, due to the technical readiness of the team. After a brief introduction, the temporary librarian started to catalog the collection and the temporary library assistant prepared the cataloged items for the scanning process.

Team spirit was another characteristic of the project. Each member played a unique role, and collaboration and communication prevailed whenever there was a crisis. There was a delay in the delivery of the final batch of scanning before the deadline for the project's completion. To complete the project within the fiscal year, by 30 June, everyone worked as if in a relay, for example, contacting the contractor to make sure the scanning job was done, processing and creating hyperlinks to the library website once an item was cataloged. During the process, there were also a number of challenges confronting LHPP. The following are typical examples.

Copyright

The issue of copyright is not a topic of this book; indeed, it deserves a whole book of its own. For the team, the dilemma of copyright lay in the paradoxical fact that, in order to faithfully preserve the photograph collection, a higher resolution was desired. In the late 1990s, web graphical applications were not as well developed as they are today, and the use of thumbnails or file saving in web resolution was not a possibility. This meant that the high-resolution items, once posted on the web, were at the disposal of end-users. To complicate the matter, not every photo in the collection was in the public domain. The solution was to stamp each item with terms of use, which were restricted by specific permission.

Over the years, SCPL has made some changes to tackle the issue of terms of use. In 2006 the assistant webmaster created a Content Bar, including a category called Restrictions on Use (*http://www2.santacruzpl.org/history/photos/pages/restrict.shtml*), to cover digitized graphical collections. Instead of stamping each item, he created a link directing interested users to the right page. For their convenience, he also added contact information and an online photograph request form (*http://www2.santacruzpl.org/history/photos/pages/photoapp.pdf*). Apparently, his solution for the utilization of historical photographs has been welcomed by both local and remote users, who are constantly submitting request forms in person, by mail, or by e-mail.

Subject treatment

Owing to the structure of Cumulus, a subject tree with main subject headings (categories) and subheadings (subcategories) was needed before the actual cataloging could start. It was decided from the very beginning that subject headings should be adopted from a standardized source, namely, Library of Congress's (LC) Thesaurus for Graphic Materials I: Subject Terms (TGM I). How could we reconstruct a unique local history using uniform subject terms? The question presented itself as another challenge.

The cataloger was entrusted with the task of drafting a subject tree after browsing through the first batch of photographs. Soon, a draft outlining 27 subjects was ready for group discussion:

Agriculture	Ocean
Amusements	Parks
Beaches	People
Buildings	Piers and wharves
Church	Politics
Cities and towns	Portraits
Commerce	Railroads
Festivals	Recreation
Forests	Roads
Frontier and pioneer life	Schools
Hotels	Sports
Industries	Universities and colleges
Libraries	Wildlife conservation
Mountains	

The draft list was based on two considerations: observation of TGM I, and the color of local history. A strong emphasis can be seen on agriculture, industry (namely lumber and mills), railroads, beaches, hotels, and amusement – typical historical elements reflecting the period from the 1850s to the turn of the twentieth century in Santa Cruz County. However the list lacked a fine balance between LC's subject terms and local appropriateness. After a series of intense discussions among the project manager, head, and team members, a working version of major subject headings was finalized as follows:

Agriculture	Frontier and pioneer life
Architecture	Industries
Arts and entertainment	Law and public safety
Business	Libraries
City panoramas and aerial views	Medicine
Disasters	Nature
Ethnic and racial groups	Organizations

Parks	Religion
Piers and wharves	Roads and streets
Politics	Schools
Portraits and governments	Tourist attractions and special events
Public accommodations	Transportation
Recreation and sports	

This second version successfully translated TGM I to the historical environment of Santa Cruz County. It was not only comprehensive in subject coverage, but also very intuitive in using LC principles to describe such features as city panoramas and aerial views. It incorporated LC subject terms and regrouped likely concepts. Today, the final version on the SCPL website has been further customized and modified to more appropriately accommodate the enlarged collection.*

Reconstruct a complete history in words. Many of the digitized photographs were original, in the sense that they had never been mentioned in any of the available sources, either in print or online. Take photograph #0125, for instance: this undated photograph was described by just three words written on its face: "Laurel Bull Donkey." Apparently this was far from sufficient for picture reviewers, especially for the younger generations. To provide concise but essential information, a footnote was composed to explain that this was an engine used to hoist logs onto flatcars bound for the mill. Cables would be extended on spools run through the woodland for a distance of up to several miles. In addition, "1890s" was entered in the Date field, for this was the decade in which the bull donkey was invented and adopted in the logging industry.

So as to be standardized and consistent, LHPP derived not only its main subject headings (or categories) and new subheadings (or subcategories) from TGM I, but also the majority of words used in the Keywords field or for tagging in Library 2.0. This was of great importance, because it provided additional capabilities for users to search for related objects not mentioned either in the main subject headings or in subheadings or in the Note field. Moreover, the standardized and uniform usage of terms or keywords enables users to retrieve all likely hits in a consistent manner. A related problem is that sometimes a term that fits a situation is not yet recognized by LC subject authority, for example, the guard

---

* See Appendix 2.

Figure 21 Laurel bull donkey. A donkey was an engine used to hoist logs onto flatcars bound for the mill. Cables could be extended on spools run through the woodland for a distance of up to several miles, ca. 1890s

Source: Title_0125.v3.jpg. Courtesy of Santa Cruz Public Libraries.

rail (on old Highway 17), which can be significant in determining the era or location. One possible solution is to use terms not in TGM I, but to capitalize them so as to distinguish them from the TGM I terms.

Retell a vanished history through images. During the process of organizing and making available hundreds of historical photographs, LHPP members had relived and revisited times and places that no longer exist. It was their wish to reconstruct history in a continuous and seamless manner. Here are some memorable details.

Santa Cruz's lost industries

Logging and lumber milling were once established industries in Santa Cruz County. Since the 1950s, especially since the 1970s, a number of publications have been devoted to the subject. However, the visual coverage conveyed to the general public was very limited.

Figure 22   **Ox team pulling wagonload of lumber in the Santa Cruz Mountains, undated**

Source: Title_0044.v3.jpg. Courtesy of Santa Cruz Public Libraries.

The SCPL presents a wide spectrum of historical portraits of these industries which were once active in the region, for example, Ox teams hauling lumber (0044), Molino Timber Company (0050), The Loma Prieta Lumber Company's motorcar (0046), Grovers Mill (0096), and Laurel Station (0029) – which played a critical role in rebuilding San Francisco by supplying much of the lumber in 1906.

Another important industry in the area is mining. Take the Henry Cowell Lime and Cement Company, for example. The company had been referred to on numerous occasions, but was seldom illustrated with actual photographs of the mining site. Therefore it was extraordinarily powerful to view a group of photographs such as Ox teams hauling rocks from the Cowell Ranch quarry (0095), Wagons being loaded with bituminous rock on the Cowell Ranch (0041) and Quarrying rocks (0084).

Figure 23 The Loma Prieta Lumber Company's motorcar #3 pushing a flatcar loaded with supplies from Molino to the base of the Molino Timber Company's incline, undated. The Molino Timber Company was incorporated in 1911 as a subcontracting company of the Loma Prieta Lumber Company

Source: Title_0446.v3.jpg. Courtesy of Santa Cruz Public Libraries.

| Figure 24 | Grovers Mill, undated. In 1861, three Grover brothers plus three other men established a lumber company called Grover and Company. They purchased land about two miles north of Soquel on Bates Creek and the area came to be known as Grovers Gulch |

Source: Title_0096.v3.jpg. Courtesy of Santa Cruz Public Libraries.

An equally important presence at that time was the railroad, both as an industry and for transportation. For the first time, the LHPP has systematically organized photographs of the various railroads that were active in the area, such as the Santa Cruz Railroad (0014), the Ocean Shore Railroad (0022), the South Pacific Coast Railroad (0251), and the Southern Pacific Railroad (SCM093). By using "Search the Gallery," users are able to retrieve images of the relevant facilities, such as the first depot in Santa Cruz (0003), and the well-known Wright's Station near Felton (0037).

Figure 25 Quarrying rocks, undated. Quarrying limestone was done by hand labor on the Cowell Ranch

Source: Title_0084.v3.jpg. Courtesy of Santa Cruz Public Libraries.

Figure 26 Wright's Station was used to ship fruit to canneries in San Jose (1895). Wright's was also a tourist destination, bringing visitors to resorts in the area

Source: Title_0037.v3.jpg. Courtesy of Santa Cruz Public Libraries.

Santa Cruz's lost land area

LHPP came across a reference to an area of land lost from Santa Cruz County to San Mateo County in 1868, namely, Punta de Ano Nuevo or New Year Point. To provide users with a complete history, LHPP team members consulted authoritative histories and experts. They succeeded in portraying the past through photographs of Flora Steele Ranch (0136), Green Oaks Ranch (0168), Pigeon Point Landing (0172) and Pigeon Point keepers gate (0135). To provide further facility for users, the team also entered consistent reference points, such as variations of the place name Punta de Año Nuevo, in the Keywords field.

Figure 27 — The lighthousekeeper's house at the Pigeon Point Lighthouse (later Pigeon Point Lighthouse State Historic Park), undated

Source: Title_0135.v3.jpg. Courtesy of Santa Cruz Public Libraries.

Santa Cruz's lost architecture

One of the main features of the available photograph collections was architecture, including buildings, bridges, and private homes. Most of these structures are still standing, but some are lost forever. Through LHPP's efforts, the public is able to view buildings that were consumed by fire, such as Sea Beach Hotel (0425), the first Santa Cruz High School (0192), and Neptune Casino, built by Fred Swanton in 1904 as part of the Beach Boardwalk, but burned to the ground 22 June 1906 (0176); or those demolished by the Great Earthquake of 1989, like Cooper House (0120). The architecture section also includes some private homes, such as the F. A. Hihn Mansion, built in 1872 and once leased to the City as the old City Hall (0131). Photos of Knight Opera House (0063 and 0216), both in its prime and at the end of its life, also provide another good complete story.

Figure 28

Neptune Casino, built by Fred Swanton in 1904 as part of the Beach Boardwalk. It burned to the ground 22 June 1906. After the fire, Swanton erected a circus tent to house the casino for the summer season

Source: Title_0176.v3.jpg. Courtesy of Santa Cruz Public Libraries.

Santa Cruz's lost politics

The historical photograph collection created by SCPL is also rich in past politics, especially World War I (0072).

There is a photograph of a convention held in Santa Cruz by the Native Sons of the Golden West (0075). As it was undated, LHPP members went through available references on political conventions in California, including Margaret Koch's *Santa Cruz County: Parade of the Past*, which lists a similar photograph but with no date specified either. Thanks to the help of a member of the Genealogical Society of Santa Cruz County (GeneSoc), the team discovered that the event depicted was described in an article in the *Santa Cruz Surf* newspaper dated 9 September 1891.

Figure 29

The Santa Cruz Aerie 460 (Fraternal Order of Eagles) band playing for a crowd in front of the Santa Cruz Post Office, 14 April 1917. A row of men in sailor uniforms stands opposite the band, in the center of the picture. Handwritten notes on the original mounting say: "Departure of Santa Cruz Troops"

Source: Title_0072.v3.jpg. Courtesy of Santa Cruz Public Libraries.

Figure 30 | The Grand Arch of the Native Sons of the Golden West on Pacific Avenue, 9 September 1891. For several years, Grand Parlors were held in Santa Cruz

Source: Title_0075.v3.jpg. Courtesy of Santa Cruz Public Libraries.

Postcard project

The digitization project Postcards of Santa Cruz County was sourced from a four-volume set of binders, together with three volumes of indexes, containing 521 historic postcards from or about the county of Santa Cruz by various local artists and publishers. The original set had been collected and donated to SCPL by community members such as Dick and Lynne Lowe, and the fourth volume was donated by Sally Coen and Jules M. Heumann. Because of its rarity and comprehensiveness, and constant usage, the set was at risk of theft and physical deterioration. It became increasingly clear that the solution for preserving this local resource was to digitize it and make it accessible online.

Gary Decker planned and organized the project. However, owing to the interruption of his retirement in 2004, the project was shelved for a few years until the webmaster, Ann Young, and her assistant decided to resume some long-delayed digital projects. Chosen as part of the SCPL Local History Gallery, the project was completed in 2008.

All the online postcards are accessible and searchable via keywords, date, place, source of information, and hyperlinks to related articles, in

Figure 31   The Capitola Hotel in Capitola, with sunbathers and children playing in the foreground, undated

Source: 072012_0001.v3.jpg. Courtesy of Santa Cruz Public Libraries.

Figure 32   The Cooper House, located in downtown Santa Cruz, was the Court House at the turn of the century (undated). It has now been converted into shops and restaurants with daily local entertainment

Source: 072012_0002.v3c.jpg. Courtesy of Santa Cruz Public Libraries.

addition to appropriate subject headings. To further meet end-users' needs, the images are provided in two sizes, original and screen. Users are invited to leave their comments.

New Scotts Valley Branch Library

The album entitled "New SV Branch – From Roller Rink to Library" went online on the occasion of the 2011 grand opening of the new Scotts Valley Branch Library. The opening of the new branch was a dream project 60 years in the making. Founded in February 1953, the Scotts Valley Branch Library survived Proposition 13 closures in 1978, earthquake damage in 1984, and relocation in 1985. The relocation to a storefront in the Kings Village Shopping Center turned out to be eventful. In December of that year, a car crashed through the front window of the branch. Both the vehicle's passengers and the branch manager were slightly injured; the circulation desk and other library equipment were demolished. In 1989, the City of Scotts Valley and the Library System planned to expand library services and space. The plan was temporarily interrupted by the October 1989 Loma Prieta earthquake in San Francisco Bay Area, but was carried through nonetheless. By the fall of 1998, the Scotts Valley Branch Library had become bigger and brighter and had been expanded to 5300 square feet with the addition of public restrooms, a Homework Center for young people, and a quiet place for young children and their parents.

The true makeover did not happen until 2009, when the City of Scotts Valley acquired the property and building of the former Scotts Valley Roller Rink on Kings Village Road for $4.5 million. Shortly after the acquisition, blueprints were drafted for a 13,000 square foot branch library, with a final total area of 13,150 square feet. On 14 August 2010, a ground-breaking ceremony was held at the site of the new library. The new library opened on 18 June 2011, with a new children's section, teen area, group study facility, two computer banks, a multipurpose space, meeting rooms for the community, an outside patio, and additional shelving space for library materials. The conversion from indoor roller rink to library was listed by *Library Journal* as one of the architectural wonders of 2011 – for the diner-style booths complementing the teen space, the solar tubes and skylights for natural light, and a cushioned story-time platform.[8] It has also been listed in the *American Libraries* AL Focus in the category Reuse and Restoration.[9]

Designed by Group 4 Architecture, Research + Planning, Inc. (*http://www.g4arch.com/*), the new library has been complimented for being

Figure 33 A lively place for young children with the friendly companionship of both library staff and feline giants inside Scotts Valley Library, 2012

Source: DSC_1506.v3c.jpg. Courtesy of Titangos Photography Studio.

Figure 34 The former Scotts Valley Roller Rink has been turned into Scotts Valley Branch Library, 2012

Source: DSC_1485.v3c.jpg. Courtesy of Titangos Photography Studio.

"the first civic project in the city's new town center. Suspended polycarbonate 'lanterns' introduce natural light into the library and define programmatic spaces. The roller rink's raised platform and booth seating inspired the teen space, providing space for both independent and collaborative work."[10]

Local online databases

Gary Decker was also instrumental in leading a number of significant local digital projects, including the Community Information Database (CID) and Sheet Music Catalog (SMC), two databases widely used by library professionals and the general public. From the late 1990s, when the first web application appeared, they began to migrate to the internet. With the rapid development of information technologies, the webmaster at SCPL completely rewrote the code on a web programming platform in 2007, using MySQL for all the local databases and applications.[11]

Community Information Database

As one of the modules in the DRA (Data Research Associates, Inc.) library system, the CID (*http://www2.santacruzpl.org/cid/public*) was first developed in 1985 to meet the increasing needs of local community members seeking local social services and organizations. Prior to its digital form, it was available only in printed format, issued annually by the county government. More often than not, annual updates were irregular and unpredictable. Under the circumstances, Gary Decker decided to make it accessible via the library OPAC (Online Public Access Catalog), with the help of a grant from the Library Services and Construction Act. The CID project took off as a collaborative project by five local public agencies, namely, SCPL, Santa Cruz County Human Resources Agency, Santa Cruz County Health Services Agency, United Way, and Watsonville Public Library. Its goal was to develop a comprehensive database of the human service resources available to the community in Santa Cruz County.

In 1990, SCPL became the sole agency responsible for maintaining and updating the CID. Meanwhile, the scope of subject areas was substantially enlarged, from coverage of merely human service resources to the following major topics:

Daycare and preschools	Political organizations
Environmental groups	Service organizations
Health and human service agencies	Social and fraternal organizations
Hobby clubs	Support groups

In 2004, the CID was made available online, first as part of local resources and later grouped in the categories both of Internet Resources and of Local Information. In July 2007, the content of the CID was augmented by the merger of records from HelpSCC (Help Santa Cruz County) (*http://www.helpscc.org/*), formerly owned by First 5 Santa Cruz County (*http://www.first5scc.org/*). At time of writing, the CID lists about 978 local nonprofit agencies. A form "Add Agency" (*http://www2.santacruzpl.org/cid/public/info.php?display=add_agency*) enables interested agencies to apply for a listing. The free listing is popular with nonprofit organizations because it has greatly enhanced their visibility not only locally but also regionally and nationally via channels such as the SCPL home page and 211 Information and Referral Search (*http://www.211.org/*), which makes use of local databases like the CID. The "Update Agency" page (*http://www2.santacruzpl.org/cid/public/info.php?display=update_agency*) makes it very easy for organizations to contact the Library and submit information updates.

The CID is equally popular in the community, having an easy-to-use and friendly interface. It is browsable alphabetically by subject and location. Quick Lists include categories such as:

Clubs	Legal Assistance
Disabled	Private Nonprofit
Employment	Seniors
Food	Volunteer Opportunities
Health	Youth
Housing	

Luis Chabolla, at the Community Foundation Santa Cruz County, says that "We see the CID as one of the best tools for local nonprofits to gain visibility and to let the public know what they do as well as what their wants and needs are."[12] It is interesting to see some of the usage patterns detected over the years. For example, the most-searched keyword in October 2011 was "employment," coinciding not accidentally with the county's high unemployment rate of 12.30 percent (US average: 9.10 percent)[13] or 11.7 percent (US average: 8.9 percent; California average: 11.5 percent) for the month of October 2011.[14]

Maintained and updated continuously by a dedicated information specialist, the CID has undergone a thorough makeover since its origin as a module of the Windows-based DRA library system. In addition to her other duties as a member of the reference staff, the information specialist gathers and organizes pertinent information harvested from online form submissions and from her daily readings and such varied sources as local newspapers and other publications. Once an entry has been created, she validates it for authenticity and accuracy. When changes occur, she makes sure that revisions are entered in a timely manner. She believes that compiling and providing local information on the web is something that library professionals can do well, for a library knows the local community and is in the information business – even though things have changed with the internet.[15]

Sheet Music Catalog

Developed also as a module in the DRA library system, the popular SMC (*http://www2.santacruzpl.org/sheetmusic/*) first became available online in 2000 as a web application. Unlike CID, the SMC did not receive any outside grants or financial aid. It is created and maintained by in-house talent and staff such as reference clerks and information specialists. Written originally in the Perl programming language, it has been rewritten in Ruby on Rails, an open source full-stack web application framework for the Ruby programming language.

The SMC is now accessible online in the categories "Books and More" and "Internet Resources," as an electronic index to more than 30,174 pieces of classical, popular, traditional, and folk music housed at the Central (now Downtown) Branch, with a strong emphasis on piano and guitar music. It is searchable by the following four criteria:

- Title of song or show
- Name of artist or group
- Keywords
- Phrase.

Also equipped with an easy-to-use and friendly interface, the SMC has both limiting and browsing capabilities. All records can be limited by

Category, Instrument, Language and Copyright Year, or browsed by All Categories (a total of 19) and Instruments (9).

SCPL used to have a music library, consisting chiefly of private gifts of music and books from individual collections and endowments. Established in 1936, it contained the best of world music to enrich the life of the community. "In stamping each piece of music I have been impressed, finding so much of the greatest of all composers, Bach, Beethoven, and Brahms, and all of the renowned composers of the European countries and of the United States, California and Santa Cruz."[16] The notable donations include the lifetime collection of Otto G. Kunitz (1937), gifts from Edward Leedham (1937), Charles Hadeden Parker (1938), and Hope Swinford (1947), the Monday Music Club's gift of Frank Hamlin's musical arrangements (1958), and gifts from the Martha Baird Rockefeller Fund for Music (1965), James West (1963), and the Frank McCrary Music Memorial (1966–68).

The SMC is sourced from major songbooks inherited from the former music library and from *Sheet Music Magazine* from 1977 to the present. With more than 2157 music scores available in the music collection of SCPL, the SMC provides an additional online resource serving the large music community in Santa Cruz County.

Local Ballot Measures (referenda) project

In order to anticipate the constant needs of local voters, the former internet librarian initiated the Local Ballot Measures (LBM) (*http://www2.santacruzpl.org/ref/measures/index.php*) project by gathering materials pertinent to LBMs, first in a binder, then in a clippings file, and finally, when the collection became too large to handle any other way, in a machine-readable database. To provide thoroughly researched and balanced information, she went to various city and county government offices for approved measures, and turned to local newspapers for failed ones (the election departments in Santa Cruz County do not keep any records of failed ballots).[17]

Under the guidance and coordination of the internet librarian, the LBM project has archived online all LBMs in Santa Cruz County from 1980 to the present. The list of LBMs is arranged by ballot date. Each record lists the measure name, the short text of the measure as it appeared on the ballot, and the election results obtained from the Santa Cruz County Elections Department. Also included is a page informing users "How the Library Determined Whether a Measure was Approved or Failed" (*http://www2.santacruzpl.org/ref/measures/results.php*). If the short text is unavailable, SCPL staff provide a brief annotation in brackets, based on information supplied by the County Elections Department. Users can search the measure names and short texts or annotations by keyword. The full-text LBMs are available from November 1998 to the present; for earlier LBMs, links to various sources of the full text are provided.

Formerly updated and continuously maintained by SCPL's Central Reference Department, and now by Library Information Technology, LBM is one of the most-used online resources. The following is a remote user's feedback received in October 2011 through the forum SCPL Patron Comment or Suggestion:

> Thank you very much for creating the Local Ballot Measures page. This is a great resource for those of us elsewhere in the state trying to do research on the efforts of other local agencies ... thanks again.[18]

Notes

1. Brown, Barry. "The California Powder Works and San Lorenzo Paper Mill: Introduction." *santacruzpl.org*. Santa Cruz Public Libraries, n.d. Web. Accessed 30 July 2012.
2. Lehmann, Susan. "Industrial Development: Tanneries." *santacruzpl.org*. Santa Cruz Public Libraries, n.d. Web. Accessed 30 July 2012.
3. McCord, Shanna. "Former Leather Factory Bustling with Arts." *Santa Cruz Sentinel*, 3 June 2012: sec. A1+. Print.
4. "Best Places to Live in Santa Cruz, California." *bestplaces.net*. Best Places to Live and Retire, 2010. Web. Accessed 30 July 2012.
5. Gumz, Jondi. "Median Home Price in April: $479,600." *Santa Cruz Sentinel*, 6 April 2012. Web. Accessed 30 July 2012.
6. Dayton, Lily. "Live, Work, Create." *Santa Cruz Sentinel*, 31 May 2012, Art and Entertainment section. Print.
7. Scally, Patricia H. "Digital Technology Projects Already Thriving in Public Libraries." *Public Libraries*, January/February 1999; 38(1): 49.
8. Fox, Bette-Lee. "Design of the Times: a Field of 176 Public and Academic Building Projects Bears Fruit." *Library Journal*, 1 December 2011: 30+. *General OneFile*. Web. Accessed 27 July 2012.
9. "Santa Cruz (Calif.) Public Libraries, Scotts Valley Library." *american librariesmagazine.org*. American Libraries, 2012. Web. Accessed 30 July 2012.
10. Fox, B. "Design of the Times." *Library Journal*, 2011; 136(20): 30.
11. Young, Ann. "Reply: Three Questions." Message to the author, 6 June 2012. E-mail.

12. Fairchild, Kristen. "Great Route to Community Resources." *Santa Cruz Sentinel*, 4 December 2011, Guide: 5. Print.
13. "Best Places to Live in Santa Cruz, California." *bestplaces.net*. Best Places to Live and Retire, 2010. Web. Accessed 30 July 2012.
14. "Santa Cruz-Watsonville, California Unemployment." *deptofnumbers.com*. Department of Numbers, n.d. Web. Accessed 30 July 2012.
15. Fairchild, Kristen. "Great Route to Community Resources." *Santa Cruz Sentinel*, 4 December 2011, Guide: 5. Print.
16. Finkleday, Stella (cousin of Otto G. Kunitz). Minutes of the Meetings of the Santa Cruz Library Board of Trustees, 5 October 1937: 182. Print.
17. Swedberg, Donna. "Re: Question about Newspaper Clipping File." Message to the author, 19 October 2011. E-mail.
18. "SCPL Patron Comment or Suggestion: Local Ballot Measures." Message to Santa Cruz Public Libraries Contact Us, 17 October 2011. E-mail.

6

Shanghai Library: windows to the world

Abstract: This chapter reviews the history of Shanghai Library, the City of Shanghai and Xujiahui Library, one of the early Jesuit libraries in China. Also examined are Shanghai Library's attempt to bring the community of Shanghai to the world by hosting the biennial Shanghai International Library Forum, and developing Windows of Shanghai and active partnerships with the publishing world, both internal and external.

Key words: Xujiahui Library, William Jones Boone, Samuel Isaac Joseph Schereschewsky, Gail King, St. John's College, *North China Herald*, *Shen bao*, H. G. W. Woodhead, OPAC (Online Public Access Catalog) Shanghai Library, National Library of China, Shanghai International Library Forum, Window of Shanghai.

The opening of Shanghai

Since "Current importance thus called for a more careful analysis of the local past," which describes one main reason for H. H. Bancroft's recording and analyzing the history of California in his works, we may wish to examine, at least briefly, the history of Shanghai, where Shanghai Library is located. Situated on the east coast of China, the city of Shanghai boasts several major water routes and networks, such as its 16 international container ship routes, international ocean routes, coastal route, Yangtze River route, and river trade routes, and has ambitious plans to become an international shipping center in the foreseeable future. Because of its geographical advantages, Shanghai is one of the largest cultural, commercial, financial, and technological centers in China. It has undergone a tremendous transformation, especially with the total makeover in 1990 of its new Pudong area, east of the Huangpu River, which is characterized by its prosperity and cosmopolitanism.

Despite its prosperous and cosmopolitan status today, Shanghai has a surprisingly short history. The modern city was founded as one of the five Chinese trading ports in 1842, eight years before the birth of California as a state in the United States. In the early nineteenth century, Shanghai was a major domestic port for the transportation of cotton, silk, and fertilizers. The potential of the Huangpu River and the small walled city of Shanghai first attracted the notice of Hugh Lindsay, an agent of the East India Company, in 1832. The Treaty of Nanking (1842) forced Shanghai to open up as a modern international city, thus ending its chapter as a closed fishing and textile town. In 1843 the British settlement was established, and was soon joined by the American and French concessions. In 1854 the Shanghai Municipal Council was established to serve all three settlements. After the French concession withdrew from the arrangement in 1862, the British and American settlements joined forces in 1863 to become the Shanghai International Settlement, which was later joined by other European and Japanese settlements.

Long before the Shanghai International Settlement, European Protestant and Catholic missionaries saw endless potential for the conversion and education of China's vast population. As a matter of fact,

> Christian churches are known in Chinese as "Halls of Teaching"... jiaotang.... Apart from the Northern Beitang cathedral, which played host to the missionaries from the French province of the Society of Jesus, the following three "Halls" were of significance: the cathedrals of the South and East (... Nantang and ... Dongtang, founded in 1605 and in 1655, respectively) accommodating the Portuguese Jesuits and the Western cathedral ... Xitang, consecrated in 1701, where the missionaries of the Vatican were located.[1]

The establishment of St. John's College in Shanghai is another well-known example. It was founded in 1879 by William Jones Boone (1811–64), the first Anglican missionary bishop of Shanghai, and Samuel Isaac Joseph Schereschewsky (1831–1906), an Anglican bishop of Shanghai. In 1905, St. John's College was officially renamed as St. John's University, enjoying the same status as any American university in the United States. In 1907, it became the first institution in China to grant bachelor's degrees.

The Xujiahui Library: the first library in Shanghai

The scholar missionaries (or Jesuit missionaries) recognized the importance of libraries and books to their goal of slowly but surely establishing the gospel in China through the means of making friends among the scholar-officials and themselves becoming accepted as scholars and priests, and as scholars of both the Western and the Confucian traditions. One of their creations is the Xujiahui Library (or the Bibliotheca Zi-Ka-Wei), which became part of Shanghai Library in 1956. Gail King's *The Xujiahui (Zikawei) Library of Shanghai* provides the most detailed and exhaustive account of the history of mission libraries in China in general, and of the Xujiahui Library in particular, such as its founding, management, staff, and collections, its fate and functions after the last missionaries left Shanghai in 1952, and its foundational role in the shaping of today's Shanghai Library.

According to King, the first library of European books in China can be traced back to the first Jesuit mission in 1583–89, in Zhaoqing in Guangdong Province, where Fathers Matteo Ricci (1552–1610) and Michel Ruggieri (1543–1607) housed their collection of books. In 1620, the Jesuit Nicholas Trigault (1577–1628) returned from Europe to his residence in Beijing with a collection of the latest editions of scientific books. This collection was the beginning of the Beitang Library, the earliest Jesuit library in China. After 1949, when the People's Republic of China was declared, it was integrated into the holdings of the National Library of China.

The Xujiahui Library of the Catholic Church was established at the village of Xu Jiahui, five miles southwest of the city of Shanghai, in 1847, a period corresponding to the development of subscription libraries in California. Xujiahui was the ancestral home of Xu Guangqi (1562–1633), one of the Jesuits' most influential converts. As a Ming Dynasty court official, he gave strong support to the early Catholic Church in China and collaborated with Father Ricci and other priests to translate Western mathematical and scientific works into Chinese.

After the establishment of a seminary in 1843, and the making of plans to set up village schools in the Christian communities in the area, Father Claude Gotteland (1803–56), head of the mission, decided that as soon as the mission's new building was ready he would allocate space for a library to support both the missionaries' study and work and the local scholars' pursuit of learning. In March 1847, the Church purchased a plot of land in Xujiahui to build the Jesuit residence complex. The building work was completed by the end of July and the Jesuits moved to their new quarters. Three rooms were set aside for the new library. The Xujiahui Library was thus founded as the second Jesuit library in China and the first library in Shanghai, functioning mainly as a scholarly repository.

Several wings have been added to the building since 1847:

> The present structure is a conglomeration of a two-story north wing and a three-story south wing connected like a letter L, plus a three-story western extension later added to the rear of the south wing. The three-story south wing decorated with verandas on each floor was originally built in 1867 as the residence for the priests of the nearby cathedral, while the two-story north wing was added between 1896 and 1897. According to a still visible cornerstone written in French, the western extension was added in 1931.[2]

The two-story north wing, in the Portuguese style, served as stack rooms, with the Chinese-language section on the first floor and Western languages on the second floor.

Gail King made a systematic survey of the library's collection in 1935. At that time, the library had more than 100,000 titles in 200,000 volumes, of which 80,000 volumes were in European languages, making it the biggest library in Shanghai. According to collection updates provided by both Shanghai Library and shanghai-today.com, the library now has a collection of 560,000 items, comprised of books, periodicals, and newspapers in nearly 20 different languages, such as Latin, English, German, French, Japanese, Russian, Hebrew, Greek, etc. The collection is not only impressive in size but also rich in content, covering a range of disciplines such as philosophy, literature, history, politics, sociology, and religions. In addition, the library has kept thousands of local gazetteers of China, early and rare magazines, and complete runs of newspapers, such as China's first English-language newspaper, *North China Herald*, Shanghai's first newspaper, *Shen bao*, complete sets of the Shanghai Municipal Council Gazette and Municipal Reports, the China Yearbooks edited by H. G. W. Woodhead from 1913 to 1939, early Japanese-language documents, pre-1800 Western-language rare editions, and manuscripts of early mission-related writings by the Jesuit missionaries.

King also examined the library catalogs available at the Xujiahui Library. A catalog of the Chinese books in the library up to the 1930s has disappeared; a two-volume handwritten catalog of European books, its latest entry dated 1952, has survived. It lists about 25,000 titles in the library. Unfortunately, there is no catalog for the library's many archival materials.

In 1956, the Xujiahui Library became a branch of Shanghai Library, along with several other special libraries in Shanghai, such as the Royal Asiatic Society Library, Haiguang Library, and Shang Xian Tang Library (the International Institute of China). It was closed down in 1996 and stood derelict until restoration work began in 2002. In August 2003, the library was reopened as a new local landmark and a center for academic research and study. The newly renovated Xujiahui Library has a 200 square meter exhibition hall on the ground floor. The second floor has a public reading area with 30 seats and open-shelf reading services. Other services include an OPAC connected to Shanghai Library, photocopying, and reference desk.[3]

The Shanghai Library

The Shanghai Library opened at 325 Nan Jing Xi Lu (Nanjing Road West) on 22 July 1952, following a citywide campaign in 1950 by the Shanghai Cultural Heritage Managing Committee to collect donations of books for a new municipal library. By the time of its grand opening, Shanghai Library had a collection of 700,000 volumes, of which 200,000 were gifts from citizens, including scholars and celebrities. In October 1958 the Shanghai Library was merged with the Shanghai Municipal Library of Science and Technology, the Shanghai Municipal Library of Historical Documents, and the Shanghai Newspaper Library. Following these mergers, the Shanghai Library was China's largest public library, and the second-largest library in China after the National Library of China in Beijing.

To begin with, the Shanghai Library was located on the site of the former Racecourse Building and had a floor space of 30,000 square meters and 150 employees. With the rapid increase of its holdings, the library outgrew its accommodation in the 1970s. Plans were made for a new library building at 1555 Huai Hai Zhong Lu (Central Huai Hai Road) and the foundation stone was laid on 1 September 1993. The new building was opened to the public in 1996. It is a Shanghai landmark, built in the shape of a pyramid composed of cubic blocks to symbolize the solid foundation of the cultural heritage and the human pursuit of

Figure 35   The pyramid-shaped structure of Shanghai Library, 2006

Source: P8180231.v3c.jpg. Courtesy of Titangos Photography Studio.

knowledge. The library covers an area of 83,000 square meters and houses approximately 50 million items. Its conference center holds international arts and scientific exhibitions and seminars all year round.[4]

The library provides services to the general public, businesses, and government departments. It maintains the Union Catalog of Chinese Books, publishes its own reference books, provides professional training to smaller libraries, and has outreach programs such as interlibrary loan, exhibitions, book discussions, and seminars. The Shanghai Library and the Institute of Scientific and Technical Information of Shanghai were joined together in October 1995, in a pioneering merger of public library services with special services to the scientific, technological, industrial, and information research communities. The combined resources and collections of the enlarged library serve the general public, academia, and the government.

Initiated at the end of 2000 and officially inaugurated in 2001, Shanghai Central Library System consists of a central library (Shanghai Library), branch libraries (district public libraries, academic libraries, and special libraries), and neighborhood service points. It is a new type of library model, enabled by the internet, with knowledge navigation as its motivation and resource sharing as its mission. By working closely together, the branch libraries have succeeded in extending their services to all the districts, counties, and communities of Shanghai.

Figure 36   **Approaching the entrance of Shanghai Library, 2006**

Source: P8170131.v3c.jpg. Courtesy of Titangos Photography Studio.

Figure 37   **An interior courtyard of Shanghai Library, 2006**

Source: P8170118.v3c.jpg. Courtesy of Titangos Photography Studio.

On 28 December 2010, a symposium was held to review a decade of development of the Shanghai Central Library System. To date, millions of readers' cards have been issued and there is an annual growth rate of 20 percent in book and document circulation. The system provides Shanghai residents with convenient access to neighborhood libraries.

Since 2 June 2001, when the first four branch libraries were dedicated in Huangpu District, Jingan District, Nanhui County, and Shanghai Conservatory of Music Library, the system has now 261 participating libraries and six service models: one-card-through service (user's card valid for all 261 libraries), e-card service, collaborative online reference service, "online entrusted loans," interlibrary loans, and public lectures.[5]

Figure 38   Another interior view of Shanghai Library, 2006

Source: P8170113.v3c.jpg. Courtesy of Titangos Photography Studio.

Shanghai International Library Forum (SILF)

One of the key elements in the success of the Shanghai Library is the stability of the administrative, personnel, and financial structures of the participating libraries. Dr. Wu Jianzhong has been the director since 2002. Fluent in Chinese, English, and Japanese, Dr. Wu graduated with a BA in Japanese Studies in 1978, and MA in Library Science in 1982, both from East China Normal University, and a PhD in Library Science from the University of Wales (Aberystwyth, UK) in 1992. Under the leadership of Dr. Wu, Shanghai Library has been promoting itself as a new leader in the twenty-first century. Since 2002 it has hosted five international library conferences, namely, the SILF, a biennial international event aimed at promoting professional and academic exchange among librarians and information professionals from around the world.

The first SILF (15–18 July 2002) focused on four major subject areas: knowledge management, reference services, interlibrary cooperation, and digitization. More than 100 delegates from 12 countries attended the forum. Seventy-seven papers were published in the 2002 Proceedings and 53 library and information professionals presented papers at the meeting.

The second SILF (12–16 October 2004) was on the theme of City Development and Library Services, with four sub-themes: the library and lifelong education; reference service and research; the library and city's knowledge infrastructure; and the library and the World Expo. Eighty papers and 25 abstracts were published in the 2004 *Proceedings*.

The third SILF (17–19 August 2006) was on the main topic of Management Innovation and Library Services and the subtopics were corporate culture; marketing and promotion; crisis management; performance measurement; and user services. More than 300 library professionals and specialists attended from 28 countries. Seventy-five papers were presented at the conference.

The fourth SILF (20–22 October 2008) had Intelligence, Innovation and Library Services as its main theme and the sub-themes were library and information services in the digital age; Library 2.0 and Web 2.0; core competences of the library and its professional future; the digital gap and the responsibilities of the library; and the digital library and cyberinfrastructure. The conference registered 124 delegates from 20 countries.

The fifth SILF (24–27 August 2010) was a collaboration between Shanghai Library and Hangzhou Public Library. It coincided with the World Expo 2010 in Shanghai and echoed the expo theme of Better City,

Better Life. More than 200 scholars and experts from 26 countries and regions attended the conference and contributed over 100 papers. Forty-six presenters explored topics in the sub-themes of libraries and multicultural service; libraries and community well-being; library performance evaluation; library support for innovation and strategic decisions; and library service in the cloud computing era.

The sixth SILF (17–19 July 2012) had Smart City and Library Service as its main theme. Focusing on the latest progress and future trends related to the theme, the forum encouraged dialogue in the following areas: the library as an infrastructure for research and learning; the coming of the new integrated library system: supporting cloud computing and mobile services; enabling librarians to proliferate digital reading and preserve digital memories; management and performance evaluation of the hybrid library; library technical service with semantic technologies; and the core values and competitiveness of the physical library in an omni-media age.

Reviewing these conferences, one can clearly see what an important stride the Shanghai Library has achieved through its active partnership with international, national, and local publishers. The printed and online proceedings, scholarly research papers, and presentations have enabled SILF to fulfill its aim of promoting worldwide professional and academic exchange among librarians and information professionals. Shanghai Library has been seeking partnerships not only with publishers and journals such as *Library Management* (first to fifth SILFs), *Libri* (sixth SILF), and *Chinese Librarianship*, but also with the government, the tourism sector, and international professional organizations such as the International Federation of Library Associations and Institutions and the Chinese American Librarian Association.

The Window of Shanghai (WoS)

WoS is a book donation program initiated by Shanghai Library in 2002 that goes beyond simple book exchanges by establishing libraries in Shanghai's sister cities. As part of the China Book International Project (*http://www.cbi.gov.cn/wisework/content/10005.html*), WoS aims to bring Chinese history and culture to the world, in partnership with leading publishing houses and libraries in China such as the National Library of China, the Library of the Chinese Social Academy, Peking University Library, Shanghai Library, and other libraries at various levels and of various types. The program is known for its three main goals, namely,

A) To help overseas Chinese to maintain a close link with their motherland, its language and culture;

B) To meet the world's desire to learn more and better about China and Shanghai by providing the latest Chinese publications;

C) To promote Shanghai Library itself internationally and serve as a foundation for its other cooperation with overseas counterparts.[6]

Publications on a variety of subjects are available, ranging from the arts, economics, people, philosophy, literature, culture, folk traditions, and history to nature, cooking, traditional Chinese medicine, and the architecture of ancient and contemporary Shanghai and China. Most of them are published in either Chinese or English or both; other languages are French, German, Russian, Spanish, Portuguese, Japanese, Korean, Turkish, and Vietnamese. By the end of April 2012, WoS had donated more than 40,000 books to 80 participating institutions in 48 countries and regions in Africa, Asia, Europe, North and South America, and Oceania. The goal of Shanghai Library's development strategy is to achieve 100 WoS libraries worldwide by 2015. Featured partners of the strategy include Andrei Saguna University Library; Biblioteca Argentina Dr. Juan Alvarez; Biblioteca Pública del Estado de Jalisco Juan José Arreola; Bibliotheek Rotterdam; Bibliothèques de Montreal; China Cultural Center in Paris; Cleveland Public Library; Atatürk Library; Biblioteca de Nacional Jose Marti; Biblioteca Sormani; Bibliothèque municipale de Lyon; Bücherhallen Hamburg; City Library of Salzburg; and the Confucius Institute for Scotland in the University of Edinburgh.

WoS functions in the following way: the period of cooperation typically lasts for three years, with 500 books in the first batch of donations and 100 titles per year for the next two years, so as to establish a continuous and consistent flow of literature to the partnership library. The program itself is free; however, prospective partners should observe five conditions, namely:

A) Partners should make the books catalogued properly and searchable online.

B) Partners should centralize all the books on the same open stacks with visible signs acknowledging the donation.

C) Partners should provide full and free access to the donated books for readers;

D) Partners are expected to launch promotions to provide the public with knowledge of the books, through opening ceremonies, pamphlets, library news and so forth;

E) Partners are expected to send feedback information to Shanghai Library for the latter to modify the scope of supplementary [gifts] in the following years.[7]

WoS is a successful initiative for bringing a local community to the world, for "The 'Window of Shanghai' has also been playing an active role in the foreign exchange activities of the Shanghai Municipality, attracting numerous media coverage and warmly greeted as 'a bridge of friendship' that 'not only delivers knowledge and wisdom but symbolizes friendship.'"[8] Today, WoS has its own website, which also operates as a link with the Shanghai Library website: *http://windowofshanghai.library.sh.cn/*. The website functions both as a platform for managing WoS's book donations and as a gateway to introduce its selected resources, services, and partners. News about WoS has been archived since September 2004.

Notes

1. Laamann, Lars. "The Current State of the Beitang Collection. Report from a Fact-finding Mission to the National Library of China." *easl.org*. BEASL (9). European Association of Sinological Librarians, n.d. Web. Accessed 30 July 2012.
2. "The Bibliotheca Zi-ka-wei (the Xujiahui Library)." *shanghai-today.com*. Shanghai-Today.com, n.d. Web. Accessed 30 July 2012. (*http://www.shanghai-today.com/attractiondetails/print.asp?pid=12201111320*).
3. "The Bibliotheca Zi-Ka-Wei (The Xujiahui Library)." *library.sh.cn*. Shanghai Library, n.d. Web. Accessed 30 July 2012. (*http://www.library.sh.cn/Web/news/20101213/n1139775.html*).
4. "Brief History1." *library.sh.cn*. Shanghai Library, n.d. Web. Accessed 30 July 2012.
5. "Central Library System Experienced a Decade's Development." *library.sh.cn*. Shanghai Library, n.d. Web. Accessed 30 July 2012.
6. "FAQ – What Are the Purposes of the Program?" *library.sh.cn*. Shanghai Library, n.d. Web. Accessed 30 July 2012.
7. "FAQ – What Obligations Should a Partner Have?" *library.sh.cn*. Shanghai Library, n.d. Web. Accessed 30 July 2012.
8. "Profile." *library.sh.cn*. Shanghai Library, n.d. Web. Accessed 30 July 2012.

Oslo Public Library: digital efforts

Abstract: This chapter reviews the history of Oslo Public Library (Deichmanske bibliotek), the first public library in Oslo. A comparison is made between its funding system during its first 92 years and that of early public libraries in the United States. Also discussed are a number of early digital projects, the system-wide digital reference service, and innovations in the management of the library's Music Department.

Key words: Carl Deichman, Oslo Public Library, Deichman Digital Workshop (Deichmans Digitale Verksted), Kinoteket (Cinematheque), LåtLån (Borrow a Tune), Sentinel eDialog 24, SMS (Short Message Service) Bergen Public Library, Phonofile, nontraditional library services, Music Department.

History

OPL, formerly known as the Deichman Library, is the first public library in Oslo, Norway. Its history is summarized visually in a set of 48 photographs available on its Flickr site (*http://www.flickr.com/photos/deichmanske/6328695090/*). The library was established on 12 January 1785 following the bequest of a collection of manuscripts and approximately 6000 books from the estate of Chancellor Carl Deichman (1705–80).

As with the growth of any library, it has gone through many moves, from one building to another across the city, in order to accommodate its growing collections and correspondingly growing staff. When the library was first opened it was located at Rådhusgaten 13 in Oslo. Over the course of 109 years it moved 11 times, averaging approximately one move every 11 years (it managed to remain in Kristian IV Street for 39 years, from 1894 to 1933). Today it is on the move again, as its collections and current level of activity have outgrown the 1930s library building. Plans are in the works for a new central library in the vicinity of the Oslo fjord and City Hall, to be opened in 2017. In addition to traditional onsite library services, the new library aims to provide a 24/7 library and web-based services.

During its first 92 years OPL was publicly owned, but had no formal public funding to support it – a situation similar to the challenge faced by American public libraries in the middle of the nineteenth century, when the tax-supported institution was just beginning in New England. Like its American counterparts, OPL was, in effect, a social library for the community, depending on private resources for support. The two original and distinct sources of finance, proprietary capital investment and the subscription associations, became blurred in the mid-nineteenth century. The reason for this, as Ray E. Held believes,[1] lay in the fact that these early organizations were attempting to expand their services to more members in their communities, so as to gain a broader base of financial support, until they became unsustainable and had to be supported as tax-based institutions. From 1877, the OPL had a formal place in the city budget, with funding for book purchases, rent, and salaries.

As Norway's largest public library, with approximately 300 employees, OPL serves the county of Oslo, including individuals, institutions, the public school system, university faculty and students, the business community, and government agencies. In addition to six branch libraries and one main library, it has several special departments, such as the Multilingual Library with a collection in 35 languages, the Music Department, and the Children and Youth Department.

OPL is one of the pioneering libraries in promoting nontraditional library services to anticipate and meet the needs of its twenty-first-century users. At the beginning of the new millennium it completed three notable projects, namely, the Deichman Digital Workshop, Kinoteket, and Traditional Library Services in Digital Form. Recently, it has initiated the Pode Project, a ground-breaking project to enhance and revive the online library catalog. We will discuss the Pode Project in more detail in Part 3.

The Deichman Digital Workshop (Deichmans Digitale Verksted)

Financed by the Research Council of Norway, the Deichman Digital Workshop cooperated with Sony and Apple to support broadband-based services in the public sector. It developed three fully equipped studios for media production, communication, and live presentation. Situated in three different locations across Oslo, the studios were interconnected by a fiber-optical network, and had professional working environments equipped with theater lighting systems, projection equipment, and public address loudspeakers, so as to create an optimal experience for the audience.

The Digital Workshop encouraged its users to create productions in the studio and to give presentations at the end of their period of study. Lecturers, writers, actors, artists, and other users could perform or discuss their works. These events were broadcast live on the web, with advance announcements. The broadcasts were later added to OPL's media archives and made accessible through its website, where students and other interested users can retrieve them for school work and research.

The workshop aimed to stimulate efforts to educate library users in media literacy, including both specialized concepts and straightforward software training in the use of packages such as Photoshop and video-editing software. The workshops were taught by in-house specialists and guest lecturers. All of the facilities, equipment, and tutorials were provided as free services to the general public. Reinert Mithassel, the project manager, recalls that not a single piece of equipment was broken or stolen during the two years that the workshop was offered. The studios were prototypes for the planning of future library services, as well as showcases to inspire other libraries to take up nontraditional services as they work on defining new roles for the library.[2]

Kinoteket (Cinematheque)

In 2004, in collaboration with the Norwegian Film Institute, OPL initiated the Kinoteket project to establish a video-on-demand-based movie service to present the Norwegian film heritage to library users. The project was based on a commercial pay-per-view service via the internet, originally developed by the Norwegian Film Institute and Norgesfilm (Film Archive). The two organizations handled content, copyrights, and technical solutions. Participating libraries paid a set monthly fee to gain unlimited access to the archive. For end-users, the service functioned in the style of a DVD player. The central video-server was located at the main branch and supplied the same content to the four branches via a fiber-optical network. In addition to the five viewing locations, users could access content in the reception areas of the library branches, where plasmascreens and wireless headphones were provided.

The library experimented with promoting other library materials and pushing forward the development of the City of Oslo's Metropolitan Area Network. According to Olav Celius, project coordinator, the goal of this project was to establish a framework for handling and distributing digital media within the library, and in a broader context than the film archive. The main challenges were issues such as copyright, standards, and commercial incentives, and for these reasons Celius and his staff did not limit themselves to any particular media, format or supplier, but wanted to expand the service as new media or technologies became available. With foresight, they kept their service strictly web-based, as this was where the most interesting developments were taking place, and where the most efforts have been made to work on standards and services.[3]

Traditional library services in digital form

LåtLån (Borrow a Tune), an electronic lending service

On 1 March 2004, OPL inaugurated its collaborative project with the Bergen Public Library (Bergen Offentlige Bibliotek) and Phonofile, a Norwegian digital music archive and central distribution point for audio files. The project was financed by a grant from ABM-utvikling, the Norwegian Authority for Archives, Libraries and Museums.

The Phonofile database held more than 50,000 titles recorded by independent Norwegian record companies and covering music from hip-hop and electronic to traditional folk, jazz, rock, heavy metal, classical, and contemporary. Loans were made by streaming content to the user's computer. Streaming, rather than downloading, was used so as to avoid running into legal and financial problems. "In effect, 'loan' consisted of a listening experience. Each file a user began to listen to is registered in the system's statistics module as a loan, and when the file finished playing, the transaction was complete, and the file could be said to be 'returned'."[4]

Users of LåtLån must be registered library users, but applications needed to be made in person. The library staff cheerfully recollected that for a time there were long queues for the issue of library cards. The lending scheme attracted new user groups who had never given a second thought to the public library system. In the first four months of the trial period, OPL had over 4000 unique visitors in a city of a half million.

More than 15,000 unique tracks were streamed. Owing to a lack of continuing funding, the project was discontinued at the end of 2004. However, a new plan is in the works to reorganize and redesign a model based on simultaneous licenses, similar to the electronic periodicals loan system. The LåtLån model has been taken up by libraries in Sweden and Denmark, both of which have similar services.

Digital reference service

As well as the LåtLån pilot project, OPL used software called Sentinel eDialog 24 to run its digital reference service. It combined three kinds of digital communication, namely, online librarians could confer among themselves, see other online partners, and refer specific questions to appropriate colleagues. Various questions were classified for future reference, which was welcomed by both library staff and users. In 2005 alone, OPL received 5966 email reference inquiries, 3591 SMS (Short Message Service) messages, and 13,452 online chats.

Such success in nontraditional library services is by no means accidental. Ann Kunish, head of OPL's Music Department, is an example of the twenty-first-century library professional. After graduating from the University of Wisconsin-Madison with a bachelor's degree in music (French horn), she went to Norway for a year to study under a well-known horn teacher at the Norwegian Academy of Music. After earning her master's degree at the Music Academy, she played with various national music organizations, such as the Norwegian Opera, the Oslo Philharmonic, and Norwegian Radio Orchestra. Having been a performer, teacher, and organizer of band seminars, Kunish finally sold her horn. Since the end of 1999 she has been employed as head of the Music Department at OPL. Her hiring was an experiment of sorts, for it was the first time that the position of department head had been given to a music scholar rather than to a librarian with formal library school education. However, the experiment has proven successful. Kunish has been heading the projects entailing both circulation (LåtLån) and reference services (Sentinel eDialog 24) in digital format. Staffed with 10 people, the Music Department is popular both within and outside OPL and makes about 190,000 loans per year. In her "Why Does the Public Library Need a Music Department?" Kunish points out that the average Norwegian relates to music in some form or other in his or her life, be it classical, ethnic, techno, or other genres, and this constitutes the library's mission to provide a music-loving population with recordings, books, sheet music, video/DVDs, and information relevant to the genres that patrons wish to explore and enjoy. In addition, she emphasizes the reason why personnel qualified in music are needed in the Music Department:

> Our department's material is available because the library has personnel qualified to choose, purchase and organize it. Simply providing material for circulation is not, however, enough; qualified reference personnel must be available to present, explain and recommend. This service includes answering patrons' questions and presenting material that widens their musical/cultural horizons. Good presentation can create interest in the culture of other ethnic groups, which in turn is a valuable contribution to integration and tolerance. Through the librarian–patron interaction, patrons can also find that "high-brow" culture is more accessible than they might have thought, and that popular culture is not only for the young.[5]

Both Kunish's viewpoint on qualified personnel and OPL's appointment of a music academic as the head of the Music Department have found an echo in two instances: Archibald Macleish (1892–1982), Librarian of Congress, and Herbert Ingram Priestley (1875–1944), Librarian of the Bancroft Library. As a matter of fact, the Bancroft is often headed by professors specialized in history and areas studies.

Notes

1. Held, Ray E. *The Rise of the Public Libraries in California.* Chicago: American Library Association, c1973. 18. Print.
2. Mithassel, Reinert. (via annk@deichman.no). "Re: Contact and Other Info Please." Message to the author. 25 September 2006. E-mail.
3. Celius, Olav. (via annk@deichman.no). "Re: Contact and Other Info Please: New ways of presenting and distributing cultural heritage." Message to the author. 25 September 2006. E-mail.
4. Kunish, Ann. "LåtLån: Circulating Digital Music Files via the Public Library." *ifla.org.* International Federation of Library Associations and Institutions, 15 July 2005. Web. Accessed 30 July 2012.
5. Kunish, Ann. "Why Does the Public Library Need a Music Department, and Why Should It Continue to Be Federally Funded?" *iasa-web.org.* International Association of Sound and Audiovisual Archives, 2004. Web. Accessed 30 July 2012.

Part 3
Present: Library 2.0

In spite of the differing views on the idea of Library 2.0, library professionals have more or less reached a consensus. Woody Evans points out that the idea of a "Library 2.0" is recent, and that it is simply a portmanteau term composed of *library* and *Web 2.0*. The idea is to apply Web 2.0 tools and values to library collections, library catalogs, and library services as a whole. He thinks that there are three predominant themes of Web 2.0:[1]

- participation, which guarantees two or more ways of communication
- tagging, which is an informal system for categorizing information objects, including files, photos, music, videos, etc.
- syndication, like RSS, to bring the web to users.

According to Tone Moseid, of the Norwegian Archive, Library 1.0 is based on the values of democracy, and "Ultimately, the Library 2.0 model for services is replacing traditional, one-directional offerings that have characterized Library 1.0. Library services will be constantly updated and re-evaluated to serve the patrons best."[2]

In her article "To a Temporary Place in Time ..."[3] Dr. Wendy Schultz defines in detail the difference between Library 1.0 and Library 2.0. According to Schultz, Library 1.0 is all about commodity. Libraries from Alexandria to the industrial era treat books as commodities: they collect, inventory, categorize, and house them within libraries. In Library 1.0, libraries represent a resource base, contributing to educating the labor force, to supporting innovation processes that fuel growth, and to informing the present and the future – whether in the neighborhood, in academia, or in business. In contrast, Library 2.0 is about product. A new mission for commodity-oriented libraries is to package their commodities, i.e., their books, as products in an environment that disintermediates, dematerializes, and decentralizes. One of the characteristics of the emerging information infrastructure is to make the library – everywhere – barrier-free and participatory. Schultz calls for a new collaboration with online book/media sites such as Amazon to provide digital downloads of books, to create a globally accessible catalog, and to invite readers to tag and comment. In a participatory environment, Schultz defines a new role for libraries: when more information becomes more accessible, people will need experienced guidance from libraries even more than ever, for Amazon's customer recommendations are notoriously open to manipulation; tag clouds offer diverse connections, not focused expertise.

The following comparison from Tim O'Reilly's website reveals some of the specific differences between Web 1.0 and Web 2.0.[4]

Web 1.0	Web 2.0
DoubleClick	Google AdSense
Ofoto	Flickr
Akamai	BitTorrent
mp3.com	Napster
Britannica Online	Wikipedia
personal websites	blogging
evite	upcoming.org and EVDB
domain name speculation	search engine optimization
page views	cost per click
screen scraping	web services
publishing	participation
content management systems	wikis
directories (taxonomy)	tagging ("folksonomy")
stickiness	syndication

Notes

1. Evans, Woody. *Building Library 3.0: Issues in Creating a Culture of Participation.* Cambridge, UK: Chandos Publishing, 2009. 3–12. Print.
2. Moseid, Tone. "Library 1.0 – Library 2.0 – Library 3.0." *Scandinavian Public Library Quarterly* 41(2), 2008 (*http://www.splq.info/issues/vol41_2/01.htm*) Accessed 10 October 2012.

3. Schultz, Wendy. "To a temporary place in time ..." *NextSpace* 2 (2006): n. page. Web. Accessed 30 July 2012. (*http://www.oclc.org/nextspace/002/6.htm*).

4. O'Reilly, Tim. "What Is Web 2.0: Design Patterns and Business Models for the Next Generation of Software." oreilly.com. O'Reilly Media, Inc., 30 September 2005. Web. Accessed 30 July 2012.

8

Santa Cruz Public Library: learning and using Library 2.0

Abstract: This chapter introduces a series of innovative library programs and services offered by SCPL in its efforts to bring a local community to the world in the era of Library 2.0. Included are its attendance at international conferences, and 23 Things @SCPL – a learning Library 2.0 program – and its effects on staff members and future library services.

Key words: language learning collection, cassettes, CDs, downloadable e-audiobooks, OneClickdigital, Library 2.0, 23 Things, blog, wiki.

In the past, SCPL relied on traditional methods for introducing its library services, programs and local community to the world. Those traditional methods include creating a library home page and attending regional and national conferences such as the Monterey Bay Area Cooperative Library System (*http://www.mobac.org/*), the Internet Librarian (*http://www. infotoday.com*), the Califa Library Group (*http://califa.org/*), the California Library Association, the American Library Association (ALA), and the Public Library Association (a division of ALA). In 2006 this regional awareness was dramatically elevated when, for the first time, the region was represented at an international conference, namely, SILF. SCPL was invited to participate in SILF in 2006, 2008, and 2010, systematically introducing to the world the community of Santa Cruz County and its library professionals, through the presentation and publication of three conference papers.

Introducing a local community

The SCPL was represented at the third SILF (2006) and presented a paper entitled "Language Learning Resources at Santa Cruz Public Libraries: An

Examination of User Services." This was published, along with 84 other papers, in the *Proceedings of the Third Shanghai International Library Forum*.[1] Taking an original research approach, the author presented the community of Santa Cruz County, one of California's 58 counties, by looking at the SCPL's development of a language-learning collection in audio format. The community of Santa Cruz County has a high concentration of artists and daily commuters to Silicon Valley. The high level of educational attainment among the residents (37.3 percent with a bachelor's degree or higher, as compared to 30.1 percent in California as a whole)[2] and their professional and personal language-learning requirements have presented a great challenge to local public libraries and their ever-shrinking library material budgets. Language learning presents multiple challenges, with language categories including major African, South and North American, Asian and European languages, as well as English as a second language.

The author of the conference paper examines how a well-rounded language study collection has been developed, modified, and maintained in different languages, formats, and levels to reflect users' changing needs. Four main areas are discussed: (1) language-learning trends and technologies; (2) maintenance of language resources, and options for replacement so as to reduce the cost of damaged/lost items; (3) essential networks with branch staff, vendors, and other government agencies, so as to provide effective and efficient services to meet users' specific needs; (4) Friends of the Santa Cruz Public Libraries book fund drives. The high level of user demand is met to a satisfactory degree, despite the small operating budget and reduction of funding in some lean years.

Anticipating and keeping abreast of user trends and new technologies is a constant challenge for library professionals. The SCPL's experience in relation to language-learning materials is described in the following sections.

Peak season vs. slow season

The circulation statistics for all media at SCPL[3] indicate that the peak season is the month of December (Table 8.1).

However, the circulation of language resources does not fit into this statistical pattern. On the contrary, November and December are the slowest months for usage of the language collection. The circulation statistics show that June is consistently the busiest month for language learners (Table 8.2). Table 8.2 indicates strongly that summer is a peak language-learning season for SCPL users. The staff need to get the language resources ready for circulation before June arrives.

Table 8.1 All non-book media circulation

Fiscal year	Month	Percentage of all media
2005–6	December	35.70
2004–5	June	32.01
2004–5	December	35.68
2003–4	June	34.87
2003–4	December	37.95
2002–3	June	33.98
2002–3	December	35.08

Table 8.2 Language resources circulation

Fiscal year	Month	CD (number of circulations)	Cassette (number of circulations)
2005–6	December	182	219
2004–5	June	199	348
2004–5	December	111	252
2003–4	June	128	371
2003–4	December	91	258

Audio resources vs. print resources

A prominent trend among today's users is a preference for audio resources over print resources such as textbooks, grammar books, etc. for language learning. For the majority of these users, their main purpose in learning a language is to acquire basic skills for work, travel, or holidays in their destination countries. To meet this need, SCPL makes heavy use of publishers such as Recorded Books, Books on Tape and Barron's Educational Series for two reasons: (1) Recorded Books has taken over many Pimsleur titles from Simon & Schuster (S&S), the former distributor. The Pimsleur system is characterized by its bookless teaching philosophy, with a great emphasis on oral drills; (2) unlike the original Pimsleur products, which were packaged as series of 16 CDs or cassettes in one large box, Recorded Books breaks a series into two parts, eight lessons per part, thus making the course of lessons very convenient to carry and to use. This is very practical for users, as the circulation period is just two weeks, plus one week's grace period (three weeks, with no grace period, as of 2011). To cover 16 lessons in 21 days would be quite impractical for the average language learner.

Audio cassettes vs. CDs

Cassettes are more durable than CDs. A cassette commonly has a life-span of 200 circulations; but a CD rarely circulates half that number of times. However, the demand for language CDs has been increasing steadily, as Table 8.2 shows. This is partly because cassette players are disappearing from today's home electronics market and also it is increasingly rare for users to own simple cassette tape players. This is partly because of the availability of CD players in automobiles, in the home, or in personal computers, but it is largely due to generational factors. The language learners tend to be much younger than those library users who want to listen to fiction/nonfiction on cassette. Their lives are busier and more mobile. They like to pursue their language studies while commuting, traveling, or at work, unlike the older users, who often are either relatively homebound or just feel uncomfortable handling CDs.

CDs vs. downloadable e-audiobooks

In theory, SCPL users can renew an item up to four times, provided that there is no waiting list for it. But for a popular language CD there is always a waiting list, thus rendering the renewal option unavailable. Today SCPL has more than 100 Pimsleur titles, more than half of which are CDs, and despite the library's purchasing efforts, it is difficult to satisfy the users' needs. For any popular language, such as Spanish, Italian, or Chinese Mandarin, there is a waiting list of at least five for checked-out items.

Even though library services are free, there is always a price, invisible to the casual observer. Dr. Michael Buckland identifies four elements in the unseen price that library users pay, namely, time, monetary cost, effort, and discomfort. His concept of time spent on delay as an expression of price is very pertinent to this case: "Other things being equal, sooner is better than later for anything one wants to have ... One prefers not to have to expend the time or incur the delay to get the service."[4] Dr. Nancy van House has conducted a detailed study on time as a cost in the use of library services.[5]

To reduce the cost of time delays to its users, SCPL embraced a new format: downloadable Pimsleur language e-audiobooks, produced by Recorded Books via Netlibrary (now operated independently as digital copies in its OneClickdigital (*http://recordedbooks.com/index.cfm? fuseaction=rb.ocd*)). The new format provides a technical solution to some of the problems that had plagued SCPL for years. First of all, a significant feature of e-audiobooks is the fact that there is no limit on simultaneous usage once the library has purchased a copy or copies of a particular title. In other words, users do not have to wait for the title they are interested in. They can check out a popular title for a loan period of 21 days and renew it once. After the due date, the encrypted data will become inaccessible. If users still need an item, they can check the title out again. Second, the format is very mobile. Users can transfer the data to their computers or any device that reads Windows Media Audio. This includes MP3 players and mobile phones.[6] Via an FM transmitter, users can study foreign languages in their home, office, or car. The ability to utilize language resources in users' automobiles, especially now, when more and more new vehicles are MP3 format-ready is a great advantage. It is illegal to use headphones while driving in the state of California, so in older vehicles a miniature FM transmitter linking the device to the car radio is an elegant solution. Third, but not the least significant, unlike language CDs, e-audiobooks do not need to be physically maintained – something that is a constant headache for media librarians.

Downloadable e-audiobooks are just another technology. Any technology improves with time and usage, if demand and supply render it sustainable. Today most libraries in the US subscribe to one or both of two major platforms, namely, Overdrive and OneClickdigital. However, these are not 100 percent perfect, and of course they are still subject to change and to replacement by future, newer technologies. For instance, Overdrive users are often faced with technical problems of either a software or hardware nature, due to Overdrive's ambitious plan to accommodate both PC and Mac, both e-books and e-audios, plus a multitude of formats and e-readers, and its lack of timely technical support.

Learning Library 2.0: 23 Things @SCPL

At the fourth SILF (2008) SCPL was invited to present a paper entitled "Learning Library 2.0: 23 Things @SCPL," a newly released staff training program for Library 2.0 based on Web 2.0. The 23 Things program manager collaborated with the author to write a working paper, which was published in the *Proceedings of the Fourth Shanghai International Library Forum*.[7] A revised version of the paper was published the following year by *Library Management*.[8] Since its publication, the revised paper has been cited by professionals and academics in the field of library and information science in countries such as Australia, Canada, Croatia, Greece, India, Indonesia, Ireland, South Korea, Taiwan, the United Kingdom, and the United States.

In 2007, the library management set "Familiarization with emerging technologies" as a goal for all library staff. To that end, it decided to implement the 23 Things learning program designed by Helene Blowers, former technology director of the Public Library of Charlotte and Mecklenburg County (PLCMC), North Carolina. Implementation of the program was assigned to the Staff Development Office (SDO). In collaboration with Network Access Services (NAS; now Library Information Technology), 23 Things @SCPL, a Learning Library 2.0 Project, was launched on 17 September 2007. The objectives included:

1. Encourage exploration of new technologies and Web 2.0;

2. Provide staff with new tools (that are freely available on the internet) to better support SCPL's mission: helping community residents meet their personal, educational, cultural, and professional information needs;

3. Reward staff for taking the initiative to complete 23 self-discovery exercises; and

4. Offer an opportunity for staff to discover, play, and learn!

23 Things @SCPL is also the largest computer-technology training project in the history of SCPL. It has changed the staff's way of thinking and working in the twenty-first century. Voluntary by nature, and open to all regular employees, it was taken up by more than two-thirds of the staff. A total of 98 out of 136 staff members signed up for the program while it was active, from 17 September 2007 through 18 January 2008.

Learning wikis and blogs

Learning a paradoxical pair of Web 2.0 applications, wiki and blog, is one of the very first exercises on the 23 Things curriculum. "A blog is very creator-centric; readers share comments, but the author controls and directs content. A wiki, by comparison, is a free-for-all where content is shaped by anyone with editing rights."[9] The introductory exercises not only ensured a good beginning for 23 Things @SCPL, but also helped all participants to gain a preliminary understanding of the difference between wikis and blogs.

Wiki

Prior to the project, any web applications were dealt with by the webmaster and other NAS staff. Staff members' knowledge of wikis went only as far as Wikipedia. When they started the 23 Things program, however, they experienced a profound change: SDO structured the program by setting up a staff wiki which enabled users to sign up for the program and to register their personally created blogs in which they documented their progress through the program. In other words, all sign-ups, notifications, exercise tracking, and tutorials were exclusively conducted in the environment of PBwiki (*http://pbwiki.com*). Owing to this full and early exposure to one of the Library 2.0 applications, participants found it quite natural to dip their toes in the water and start to swim in the sea of 2.0. Today, wikis are widely used in the daily work of the library staff, for example, in discussions on the introduction of AquaBrowser (SCPL Staff Development AquaBrowser, 2007) and for tutorials on the system-wide upgrading of DVD cases by the Processing Department.

Blog

Weblogs made their first appearance as early as 1997 (*http://www.blog. com/*). Users soon began to utilize blogs to share and publish their opinions and experiences. Prior to the 23 Things @SCPL program, there were two blogs in the whole SCPL system, one operated by the Children's Department and the other by the Adult Reference Department. For some reason, they never blossomed, and only a few librarians blogged, although invitations were sent out on many occasions. As a result of the 23 Things program, blogging mushroomed throughout the library system, with bloggers ranging from level IV librarians to library clerks. A total of 72 personal blogs have been created, at the time of writing averaging 22 entries each. Encouraged by the gradual but systematic pace of the curriculum, staff members began to tackle Blogger, creating accounts, writing and publishing posts on their weekly assignments, and gradually learning to insert live links, images, audio, and video. Assisted by the tutorial sessions, they learned how to create, design, and manage blogs. They not only customized their blogs and profiles but also added new authors and page elements. To further explore the social networking aspect of blogs, the project encouraged participants to share their blogs with their fellow bloggers and to make comments whenever a new entry was published and announced to the web. Bloggers thus had ample opportunities to visit other blogs and acquaint themselves with their owners. This interaction has proved to be very effective. From the perspective of the web, "Blogging is throwing the internet forward and backward at the same time. Forward into a new era of consumer empowerment, and backward to the grass-roots spirit of the early Web ... Blogging is the perfect antidote to highly commercialized, blandly consolidated Web sites. You can have a great site, be part of an amazingly dynamic global community, and, if you play your cards right, attract a devoted audience."[10]

Overcoming stress and learning blocks

Learning computer technologies and applications can cause severe stresses in our modern society. In order to defer or avoid learning, we blame the age factor, or excuse ourselves either for lack of time or on account of computer illiteracy, or we decline outright for the simple reason that we are soon to retire, and thus do not need to learn anything new. At the beginning, the 23 Things @SCPL project encountered all of these excuses, and many more misunderstandings, such as the notion that Library 2.0 had little relevance to one's day-to-day work. In mid-October, a month into the project, the learners' stresses came to a head. Staff members were distressed on multiple levels. Some were worried about the looming deadline of 14 December 2007, or were overwhelmed by an endless torrent of new subjects to be studied. Others ran into typical learners' blocks when they attempted in vain to learn or to apply a particular piece of software. Still others were apprehensive that mastering 23 Things and other new social networking software would become a standard objective in their annual performance appraisals, while they had not yet taken a single step.

Three strategic moves

In these circumstances, SDO made three strategic moves. The first was to consult the library management. In a message sent to all staff, the library director called on supervisors to render particular support, especially to part-time staff, to extend the deadline for course completion, and to revise the requirement of familiarity with social networking software as a standard objective for staff performance appraisals (see more below).

Second, a "lighten-up" approach was adopted by introducing humor and rewards into the project. A new tone was set: learning without tears, but with creativity, enthusiasm, and fun. When staff members were encouraged to play around with Library 2.0, and to see whose assignments were the most fun, their creativity knew no bounds.

To further cultivate a positive atmosphere, SDO followed the Charlotte-Mecklenburg model of providing incentives and awarded an MP3 player to each participant who completed the program by the deadline. It also entered the names of all participants in a draw for a laptop computer. The awards were generously funded by Friends of the Santa Cruz Public Libraries (www.fscpl.org/), a nonprofit organization that provides SCPL with advocacy, volunteer services, and fundraising support. The enthusiasm of the staff increased and peaked.

Third, all participants were reminded of the availability of weekly tutorials, known as 23 Things Discovery Sessions. The purpose of the Discovery Sessions was to provide technical assistance. During the sessions, a core group of staff acting as "23 Things guides" were available to provide tips and advice. Every Friday, from 8.00 a.m. to 10.00 a.m., September 2007 through January 2008, in the Library Headquarters building, a team of five took turns as the two-member tutorial pair. Tutorial sessions started on a very quiet and slow note, with few visitors dropping in for help. However, soon after the library director's message and the increased involvement of the staff in learning 23 Things, the tutors found themselves so busy that a sign-up sheet was needed for each session. The number of Discovery Sessions offered was doubled before the close of the program, so as to meet the pressing needs of many last-minute finishers.

With the incentive of the sure prize of an MP3 player and the possible grand prize of a laptop, and, more meaningfully, inspired by their newly acquired knowledge of Library 2.0, 43 out of 98 learners managed to overcome all the obstacles and complete the program. On 14 February 2008, over 40 people gathered in the Downtown Branch meeting room to attend a "23 Things Valentine's Day Celebration." Eating Valentine chocolates, they waited patiently to receive their Zen Stone MP3 players, 23 Things certificates of completion, and a big surprise. One absentee participant was the luckiest person on earth that day: he received the grand prize laptop.

Four keys to success

Key 1: Comprehensive curriculum

Learning Library 2.0 proved to be a humbling experience. By 2010, it was estimated that half a million applications were operating on Facebook. They have been developed in more than 180 countries. To avoid getting stressed over the ever-growing number of Web 2.0 applications, users are advised to "Start exploring. Get acquainted with what Web 2.0 has to offer. Take your time. Take baby steps – one small application at a time. Web 2.0 offers powerful applications with great potential, but you have to use them to experience their benefits."[11]

The success of 23 Things @SCPL was largely due to a comprehensive but gradual curriculum entitled "23 Things Exercises" and its coverage of essential social networking software prevalent in Library 2.0. Despite the exclusion of Second Life and Facebook, through the systematic weekly assignments the program provided participants with appropriate exposure to many of the popular 2.0 utilities. The topics covered ranged from blogging to Flickr, from RSS and newsreaders to LibraryThing and online image generators, from tagging, folksonomies, and Technorati to wikis, and from online applications and tools to podcasts, videos, and downloadable e-audio.

During the Discovery Sessions the tutors worked with students to explore various 2.0 applications, such as setting up accounts with Blogger, Delicious, Flickr, LibraryThing, and Rollyo. Because of the great amount of social networking software to be covered, the tutors tried to focus on the topic of the week. However, exceptions were greatly welcomed if students had particular problems from previous weeks, or anticipated problems with topics on the horizon. The tutors won the respect of the students, due to their patient, polite, and professional approach during these sessions.

Halfway through the program, participants who had accumulated enough first-hand experience with 2.0 were required to read a few historical and theoretical perspectives on Library 2.0 and Web 2.0 and then to record their learning progress in their 23 Things Tracker, sourced from their blogs. Through visiting and reading the live links provided, they came to realize that Library 2.0 was an extension of Web 2.0, and that to adapt Web 2.0 to the library world, library professionals used this term to describe a new set of concepts for developing and delivering library services.

Key 2: Strong leadership

The success of SCPL Library 2.0 program was certainly due to the strong leadership of the SDO coordinators and tutors at every stage of the project. They were the backbone for both emotional and technical support. Before the program was announced, SDO and NAS staff modified and finalized the 13-week curriculum of SCPL's 23 Things based on Helene Blowers' *The Learning 2.0 Program*, Stephen Abram's article "43 Things I (or You) Might Want To Do This Year" and the website www.43things.com. It is a well thought-out program, aimed at gradually introducing and spreading new knowledge in the library community within a targeted time period. In addition to the curriculum in the works, SDO recruited three young tutors, newly graduated from the School of Library and Information Science at San Jose State University. Their fresh knowledge and teaching materials from the school turned out to be a great asset to the program.

During the program, the project manager and her assistant were always one step ahead of everyone else. They closely tracked the 23 Things Trackers maintained by the participants. Every week they would go over each participant's assignment meticulously. If there were any errors, they would notify the participant and correct it accordingly. If the participants had any concerns or technical difficulties, they would step in and serve as a bridge between staff members and the library management, supervisors, or NAS. For instance, the management was on the point of announcing its decision to make familiarity with social networking tools mandatory for all staff members by including it as an objective on each employee's performance appraisal. This decision reflected a wish to build on the momentum of learning Library 2.0 that had resulted from the 23 Things @SCPL project. With SDO's timely intervention, the wording of this system-wide objective was revised and modified by members of the Staff Development Committee. Since performance objectives should be specific and measurable, the Committee devised a checklist of Web 2.0/social networking competencies in order to address some typical issues, such as heavy workloads, conflicting priorities, or technology anxiety. Staff members who faced such issues would have a year in which to explore six specific Web 2.0 tools. Thus, SCPL succeeded in providing a creative atmosphere within a learning organization in order to provide opportunities to increase staff competency in new technologies.

Key 3: Post-23 Things @SCPL – exposure to Facebook

In early 2008, shortly after the end of the learning program, SCPL started its group Facebook, namely, SCPL-Unofficial (*http://www. facebook.com/login.php*), as an introduction to future exploration of Web 2.0, with an attached self-help document written by a staff member. This page was replaced in February 2010 by an official Facebook Page (*http://www.facebook.com/santacruzpl*). This will be discussed in more detail in Chapter 16.

Key 4: Grassroots-level training on e-products

Prior to the 23 Things @SCPL project, SDO started its mandatory training of all staff on the downloading and usage of e-audios and e-books. The teaching team consisted of three selection/acquisition Level III librarians. Since learning downloadable e-audios and e-books was one of the 23 Things, the team continued its teaching and held nine sessions at various branches between August 2007 and February 2008. They taught branch staff the similarities and differences of these e-products. The courses were very necessary. More and more downloadable e-audios had been acquired and added to the library's collections, yet there was no global standard on media players for downloaded media files. Moreover, files were not necessarily MP3 or Macintosh compatible, although efforts are being made towards greater standardization in the near future. Because of this, the teaching team had been trouble shooting, and had been obliged to devote a significant amount of time and energy to dealing with problems and questions from branch libraries. The grassroots-level training not only enabled staff to familiarize themselves with the e-products through usage and experimentation but also helped to identify frequent questions and their answers, so that users could be assisted in a timely manner instead of every question having to be referred to the team.

Impact on library services and beyond

A great change has taken place at SCPL since the 23 Things program. The following are just a few notable points.

- The project acted like a storm, sweeping away mental dust and cobwebs along its route. Some staff did not participate, offering excuses such as proximity to retirement, or being "too old" to learn, or Library 2.0 lacking relevance to their daily work. After seeing 98 people participate and 43 complete the program, the rest of the staff have been persuaded that it might just be the right time to sit down and learn. A number of them quietly signed up for training after the project.

- The project has empowered staff with a systematic repertoire of Library 2.0 terminologies and applications. Instead of being confrontational or scared of new gadgets, employees actually welcome and enjoy users' inquiries on mash-ups, Facebook, YouTube, downloadable e-audios, etc. An assessment completed by participants showed that, overwhelmingly, they have a positive attitude toward emerging technologies and that they want to challenge themselves to learn new things at work. With their new knowledge and technical tools, they feel more confident in their work and are able to help the public more appropriately.

- The project has fundamentally changed the outlook of staff members. They are willing to embrace and experiment with more and newer Library 2.0 applications. In the changeable technology landscape, staff members are moving deftly to tackle the latest devices. At the time of writing, they are helping the community to learn how to use e-readers, such as the Kindle, which will be discussed fully in Chapter 12.

The project has laid a solid foundation for lifelong learning. As one participant put it: "I hope we continue to use and apply the knowledge we have acquired and that the spirit of lifelong learning continues to be supported and applied to new technologies as they emerge and become available."

Notes

1. *Management Innovation and Library Services: the Proceedings of the Third Shanghai International Library Forum.* Shanghai: Shanghai Scientific and Technological Literature Publishing House, 482–92, c2006. Print.
2. "California. Bachelor's Degree or Higher, pct of Persons Age 25+, 2006–2010." *census.gov.* United States Census Bureau, n.d. Web. Accessed 30 July 2012.
3. "Circulation of Non-book Materials 2002–2006," generated by SCPL system.
4. Buckland, Michael K. *Library Services in Theory and Context.* 2nd ed. *Berkeley.edu.* University of California Berkeley, 14 April 1999. Web. Accessed 30 July 2012.

5. Van House, Nancy A. "Time Allocation Theory of Public Library Use," *Library and Information Science Research* Winter 1983; 5(4): 365–84. Print.
6. Mears, Craig. "RE: Pimsleur Language Greek II." Message to the author. 24 April 2006. E-mail.
7. *Intelligence, Innovation and Library Services: Proceedings of the Fourth Shanghai International Library Forum.* Shanghai: Shanghai Scientific and Technological Literature Publishing House, 117–28, c2008. Print.
8. Hui-Lan H. Titangos and Gail L. Mason. "Learning Library 2.0: 23 Things @SCPL", *Library Management* 2009; 30(1/2): 44–56. Print.
9. Brooks, L. "Old School Meet School Library 2.0: Bump Your Media Program into an Innovative Model for Teaching and Learning." *Library Media Connection* [serial online]. April 2008; 26(7): 14. Available from: MasterFILE Premier, Ipswich, MA. Accessed 27 July 2012.
10. Hill, B. *Blogging for Dummies.* New York: Wiley Publishing, 2006. Print.
11. Thompson J. "Don't Be Afraid to Explore Web 2.0." *Education Digest* [serial online]. December 2008; 74(4): 19. Available from: MasterFILE Premier, Ipswich, MA. Accessed 27 July 2012.

9

Bibliotheca Alexandrina: carry forward capital of memory

Abstract: This chapter focuses on Bibliotheca Alexandrina, or the new Library of Alexandria. In the decade since it opened in 2002, Bibliotheca Alexandrina has made tremendous progress. Aspiring to be the world's window on Egypt, and Egypt's window on the world, BA has been building a series of digital projects including a digital library, Documentation of Heritage, open knowledge, and science and technology projects.

Key words: Bibliotheca Alexandrina, ancient Library of Alexandria, Egypt, Mohsen Zahran, Alexandria and Mediterranean Research Center, digital archive, Digital Assets Repository.

In the opening paragraph of *Clea*, the last volume of his Alexandria Quartet, Lawrence Durrell calls Alexandria "the capital of memory." Alexandria is indeed "An ancient city changing under the brush-strokes of thoughts which besieged meaning, clamoring for identity, somewhere there, on the black thorny promontories of Africa the aromatic truth of the place lived on, the bitter unchewable herb of the past, the pith of the memory."[1] True to Durrell's exclamation, Alexandria boasts the world's first and oldest public library, namely, the ancient Library of Alexandria, a place to store human memory and knowledge. In 295 BC, Ptolemy I declared that he wanted to collect the "books of all the peoples of the world," in order to bring the world to Egypt through the establishment of the library. Before his death, a considerable quantity of scrolls had been collected, catalogued, and shelved in the palace. His son carried out his wishes by establishing a daughter library to serve the general public. The great library flourished as one of the scholarly centers of the known world; scholars produced new editions of the works of the Greek authors, and for the first time the Old Testament was translated from Hebrew into Greek by Jewish scholars. By the third century BC, the library held more than half a million scrolls, representing the knowledge of different races and creeds in the known world.

Like so many of the vanished historical landmarks of Alexandria, during the ensuing centuries the library did not escape the ravages of fire, earthquakes, wars, and time. During the past two centuries there has been much speculation about the destruction of the library. Some believe that Julius Caesar accidentally burned the library's warehouses when throwing fire at Ptolemy XII's ships in the harbor in 48 BC. However, it remains a mystery whether it really was this fire which reduced the library and its 40,000 scrolls to ashes, or whether its destruction was the result of Emperor Aurelian's destroying the palace district while suppressing a rebellion in 272 AD. Some, like the historian Edward Gibbon, attribute the ruin of the library to Theophilus, Bishop of Alexandria (*http://en.wikipedia.org/wiki/Theophilus_of_Alexandria*), who issued the order to destroy the Serapeum (*http://en.wikipedia.org/wiki/Serapeum*) in the year 391.[2] Others claim that the fall of the library was due to the Muslim conquest of the city in 642.

However, one thing that is clear to both Alexandrians and the rest of the world is that the ancient Library of Alexandria is gone. On Alexandria's Mediterranean waterfront, a new Bibliotheca Alexandrina was inaugurated in October 2002 after 25 years of planning, fundraising, and construction by the Egyptian government and UNESCO, with contributions from countries such as France, Germany, Great Britain, Greece, Iraq, Italy, Japan, Norway, Oman, Saudi Arabia, Spain, and Turkey. The BA comprises six libraries, namely, the Main Library, the Taha Hussein Library, the Children's Library, the Young People's Library, the Arts and Multimedia Library, and the Nobel Section.

Goals

With regard to goals of the BA, Mohsen Zahran, the former project manager, states, "We are not reviving an ancient library. We are reviving the idea of the pursuit of knowledge that thrived in the ancient library. The old library encouraged the public to debate, create and invent. The new library is carrying the legacy forward."[3] Zahran and his colleagues are justified in not pursuing the old path of reviving an ancient library. Lawrence Durrell, who has experienced the hopelessness and futility in reviving the past, would concur with them wholeheartedly: "I had set out once to store, to codify, to annotate the past before it was utterly lost – that at least was a task I had set myself. I had failed in it (perhaps it was hopeless?) – for no sooner had I embalmed one aspect of it in words than the intrusion of new knowledge disrupted the frame of reference, everything flew asunder, only to reassemble again in unforeseen, unpredictable patterns ..."[4]

Mission and vision statements

To carry the legacy of the ancient library forward in the era of social networking, two steps are of great importance: bringing the world to Egypt, and bringing Egypt to the world. The following words from the BA's mission statement are a clear indication:

> To be a center of excellence for the production and dissemination of knowledge and to be a place of dialogue and understanding between cultures and peoples.

The unique role of the BA, as a great Egyptian library with international dimensions, will focus on four main features that seek to recapture the spirit of the original ancient Library of Alexandria. Its vision statement is for the BA to be

- The world's window on Egypt;
- Egypt's window on the world;
- An instrument for rising to the challenges of the digital age; and, above all,
- A center for dialogue between peoples and civilizations.[5]

It is interesting to note that immediately after the BA was opened, negative responses surfaced from many corners of the world. At one point, the BA was compared to a white elephant, a world-class fiasco; its acquisitions budget was considered paltry, and its collection obsolete. Some library experts even seriously questioned its lack of preparation for moving rapidly into the digital age. Despite all these doubts and questions, the BA has undergone a dramatic digital development in the ten years since it opened. The Alexandria and Mediterranean Research Center (Alex Med) has been particularly instrumental in promoting and preserving the heritage, the dialogue and exchange, and future development of Alexandria and the Mediterranean. Alex Med has conducted a wide range of activities, including local and international projects on urban development and the preservation of heritage, seminars, conferences, and exhibitions, as well as the development of a series of digital projects and specialized databases including maps, the arts, and architecture. The next section provides a brief review of some of the notable achievements listed on the BA's website.[6]

Digital projects

Alexandria: Old and New[7]

Documentation of the Ministry of Awqaf Drawings

The aim of this collaborative project by the BA, Alex Med and the Egyptian Ministry of Awqaf (Endowments) is to create a database of the Ministry's collection of about 450 drawings and plates of mosques, houses, and hammams (bathhouses) in Alexandria. The database, which will be made available to scholars and researchers of Alexandria's architectural history, will include scanned images and data on the location, building type, architect, and year of construction of each building.

Reconstructions

This project is a collaborative effort between the BA and Alex Med. Its aim is to reconstruct and recreate models of Alexandria's vanished or endangered structures and buildings. The data sources for the project include archaeological remains and historical records about the Pharos of Alexandria, the Bourse, Taposiris Magna, the Mosque of One Thousand Columns, the ancient city of Alexandria, the Saint Catherine Cistern, the Roman House, and the Serapeum.

The Bathhouses of Alexandria in the 19th and 20th Centuries

Between March 2006 and October 2007, Alex Med made a survey of the city's bathhouses (hammams). The survey team discovered a previously unknown bathhouse, the Hassan Abdallah Hammam. It was also able to reconstruct several extinct hammams, using descriptions in old documents, and determined the location of other lost hammams by referring to old maps.

Alex Cinema

Sponsored by the European Union, Alex Cinema is a joint project by the BA and Alex Med to trace the history of the cinema in Alexandria, beginning in 1897. Using still photographs, film footage, and historical documents, the team has reconstructed the history of Alexandrian cinema up to the era of Youssef Chahine and the Egyptian film industry's later move to Cairo. "The Birth of the Seventh Art in Alexandria," the project's final product, is available as a print publication, on CD, as a website, and as an exhibition.

Digital Library[8]
Memory of Modern Egypt

This is a collaborative project between the BA's International School of Information Science (ISIS) and the Special Projects Department. The digital repository documents the last 200 years of Egypt's modern history and comprises tens of thousands of items, such as documents, pictures, audio and video recordings, maps, articles, stamps, coins, etc.

Eternal Egypt

This is the BA's effort to bring the experience of Egypt to the world. The project is a collaboration between the Egyptian Center for the Documentation of Cultural and Natural Heritage, the Supreme Council of Antiquities (SCA) and IBM. It uses innovative technologies to present an interactive, multimedia experience of Egyptian cultural artifacts, places, and history to a global audience. The website includes descriptions of more than 2000 artifacts, key historical characters, and archeological sites, all of which is presented through a variety of stories and virtual tours of famous sites and museums.

Description de l'Egypte

The BA has digitized and made available online for free the original *Description de l'Egypte*, a 20-volume work that was produced as a result of Napoleon Bonaparte's military expedition to Egypt in 1798.

L'Art Arabe

The four-volume *L'Art Arabe* is one of the most important books on the Islamic monuments of Egypt. Compiled by Prisse d'Avennes, it was first published in 1869. The three plate volumes (222 plates) and the text volume (388 pages) have been scanned and processed in high resolution. Using optical character recognition (OCR), a full-text search capability has been provided for the text volume. The website was completed during the 34th session of the General Conference of UNESCO in October 2007.

Documentation of Heritage[9]

Digital Manuscript Library

This is a project to publish the manuscript treasures of Arabic heritage in digital form. In 2007, the fifth and sixth sets of the Digital Manuscript Library, namely, the St. Catherine's Monastery and the National Library of Sweden (KB) collections, were released. Each set comprises seven manuscripts and an introductory booklet.

Arabic Papyri Collections at the National Library of Egypt

In collaboration with the National Library of Egypt, CultNat (the Center for Documentation of Cultural and Natural Heritage) has completed the digitization of two archival collections of approximately 10,000 maps and 3500 papyri. The databases are available to visiting researchers and scholars. *Egypt in the Cartographic Heritage (1595–1840 CE)* is an English/Arabic publication about the map collection.

Al-Hilal Digital Archive

Al-Hilal is the oldest cultural journal in the Arab world, first published in 1892. It covers the history of the Arab world in general and of Egypt in particular. The BA has digitized the whole collection of 114 issues and stored it on 12 DVDs, and has provided it with the necessary browsing tools and search facilities in a user-friendly interface.

The 100,000 Manuscripts Project

This project was initiated in 2005 to acquire the largest possible number of microfilmed and digital copies of manuscript collections worldwide, especially works pertaining to the history of science and the contributions of the Arab-Islamic civilization to humanity. The initial target of the project was to collect 100,000 manuscripts. In 2011 alone, 5298 manuscripts were added to the collection.

Open Knowledge[10]

Access to Knowledge (A2K)

To promote innovation and creativity, and to stimulate the development of an inclusive knowledge society in the Arab world, the BA has initiated several activities to spread the A2K philosophy and build the local capacity of researchers, librarians, and others to effectively implement A2K tools and practices. The A2K movement aims to promote access to knowledge and to situate it within the contexts of social need and policy platforms.

The Beacon for Freedom of Expression Database

This international bibliographical database on censored books and newspapers and literature on censorship and freedom of expression was a gift to the BA from the country of Norway in May 2003. The BA has organized a series of conferences on freedom of expression, freedom of speech, and access to information.

Science and Technology[11]

BA Supercomputer

To foster educational research and development in multiple scientific fields, the BA and the Ministry of Communication and Information Technology have jointly acquired a high-performance computing cluster, known as the Supercomputer. It is used in specialized research applications that require highly accurate results from extremely large mathematical calculations, typically involving trillions of calculations per second.

Science Supercourse Project

Initiated by the University of Pittsburgh and mirrored at the BA, the Supercourse is an online repository comprising more than 3600

PowerPoint lectures on epidemiology and preventive medicine. It includes the New Science Supercourse, an online repository of lectures in the fields of public health, computer engineering, agriculture, and the environment that is freely available online for use by academic faculty and graduate students.

The BA has developed a new interactive platform so that the Science Supercourse can be equipped with more functionality, including personalized experience and interactive features. The new interface provides users with access to more than 169,000 searchable PowerPoint lectures, and permits registered users to customize their personal access to the repository according to their interests.

The Universal Networking Language (UNL) Project

Initiated within the United Nations and devised by the Universal Networking Digital Language Foundation, the UNL Project enables all peoples to have access to cultural knowledge in their native languages. By using an artificial language, it attempts to replicate the functions of natural language in human communication by addressing the obstacle of linguistic diversity among different nations. The applications will include multilingual web pages, UNL encyclopedia, etc.

Hypertrophic Cardiomyopathy (HCM) Project

HMC is a genetically based disease that can cause sudden death in young adults. In collaboration with the Magdi Yacoub Research Institute in London, Imperial College London (UK), the University of Florence (Italy), and other national institutes, the HCM Project promotes at a national level the early detection of HCM through the establishment of community-level services. An advanced Molecular Genetics Laboratory is currently operational at the BA's Shallalat premises, and 50 index patients have been referred by cardiologists nationwide.

The Encyclopedia of Life (EOL)

This is a global collaborative effort to compile and organize information on the approximately 1.9 million species of plants, animals, and microorganisms on Earth. The aim is to provide the world with a freely accessible knowledge base. Currently it is available in three major languages: English, Arabic, and Spanish.

Webcast

This is a dedicated site for providing both live and archived access to all the conferences, lectures and presentations held at the BA as a part of its role as an incubator of knowledge and culture.

Digital Assets Repository (DAR)

DAR is a system developed by the BA and ISIS to create the library's digital collections. The content of out-of-copyright books is fully available on the internet. For in-copyright books, users can obtain simultaneous access to those books that are available in the library as physical copies, subject to a restriction that only 5 percent of the digital copy may be consulted. DAR's functionalities include a range of viewing and searching options, tagging, sharing, and interaction with other users.

DAR's technical features include several modules, namely:

1. The Digital Assets Factory (DAF) provides flexible management of the digitization workflow, and a unified means of ingestion into the system. It supports both physical and born-digital materials of different media types.

2. DAM (Digital Assets Metadata) manages the metadata of the objects within the repository. It consists of a metadata store for METS (Metadata Encoding and Transmission Standard), and uses Fedora for metadata management. The system provides flexible metadata editing via XML templates and dynamic forms.

3. The Digital Assets Keeper (DAK) is a storage layer for digital objects and is responsible for caching, versioning, and load balancing.

4. A RESTful API builds applications on top of the Repository. This constitutes the Digital Assets Publishing layer (DAP).

5. A Discovery Layer provides full-text search across the whole collection and is based on the access rights granted to the user.

6. OCR capability.

7. The Book Viewer provides full-text (morphological) search within the book's title, subject, keywords, and content, highlighted search results, single- or two-page view, annotation tools, streaming, and a multilingual interface.

8. The Digital Lab is available for the digitization of materials that have been acquired by the BA, as well as materials belonging to other institutions. The complete cycle of the workflow to produce digital objects has been automated, and integrated with the BA Library Information System.

In the course of a little over a decade, the BA has miraculously carried forward the legacy of the ancient library, through a combination of internal talent and worldwide contributions. By emphasizing the city of Alexandria, a unique community, not only has it entered boldly into the digital age, but also, more importantly, it has once again become the leader and center of knowledge and intellectual pursuits in the region.

Notes

1. Durrell, Lawrence. *Clea*. New York: E. P. Dutton & Co., 1960. 11. Print.
2. Gibbon, Edward. *The Decline and Fall of the Roman Empire*. 3. Print.
3. Watson, B. "Rising Sun." *Smithsonian*. 2002; 33(1): 78. Print.
4. Durrell, Lawrence. *Clea*. New York: E. P. Dutton & Co., 1960. 11–12. Print.
5. "About the BA Libraries. Vision and Mission Statements." *bibalex.org*. Bibliotheca Alexandrina, n.d. Web. Accessed 30 July 2012.
6. "Home." *bibalex.org*. Bibliotheca Alexandrina, n.d. Web. Accessed 30 July 2012. (*http://www.bibalex.org/home/default_EN.aspx*).
7. "Projects. Alexandria: Old & New." *bibalex.org*. Bibliotheca Alexandrina, n.d. Web. Accessed 30 July 2012. (*http://www.bibalex.org/Project/Category Projects_EN.aspx?CatID=6*).
8. "Projects. Digital Library." *bibalex.org*. Bibliotheca Alexandrina, n.d. Web. Accessed 30 July 2012. (*http://www.bibalex.org/Project/Category Projects_EN.aspx?CatID=2*).
9. "Projects. Documentation of Heritage." *bibalex.org*. Bibliotheca Alexandrina, n.d. Web. Accessed 30 July 2012. (*http://www.bibalex.org/Project/Category Projects_EN.aspx?CatID=5*).
10. "Projects. Open Knowledge." *bibalex.org*. Bibliotheca Alexandrina, n.d. Web. Accessed 30 July 2012. (*http://www.bibalex.org/Project/Category Projects_EN.aspx?CatID=14*).
11. "Projects. Science and Technology." *bibalex.org*. Bibliotheca Alexandrina, n.d. Web. Accessed 30 July 2012. (*http://www.bibalex.org/Project/Category Projects_EN.aspx?CatID=9*).

10

Oslo Public Library: rejuvenated OPAC

Abstract: This chapter introduces the Pode Project launched in 2008 at OPL, which has become an ongoing project within its Digital Services Department. The project is a big step towards the rejuvenation of the existing online library catalog. It involves conversion of the bibliographic data to RDF and then making it available as Linked Data, so as to ultimately turn the library catalog into an open and flexible API. To date, two prototypes have been completed, namely, the Trip Planner and Music Mash-up.

Key words: Pode Project, Resource Description Framework (RDF), Application Program Interface (API), Z39.50/ISO 23950, Search and Retrieve URL (SRU), Linked Data, Open Data, Functional Requirements for Bibliographic Records (FRBR), mash-up, Project Gutenberg, MARC, SPARQL.

The Pode Project

Headed by project manager Anne-Lena Westrum, the Pode Project was launched in 2008–10, with partial funding from the Norwegian Archive and Museum Authority.[1] It is now an ongoing project of the Digital Services Department at OPL, with a national focus on public libraries. OPL's Pode Project goes a step further than most by converting bibliographic data to RDF (Resource Description Framework) and then making it available as Linked Data, in order to ultimately turn the library catalog into an open and flexible API (Application Program Interface), for a good API makes it easier for everyone to develop a program or create their own mash-ups based on the building blocks or the open semantic data. So far, the project has converted the catalog of the whole of the nonfiction collection in the Multilingual Library to RDF, equipped with OCLC's Dewey Summaries. OPL plans to convert the whole library catalog to RDF. After performing a search and obtaining the results, the user can click on the "Location" option to browse all the retrieved titles in the Dewey arrangement, thus creating a virtual browsing experience.

The Norwegian word "pode" translates as "graft." It is a term used in both horticulture and medical surgery for the joining of one part onto another for adhesion and growth. As its name suggests, the Pode Project's main goal is to combine internal data with external data, and then to utilize the metadata to provide better library services. By adopting the protocols Z39.50/ISO 23950 (*http://www.niso.org/standards/resources/ Z39.50_Resources*) and SRU (*http://www.loc.gov/standards/sru/index. html*) (Search and Retrieve URL), the project utilizes social media technologies like mash-ups, together with FRBR (Functional Requirements for Bibliographic Records) and Linked Data (*http://linkeddata.org/*), to inject new life into the traditional OPAC. Z39.50 is a computer protocol that can be implemented on any platform, and establishes a standard for two computers to communicate for the purpose of information retrieval. SRU is a newly emerging protocol for querying remote databases; to a large extent, it is a descendant of the Z39.50 protocol. As it is based on XML and HTTP, SRU has significantly reduced the complexity of Z39.50.

Two phases

The Pode Project has two phases. The first stage was the prototyping of two services, the Trip Planner and Music Mash-up. The former provides users with information on country, language, place, time zone, and currency when they search for geographic names against GeoNames (*http://www.geonames.org/*), a free geographical database covering all countries in the world and with more than eight million place names. When the information is retrieved it is organized under clear and explicit headings so that users can browse through it or check out relevant materials from the OPL's huge travel collection.

The Music Mash-up uses Last.fm (*http://www.last.fm/*), a free music-recommendation service based on users' preferences for similar artists and albums. The search function in Music Mash-up performs a dual role: it connects artists, albums, and tracks to Last.fm, which returns images, biographies, and cover art if the search is successful. In addition to displaying library holdings of a music group's releases, it goes a step further by searching and displaying all related DVDs, music scores, and books about the group and its artists. According to Anne-Lena Westrum,

"This list gives the user a unique opportunity to discover new music through further exploration of the OPAC."

OPL has demonstrated for the first time the expanded potential of the online library catalog that can be achieved by integrating relevant internal and external data. It not only enhances users' library experience, but increases the circulation of library materials because users can see that their library is providing them with appropriate information in a timely manner and is thus a real provider of information. The results of the Pode Project are a powerful response to the pessimistic view that the library catalog is a thing of the past because 85 percent of library users no longer use it for searching, but resort to shelf browsing and online book stores like Amazon.

The second phase of the Pode Project is to convert traditional bibliographic data into semantic data by the application of automated FRBRization of catalog records. There are three groups of entities in the FRBR model:

- Group 1 entities consist of work, expression, manifestation, and item.

- Group 2 entities consist of persons and corporate bodies that are related to Group 1 entities through specific relationships.

- Group 3 entities consist of subjects of Group 1 or Group 2. They can be names, concepts, objects, events, and places.

The Pode Project uses Group 1 in the FRBR model to cluster under one *work* or title with different *manifestations*, or types of bibliographical records related to the same *expressions*, an equivalent to Amazon's Formats display. This results in the retrieval of a concise and non-duplicated title list for a specific author's works, which proves that bibliographical records can be grouped and browsed by all Group 1 entities.

Experimentation with FRBR

In addition, the Pode Project has experimented in using FRBR with Semantic Web technologies to connect FRBRized records with sources like Linked Open Data, by first converting the data sets to RDF and then linking the data to other sources for a semantic mash-up. The project tied in both DBpedia (*http://dbpedia.org/About*), a community effort to extract and make available structured information from Wikipedia, and Project Gutenberg (*http://www.gutenberg.org/*), a website that provides access over 36,000 free e-books that are in the public domain. The successful results show that the application enables users to retrieve biographical information on authors and their digital full-text works.

To summarize, there are several significant aspects to the Pode Project's work. MARC (MAchine-Readable Cataloging), a product of Library 1.0, has been with us for more than half a century since it was first developed by Henriette Avram at the Library of Congress in the 1960s. Through the testing of time and practice, especially since the advent of the internet, MARC has revealed its weaknesses, which can be overcome by its descendants such as RDF. The following is a listing.

1. Semantic data sources promise more opportunities for solving some historically tough questions, such as limiting search results to a book with certain pagination. By using SPARQL query language for RDF data, one can certainly come up with a quick answer. Instead of fragmentation of bibliographic data, the relationship between different data sets can produce endless potential for complex queries. The MARC format resides somewhere between human and machine readability, which presents an obstacle by itself. As Westrum aptly puts it, "The linked Open Data movement is a democratic one, and we want the library catalog to be a significant part of it. The key to the future of the library catalog is openness!" To realize such openness, we need to replace library-specific formats and protocols and let our users create their own services from our public and open data.

2. Mash-ups of internal and external data are of great importance if we want to utilize related internet resources for our users, such as Last. fm, GeoNames, etc. The Trip Planner and Music Mash-up, the two prototypes created by the Pode Project, are two telling examples. We need to enhance our library catalogs through easy and accurate access to related internet resources. Relying solely on the library's home page and index provides only a partial solution.

3. Data need to be organized relevantly and discretely. During the Pode Project, Westrum learned quickly to avoid information overload: "Our experience is that too much information puts people off. There is no point in adding more just because we can. Targeted information is definitely preferable. Furthermore, it is crucial for the users to be able to distinguish between the library's data and data provided by others."

4. Apparently, the library catalog has not yet reached the point of being a thing of the past. There is still tremendous potential to be harvested from the existing bibliographic data. Judging from the Pode Project's experiments in travel and music, we can explore further in other collections such as DVDs, audiobooks, art and literature, foreign languages, the sciences, and home improvement.

5. Librarians will not be superannuated yet! Their responsibilities have reached a much higher level, for there will be a pressing need for human interaction if we want to adopt Google's mission to organize the world's information that exists in non-standardized and varied media and formats. Existing hardware and software by themselves may not be able to process everything to meet the particular needs of our local communities.

Note

1. Westrum, A. "The Key to the Future of the Library Catalog Is Openness." *Computers in Libraries* [serial online]. April 2011; 31(3): 10. Available from: MasterFILE Premier, Ipswich, MA. Accessed 27 July 2012.

Part 4
Social Media for Local Community

11

Using social tools: Staff Picks in blogs

Abstract: This chapter discusses in detail how the blog, one of the social media, has been used in the context of SCPL's services for its community. The blog has remained a favorite medium with both staff and community members, due to its unique combination of attributes, such as advocacy, currency, relevancy, two-way communication, and promotion.

Key words: Staff Picks, book discussion kits, academic librarians, public librarians, book reviews, blogs, comments.

SCPL Staff Picks: publishing opportunity for librarians

In February 2008, SCPL announced a new feature entitled SCPL Staff Picks. The purpose of introducing Staff Picks was twofold. As an addition to the available book discussion kits, guides, and reads, it aims to provide the community of Santa Cruz County with online book selections and reviews written by library professionals. Over the years, local residents have formed various book clubs, most notably, Downtown Branch Book Discussion Group, La Selva Beach (LSB) Book Discussion Group, LSB Passionate Readers Book Discussion Group, and Bookshop Santa Cruz Community Book Group.

Another purpose of Staff Picks is to encourage library professionals to write and publish book reviews, so as to contribute to the excellence of library and information literature. It is not an entirely new idea for library professionals to publish book reviews in blogs. What distinguished SCPL Staff Picks from other libraries' online book reviews was its new mandate. Unlike their academic counterparts, public librarians do not have the pressure of "publish or perish," an effective but sometimes relentless metric for academia and academic librarians to observe if they are to survive in their professions. Professional publications by public librarians are therefore often outnumbered by those of academic librarians. For the fiscal years of 2009 and 2010, SCPL formally adopted a mandate for librarians to contribute three times a year to Staff Picks, and made it a new requirement for annual performance appraisals.

Despite the initial fears or misgivings of some librarians as to whether they could complete their annual quota, the Staff Picks program has enjoyed unprecedented and unexpected success. Its success was largely due to the 23 Things crash course in Library 2.0 (described in Chapter 8). Through this course and subsequent ongoing training, staff members underwent systematic exposure to a series of social media technologies. They came to the realization that:

> The choices available for libraries to adapt, remain relevant, and make unique contributions in this rapidly changing virtual universe are obvious: Understand the power of Web 2.0 and take advantage of the opportunities available to use this technology and provide innovative and user-centered services to tech-savvy information consumers.[1]

SCPL Staff Picks started with a monthly frequency of publication. In October–November 2008, two pilot book reviews were published. Up to the time of this writing, 105 titles have been reviewed by staff.

The SCPL Staff Picks was introduced and developed during one of the most difficult and turbulent periods in the history of SCPL. A change of top management coincided with continuous budget shortfalls, which resulted in furloughs that lasted more than three years, staff layoffs, and reductions in materials and services. Staff morale was at one of its lowest points. Perhaps it was the hard times that inspired those 105 Staff Picks. Perhaps the mandate of an annual quota did have an effect. But a closer examination of the Staff Picks in question tells us that the development of the program embodied something more than these two possible stimuli. In his *Outliers: The Story of Success*, Malcolm Gladwell discusses the key to success by testing and proving true a magic number: 10,000 hours needed to practice and achieve the desired mastery:

> We pretend that success is exclusively a matter of individual merit. But there's nothing in any of the histories we've looked at so far to suggest things are that simple. These are stories, instead, about people who were given a special opportunity to work really hard and seized it, and who happened to come of age at a time when the extraordinary effort was rewarded by the rest of society. Their success was not just of their own making. It was a product of the world in which they grew up.[2]

Following Gladwell's path of reasoning, the program of SCPL Staff Picks provides public librarians with exactly such a special opportunity. Before the advent of Library 2.0, public librarians were more accustomed to expressing their professional views or recommending potential titles to their users in a format other than online book reviews. They felt more at home doing book displays, and offering book recommendations during their reference interviews. But now Staff Picks has become an effective forum for public librarians to start their 10,000 hours of writing practice, and to improve and publish their writing, without having to suffer the traditional intimidations of publishing. This is one of the hidden keys to the success of Staff Picks. To fully seize the opportunity to make the program a success, the Staff Picks Committee and Coordinator drew up the following guidelines.

Policy to encourage writing practice

Under the guidance of three committee members, Staff Picks was coordinated by a young librarian who was responsible for receiving, revising, scheduling, and publishing the contributed articles. From the very beginning, an inclusive policy was declared, that is, everyone was welcome to participate in Staff Picks, regardless of ranking or position. This welcoming and fostering policy played a dual role: it not only encouraged more participants to join, but also helped to eventually bring all librarians on board by overcoming their initial fears and their misgivings that they could not write because of lack of time or practice. By studying published reviews, many librarians greatly boosted their self-confidence. The flexibility of template, format, and subject matter also assisted them in their writing. After the publication of one or two book reviews, they found the seemingly formidable writing quota to be manageable and that they had conquered the mystery of writing. Soon, many librarians had fulfilled their annual quota. A stable group of contributors was formed, and was infused from time to time with newcomers who tended to stay and who actually enjoyed the gratification of seeing their articles published and featured for a specific period of time. Due to the great number of book reviews submitted, the coordinator had to increase the frequency of Staff Picks more than twice.

Encourage freedom of writing

Staff Picks selects printed books geared toward an adult audience. "Reviews may be of books associated with assigned selection categories or focus on subject of your expertise or interest,"* and librarians are not restricted by the boundaries of their collection development areas, which may be or may not be in their particular subject strength or expertise. This was an especially important policy in encouraging more writing from them. It was up to writers to choose a fiction or nonfiction title, even though the tendency was to write about something with which they were familiar and or about which they were enthusiastic. A now retired science librarian had taken flying lessons for three years. One day, she found *The Complete Guide to Flight Instruction* (1994), a neglected book in the section on "Flight training." Leafing through a few pages, she discovered that it was one of the best flying instruction books available. "Learning to fly" was her first – but successful – book review. Through her review, spiced with humor and her own flying experience, she literally revived this all-but-forgotten title. The total loans of its two copies were impressive. One copy had 116 unique loans and the other copy 18 loans – although, over time, the DRA library system was unable to track their total circulation numbers following the review's publication in August 2009.

Encourage the public to read through quality picking and reviews

Staff Picks encouraged the public to read by picking a good book that it was worth their time to read. At the beginning, one contributor misunderstood the guideline and dwelled heavily on the negative aspects of the book as compared with other similar books. The review was returned to the writer with a detailed explanation from the coordinator, who pointed out the desired way to pursue picks. The author rewrote her review and later it was well received by readers.

Staff Picks did have certain required stylistic standards. The coordinator checked all reviews before publication and corrected all grammatical and spelling mistakes. Through her efforts, the 105 Staff Picks were all branded by their catchy titles, in addition to the original book title, and concise and informative review content, even though they might vary in length.

Encourage technical and team support

Staff Picks received support from various departments. It was the webmaster who recommended the Staff Picks feature. It was also she

---

* See Appendix 3.

who designed the SCPL website "Administration," a homegrown content management system where the Staff Picks were received, scheduled, and published. As the project progressed, new challenges emerged beyond those initially anticipated by the creators of Staff Picks. Therefore, a how-to guide was prepared for prospective writers.*

After the book review of *Lime Kiln Legacies: The History of the Lime Industry in Santa Cruz County* was accepted, the writer was informed that, unlike other Staff Picks, this review would not be illustrated with cover art. Because it was a local publication, its ISBN was not connected to available commercial metadata packages. Frustrated by this technical limitation, the writer and coordinator turned to the webmaster for help. A reply came two days later, with a positive solution.[3] The technical breakthrough was of great significance on several counts. There was indeed a solution to displaying cover art for local authors' publications that were not covered by commercial cover packages. The result was a great public relations promotion to the community of Santa Cruz County, which is active not only in reading, but also in writing and publishing. By displaying the book's distinctive cover, instead of a generic book icon, on the Staff Picks web page, SCPL succeeded in attracting and holding the attention of many a reader.

Another important enhancement for SCPL Staff Picks was that the reviews were made accessible not only through the library website, but also through the library catalog. The Cataloging Department provided all staff-picked titles with an additional Electronic Location and Access field (856) so as to provide a URL or URLs to link to the reviews. One cataloger was in charge of updating all links to Staff Picks. At present, the links work effectively in Evergreen, a newly installed Open Source integrated library system (ILS).

Ideal Web 2.0 participatory environment

Apart from the original twofold purpose mentioned above for introducing Staff Picks, Staff Picks soon found a new purpose in its mission, namely, enlisting the active participation of the public, for it is created in the blog environment, one of the innovative and user-centered Library 2.0 social media applications. Why was the medium of the blog chosen for the Staff Picks environment? The reason is obvious:

---
* See Appendix 3.

> The big win when it comes to blogging and indeed any Web 2.0 applications is that it gives you a voice, it puts you where your users are and to provide examples of where this has worked to great effect I have, I regret, to look overseas.[4]

One major advantage of Staff Picks is its two-way communication feature, which is missing from our traditional book displays, reference interviews, or book reviews. Because it is in blog format, readers are able and free to leave their comments on staff reviews in real time, anytime. Apart from the necessary monitoring and filtering for spam, Staff Picks elicits points of view from readers. In October 2009, "Ever Worked a Weird Low-level Job?" (Review for *Nickel and Dimed: On (Not) Getting by in America*) was published. A few days later, a reader responded to the review with an entirely different viewpoint, which was supported by three more comments.[5]

Staff Picks is able to foster library advocacy and promotion from an enthusiastic community. A notable example of this was "Correspondence from the German Occupation," a book review of *The Guernsey Literary and Potato Peel Pie Society*. Since its publication in February 2009, it had received a number of lively comments from readers offering their experiences and values in response to the reviewer's original views, and comparisons on a similar theme. As a serendipity of book reviews, many relevant library titles on the same subject have thus been discovered and promoted. Here is a recent comment from a reader:

> Thank you for doing these staff picks. I always like the books. It's a big help in finding something good to read![6]

The results that Staff Picks have achieved so far have fully validated the five key elements of blogging that are summarized by Hammond,[7] namely,

1. find an advocate;
2. currency;
3. relevance;
4. two-way communication; and
5. promotion.

Users' comments and feedback are also valuable tools for library professionals in order to record, measure, and analyze the particular needs of the local community at a given period of time. In doing so, we library professionals can serve the community more appropriately and efficiently, without the need to start from scratch.

Second chance for non-bestsellers

Upon close examination of the 105 picked titles, one finds that, with the exception of *Help* and *The Guernsey Literary and Potato Peel Pie Society*, two bestsellers in 2009 and 2008, the other 103 titles can hardly be considered blockbusters. On the contrary, most of them had either been ignored or languished on the shelves. In his *Free for All: Odd Balls, Geeks, and Gangstas in the Public Library*, Borchert states:

> Once a book hits the shelf, the library is loath to get rid of it no matter what outrage it causes. The only way a library will discard a book is if it is ignored. The scandalous ones do not get ignored until they are passé.[8]

Borchert might have been exaggerating. He is, however, not too far from the truth in describing library weeding policies. At SCPL there were two fates awaiting an uncirculated title: reassign it to another branch, or discard it after no improvement from reassigns. Take, for instance "A colorful history" (book review of *Color: A Natural History of the Palette*). Before the Staff Pick, the circulation of the two existing copies had been sluggish. After the Staff Pick in May 2009, SCPL added a third copy to meet the needs of a long request list. As both an artist and a librarian, the review writer captured readers' interest with her personal artistic expertise and experience. The title gained a second chance. The circulation statistics for all Staff Picks have been consistently high.

Future means more improvement

With over five years' practice, Staff Picks is still relatively young for SCPL professionals. There is still room for improvement: basic information on Staff Picks and its regular management is needed, for after an existence of more than five years Staff Picks still has not published its official guidelines. In contrast, the book discussion kits program is more systematic in its approach, with a dedicated web page.[9] Stylistic revisions are needed for some contributed articles. Without such revision, readers would have the impression that Staff Picks are published as is. A guideline on the length of reviews might be useful, in the interests of readers, who are never told how long the reviews will be. A regular frequency might be desirable, so that users will know when to expect new reviews to be published. Consistent quality control is another area for improvement. Some reviews are extremely well written, others are less than satisfactory. More staff members need to be encouraged to participate, so as to obtain a larger pool of contributions.

Despite the above wish-list of improvements, Staff Picks has demonstrated the validity of Library 2.0 by its popularity among both staff and the public. It is innovative in the sense that, for once, public librarians are encouraged to write and publish. Their practical research work has benefited not only their own promotions and appraisals but, more importantly, the lives of the public whom it has touched. Owing to this main factor, Staff Picks has survived various changes and reorganizations during the last five years. A detailed report on Staff Picks was published in *City Life and Library Service: Proceedings of the Fifth Shanghai (Hangzhou) International Library Forum (SILF)*,[10] and a revised version of the paper appeared later in *Library Management*.[11]

Notes

1. Peltier-Davis, C. "Web 2.0, Library 2.0, Library User 2.0, Librarian 2.0: Innovative Services for Sustainable Libraries." *Computers in Libraries* [serial online]. November 2009; 29(10): 16. Available from: MasterFILE Premier, Ipswich, MA. Accessed 27 July 2012.
2. Gladwell, M. *Outliers: The Story of Success.* New York: Little Brown and Company, 2008. 67. Print.
3. Young, Ann. "RE: Cover Art for Lime Kilns Legacies." Message to the author. 25 June 2009. E-mail.
4. Hammond, S. "Public Library 2.0: Culture Change?"*Adriadne* 64 (2010). Web. Accessed 30 July 2012.
5. "Ever Worked a Weird Low-level Job?"*santacruzpl.org.* Santa Cruz Public Libraries, 4 October 2009. Web. Accessed 30 July 2012. (*http://www. santacruzpl.org/readers/blog/2009/oct/04/ever-worked/*)
6. "Madensky Square – A Year in the Life." *santacruzpl.org.* Santa Cruz Public Libraries, 9 June 2011. Web. Accessed 30 July 2012. (*http://www. santacruzpl.org/readers/blog/2011/jun/09/madensky-square-year-life/ #comments*)
7. Hammond, S. "Public Library 2.0: Culture Change?"*Adriadne* 64 (2010). Web. Accessed 30 July 2012.
8. Borchert, D. *Free for All: Odd Balls, Geeks, and Gangstas in the Public Library.* New York: Virgin Books, 2007. 14. Print.
9. "Reader's Link – Book Kits." *santacruzpl.org.* Santa Cruz Public Libraries, n.d. 2009. Web. Accessed 30 July 2012.

10. *City Life and Library Service: Proceedings of the Fifth Shanghai (Hangzhou) International Library Forum (SILF)*. Shanghai: Shanghai Scientific and Technological Literature Publishing House, 256–66, c2010. Print.
11. Titangos, Hui-Lan H. "Promote Staff Publications: Library Performance Evaluation at Santa Cruz Public Libraries," *Library Management*. 2011; 32(4/5): 290–301. Print.

12

YouTube: the power of crowdsourcing

Abstract: This chapter discusses in detail why YouTube, one of the social media sites, remains popular with library services for their local communities. Despite differences in cultures, languages, and softwares, YouTube has been employed for a variety of library outreach programs and teaching and learning tools, due to its unique crowdsourcing power.

Key words: crowdsourcing, Khan Academy, BAChannel, video tutorial, Overdrive, e-books, Kindle, Tales to Tails, Read to Me, Battle of the Bands.

History

Founded in February 2005, YouTube (*http://www.youtube.com/*) provides a social website for users to connect with, inform, and inspire other users around the globe by uploading and sharing videos. It also acts as a distribution platform for creators of original visual content and advertisers. YouTube is a successful shift from professional-powered content to crowdsourced content, which facilitates opportunities for show-and-tell, as Todd Kelsey defines it in his *Social Networking Space*. People visit YouTube for at least three reasons: to watch a video, or to make a comment after the viewing; to share their own or other people's videos with family, friends, or colleagues; and in search of American-idol fame, for YouTube possesses a magical power to make someone famous overnight.

The Khan Academy (*http://www.youtube.com/user/khanacademy*) is one of the most-viewed video channels on YouTube. At the time of this writing it has been viewed more than 166,642,642 times and has 359,576 subscribers. It has archived more than 3152 videos catering to the needs of high school students, such as mathematics, science, finance and economics, humanities, and test preparation. On 11 March 2012,

60 Minutes on CBS ran a review on the academy entitled "Khan Academy: the Future of Education"(*http://www.youtube.com/watch?v=zxJgPHM5NYI*)[1] to report a success story in education. The academy started accidentally after Salman Khan began helping his cousins remotely with their high school homework, via YouTube. The YouTube videos were picked up by other users, including Bill Gates' children. With backing from both the Bill and Melinda Gates Foundation and Google, the Khan Academy's free online educational videos have not only been used by individual students, but also moved into classrooms around the globe. Khan's goal is to revolutionize the traditional model of education. In the case of the Khan Academy, stardom is based on a series of videos that are beneficial to the community and to future generations.

Reaching out to local communities

In addition to the Khan Academy, YouTube EDU (*http://www.youtube.com/education*) is another great educational resource for reaching out to a broader audience of local communities. It is a free site for videos and channels maintained by college and university partners, and for educational TV or radio programs like National Geographic and NPR (National Public Radio). It enables members of the community to learn for free and for a lifetime; it also provides lecturing opportunities for new professors as well as for the famous ones. YouTube EDU is divided into three major sections:

1. Primary and secondary education, consisting of lectures on history and the social sciences, sciences, mathematics, etc., with a heavy contribution from the Khan Academy;
2. University level, consisting of lectures on the sciences, mathematics, engineering, social sciences, history, business, the humanities, medicine, the arts, law, education, languages, etc.;
3. Lifelong learning, consisting of free-form content.

Unlike some social networking sites, which are not searchable or browsable, YouTube is well organized and indexed, with 12 popular categories and prominent featured sections such as "Most Viewed Today" and "All Time Favorites." In addition to videos, it includes music, movies, shows, trailers, live events, sports, education, and news. The "Browse" button and the "Search" box enable users to search and browse its rich and huge range of content. Users can add channels to their home pages and embed video clips into their blogs or websites. Because of YouTube's popularity and its friendly user interface, libraries around the world have utilized the site since its early days.

BAchannel

The BA joined YouTube in August 2008. In order to provide "everyone with the chance to share knowledge and culture through this gateway to one of the leading institutes in the region," BAchannel (*http://www. youtube.com/user/BAchannel*) has uploaded 107 videos to YouTube. It has 608 subscribers and has had 201,426 views at the time of this writing. YouTube serves as a visual archive for most of the conferences, lectures, and presentations that have taken place at BA. The BAchannel's Featured Playlists are divided into five sections:

- Dr. Ismail Serageldin presentations
- BA Conferences
- Other Presentations
- BA Projects
- BA Celebrations

The Featured Playlists include videos of American filmmaker Martin Scorsese's two visits to BA, *Martin Scorsese in BA* and *Martin Scorsese: Cinema as an Art Form*; Rotaract's special project to *Kick Polio out of Africa*; and the presentation of the *Millennium Excellence Award 2010* to Dr. Ismail Serageldin for his scientific research in Africa. For the latter, the official prize ceremony was held on 4 December 2010 at the State House, Accra, Ghana, by Ghana's Excellence Awards Foundation, a private institution that presents the award every five years to recognize outstanding achievement by individuals who have selflessly served the continent of Africa and contributed to its socio-economic development. Previous recipients are Kofi Annan, Former UN Secretary General (2005), and Jerry Jon Rawlings, former President of Ghana (2000).

SCPL on YouTube

SCPL joined YouTube on 24 August 2011. The SCPL YouTube site (*http://www.youtube.com/user/santacruzpl*) lists the library's new outreach activities, such as Stuffed Animal Sleepover at branch libraries, reading programs like Tales to Tails and Read to Me, and the annual Battle of the Bands. On 14 January 2012, SCPL posted its first YouTube video tutorial, entitled "Library eBooks for Amazon® Kindle," in response to an overwhelming local demand for instruction in how to use the Kindle e-reader. The video, which has now totaled more than 197,500 views, teaches users how to browse, checkout, and access library e-books on the Amazon Kindle. OverDrive (*http://overdrive.com/ About/*), founded in 1986 in Cleveland, Ohio, is one of the leading distributors of e-books, e-audiobooks, and other digital content to more than 15,000 libraries, schools, and colleges worldwide. It currently hosts 650,000 premium digital titles from over 1000 publishers, including Random House, HarperCollins, BBC Audiobooks America, Harlequin, and Bloomsbury. Amazon Kindle e-books are one of its four major collections, and libraries, especially public libraries, have been purchasing Kindle e-books for quite some time. So why the sudden surge of the Kindle's popularity among library users, particularly among the elderly? It turns out that many people received Kindle readers as Christmas presents from their children or grandchildren in 2011. To learn how to use their Kindle readers, they have turned en masse to libraries for help. A marriage made in heaven was thus consummated between Overdrive and Kindle e-books, between technology and traditional library users, and between social networking and local communities.

YouTube is still a new territory at SCPL, with only nine subscribers and 783 views at the time of writing. However, it has potential, and the coordinator of the virtual library has new plans for videos, such as instruction for the public in how to use the new library catalog, how to use various e-readers, and library tours of different branches, possibly using UCSC student interns.

Note

1. "Khan Academy: The Future of Education?" *cbsnews.com*. CBSNewsOnline, 11 March 2012. Web. Accessed 30 July 2012.

13

Using social tools: RSS feeds

Abstract: This chapter discusses RSS feeds in detail. RSS is a favorite social media tool with libraries for reaching their local communities by automatically syndicating their web content, such as the community calendar of events, exhibitions and lectures, and news of newly acquired titles and resources. Despite differences in cultures and languages, RSS has been extensively utilized to publish library programs and services, due to its unique power of delivering changing content to interested users.

Key words: RSS feed, RDF Rich Site Summary, web feed, aggregator, syndicated content, calendar of events, exhibitions, lectures, seminars, Canton Public Library.

What is RSS?

RSS (*http://rss.softwaregarden.com/aboutrss.html*) is a means for interested users to keep up with a website's changing content by subscribing to the site's RSS feeds, and to be alerted to changes through an aggregator or RSS reader. It was created by Dan Libby and Ramanathan V. Guha at Netscape in March 1999. Known as RSS 0.9, it was used as My.Netscape.Com portal. In a newer version, RSS 0.91, issued in July of that year, Dan Libby made two significant changes to simplify the format by removing RDF elements and incorporating elements from Dave Winer's scriptingNews syndication format. RSS 0.91 was later named RDF Rich Site Summary or RSS Rich Site Summary. Winer continued RSS development by creating RSS 0.92 in 2000, and RSS 2.0 in 2002. Since 2006, the icon of an orange square with white radio waves has become the industry standard for RSS feeds, following announcements by Microsoft and Opera Software that they would adopt the feed icon.

RSS is part of web feed, or news feed, which is a data format to provide users with constantly updated content. By utilizing web feeds, web syndication provides users with a summary or update of the recently added content on a provider's website. Content syndication is often used by webmasters to add greater depth and immediacy to their sites:

> In order to attract search engines and site visitors, webmasters rely heavily on providing new, innovative and fresh content. If the web site content is rich, visitors will come. If the website content is updated regularly, visitors will return. When evaluating a website's traffic it is easy to see that the low cost of syndicated content can increase a website's value. Sites that contain multiple pages related to a specific topic increase the likelihood of being 'found' when a variety of search phrases are used for that topic.[1]

RSS at BA, Shanghai Library, and SCPL

RSS feeds are one of the favorite tools adopted by the libraries examined in this book. BA utilizes the RSS feature to disseminate and distribute BA Events, BA News, and BA Press in both English and Arabic. Shanghai Library publishes its home page in four languages, namely, English, Japanese, Simplified Chinese, and Russian. Interestingly, only its Chinese page has adopted RSS, for the categories of "Trends" since May 2011, and of "Lectures at Shanghai Library" since February 2012.[2]

SCPL was one of the first public libraries in California to utilize RSS. At present, it uses RSS to feed seven syndicated content streams in two major categories, "General," and "Newly Inventoried Items." Of the two categories, the latter has been especially popular with the local community. It not only notifies subscribers about what is new in the library catalog, but also helps nonsubscribers to find new items by conducting an instant search.

The "General" category (*http://www.santacruzpl.org/rss/*) has the following sections:

- SCPL News
- Checking In: The Future of SCPL
- Calendar of Events
- Small Business Brown Bag Seminars

- Staff Picks
- Kids Page Blog

"Newly Inventoried Items" (*http://www.santacruzpl.org/evergreen/newitems/*) lists new materials under the following headings:

- New Adult Items
  - Fiction
  - Mysteries
  - Non-fiction
  - Large Print
  - Audiobooks
  - Videos and Other Media
- New Kids and Teens Items
  - Y[oung] A[dult] Books
  - YA Media
  - J[unior] Fiction
  - J Non-fiction
  - J Media
  - Picture Books

More extensive usage of RSS at Canton Public Library

In general, BA, SCPL, and Shanghai Library all utilize RSS in a similar way, namely, they tend to use it as a broadcast medium to announce news, events, lectures, or new resources. Many libraries, however, have applied it much more extensively. One notable example is Canton Public Library in Michigan (*http://www.cantonpl.org/*). On its page "Books and More" (*http://www.cantonpl.org/books-more*), RSS is built into categories such as *New York Times* Bestsellers, Genre Blogs, On Order, New Arrivals, Dewey Call Numbers, and subcategories such as Kits, Teens, and Books on CD. With the orange RSS button inserted into different library resources, it makes the library catalog friendly, lively, and easy to navigate.

Notes

1. Housley, Sharon. "Content Syndication." *feedforall.com*. NotePage, Inc., n.d. Web. Accessed 30 July 2012.
2. "上图讲座 - 最新讯息" (the Latest Updates on Shanghai Library Lectures) *library.sh.cn*. Shanghai Library. July 2012. Web. Accessed 30 July 2012. (*http://feed.feedsky.com/jiangzuo*).

14

Using social networks: Pinterest

Abstract: This chapter discusses Pinterest, one of the fast-growing social media, favored mainly by female users, especially in the Central and Midwest United States. Owing to its variety and flexibility in usage, it is an ideal platform for public libraries to connect to their local communities.

Key words: Pinterest pinboard, connecting people, Oprah Winfrey, Martha Stewart, Dr. Phil, Rachael Ray, self-helps, DIY, uncluttering.

What is Pinterest?

Pinterest (*http://pinterest.com/*) is one of the rapidly growing social media. Developed in December 2009, the Pinterest site was officially launched in March 2010 with 5000 users – a number that doubled within nine months. In April 2012, Alyson Shontell of *Business Insider* reported, "Pinterest's traffic was up almost 50% from February to January 2012 and Pinterest's unique visitors increased from 11 million to 17.8 million. One week during January yielded 21.5 million Pinterest visits, which is 30 times what its traffic was six months prior."[1] When Barbara Ortutay reported on Pinterest in detail in March 2012, very few people had heard of it, let alone used it.[2] In her article, Ortutay attributed its phenomenal success to female users: "What makes Pinterest's surge unusual is that it's driven not by the usual geek crowd of young men from New York and San Francisco, but by women, many of whom live in the Midwest and Central US. They use the sleek, photo-heavy website for fashion ideas, wedding planning and home design, or just to share photos of puppies." Owing to its ascent to 10 million monthly visitors, Pinterest is now ranked right behind Facebook and Twitter.

Why is Pinerest so successful, apart from the reason given above that many women in the Midwest and Central United States are the driving force behind its rapid rise? According to the brief description on its website,

Pinterest is a virtual pinboard that enables users to organize and share all the beautiful things that they find on the web. Typically, they use pinboards for planning and organizing weddings, home decorations, and favorite recipes. Users are also encouraged to browse the pinboards created by other people, and to discover new things and get inspiration from people who share their interests. To summarize from this description, at least four winning elements are driving the phenomenal success of Pinterest: people connecting, content sharing, simple designing, and real-life problem solving.

People connecting

Pinterest states that its goal is to connect everyone in the world through the "things" they find interesting. A favorite book, toy, or recipe can reveal a link between two people. With millions of new pins added every week, Pinterest is connecting people all over the world, particularly women in our local communities, on the basis of shared tastes and interests. It is hardly an overstatement to say that Pinterest is the first social network to have succeeded in helping women in their reaching out for sisterhood, friendship, and sharing of common interests – which somewhat reminds one of the unparalleled popularity of Oprah Winfrey, Oprah Book Club and O, *the Oprah Magazine.*

Content sharing

Pinterest is another successful site for crowd-created content. It started small but has become increasingly popular within a short period of time. Two interesting characteristics are unconsciously reflected in our social behavior: people like to comment on other people's creations; and people welcome the opportunity to share their own creations, as well as other people's creations that match their tastes or interests. This is the formula that has sustained the success of blogging and YouTube. It also demonstrates that it is a successful model as long as we follow the formula; format is secondary, whether it be blog, video, or pinboard.

Simple designing

Stylistically speaking, Pinterest's design is very clean and simple to use, employing bright and light colors. In What Can You Do with Pinterest?

(*http://pinterest.com/about/*) Pinterest uses five pinboards to illustrate five popular areas in which most people, especially women, are interested, namely,

- Redecorate your home!
- Plan a wedding!
- Find your style!
- Save your inspirations!
- Save your recipes!

This simple design and overall layout is a very attractive to people who need to organize the chaos of internet-age information overload.

Real-life problem solving

Compared with other social networks and sites that are aimed at connecting people to people and sharing their life stories, Pinterest chooses a surprisingly practical approach in our real social life: offering visual DIY (do it yourself) online help, and sometimes solutions to deeply rooted social issues, such as the clutter in our life. Like any consumer society, "We live in a world of things, of junk, of things," as Kathleen Parrish writes so indignantly in her *Curing the Clutter Epidemic*.[3] She questions why Americans have so much "stuff," and traces the causes, such as an abundance of cheap goods, instant credit, and the constant and persuasive power of the advertising industry. Therefore buying and acquiring have become a national pastime and obsession. To cure this national obsession, many people go to libraries for books on how to unclutter, read articles like Parrish's for practical tips, or hire professional organizers to come into their houses to organize their space and life. In this sense, Pinterest is like a composite of Oprah Winfrey, Martha Stewart, Dr. Phil, Rachael Ray and self-helps, ongoing classes and programs, and hiring professionals. Through its visual cues, Pinterest helps its users to apprehend the uncluttering concept, which is an effective first step toward curing the clutter. In a webinar entitled "Putting Yourself in a Marketing Mentality,"[4] Canton Public Library reported its resounding success in using Pinterest to help its community to obtain a full control of their lives. So far, the library has set up eight pinboards for Education, Book Places and Spaces, Literary Accessories, Favorites, Movies, Books Worth Reading, DIY, and About Libraries. The community cannot have enough of those pinboards and pins.

Today, Pinterest has gained a much wider user circle than was the original intention for it. Websites like Amazon have used it to remind visitors about pinteresting any good titles to their pinboards. Along with Facebook and Twitter, Pinterest is one of the three major social media for sharing information.

Notes

1. Shontell, Alyson. "Chart of the Day: If You Don't Understand Why Pinterest Is a Big Deal, Look at this Chart." *businessinsider.com*. Business Insider, Inc., 6 April 2012. Web. Accessed 30 July 2012.
2. Ortutay, Barbara. "Pinterest Use Is on the Rise: Here's Everything You Need to Know about the Internet's New Darling." *huffingtonpost.com*. TheHuffingtonPost.com, Inc., 12 March 2012. Web. Accessed 30 July 2012.
3. Parrish K. "Curing the Clutter Epidemic." *Saturday Evening Post* [serial online]. July 2010; 282(4): 45. Available from: MasterFILE Premier, Ipswich, MA. Accessed July 27, 2012.
4. Golden, Lori. "Putting Yourself in a Marketing Mentality (webinar to SCPL)." *gale.cengage.com*. Cengage Learning, 12 March 2012.

15

Using social sites: Twitter and Weibo

Abstract: This chapter discusses Twitter, which is one of the prevailing social media adopted by libraries for sharing information with their local communities, and which is likely to be with us for a while, based on its omnipresence and increasing popularity. With its simplicity and ease of communication, it is certainly an ideal tool for sharing one's community with the rest of the world. Its limit of 140 characters per message has not deterred enthusiastic users. On the contrary, users find themselves becoming more creative in composing messages that use texting abbreviations, shortened words, and leetspeak.

Key words: Twitter, information stream, tweet, followers, Weibo, information network, texting abbreviations, leetspeak.

What is Twitter?

Created in 2006 and based in San Francisco, Twitter (*https://twitter.com/*) is a real-time information network. It plays two main roles: providing its users with a forum on which to post updates of no more than 140 characters; and serving as a platform for broadcasting and other applications. It can be used on both PCs and mobile devices. Twitter and Facebook share a number of similarities. As in Facebook, the heart of Twitter is an information stream, a Tweet or a message of up to 140 characters. Instead of feeling inconvenienced or frustrated by this limit on message length, Twitter users have found the limit a delightful challenge to their boundless creativity. They adopt many creative methods to circumvent the character limit, such as using texting abbreviations, shortened words, and leetspeak – or leet for short, a vernacular form of the word "elite." Leet is a type of online jargon in which computer users substitute other characters, letters, or numbers to represent a letter or letters in a word, for example, "f" in the place of "ph." In the context of Twitter, leetspeak is borrowed to overcome its character limit. Leetspeak lacks standardization as a formal language and has few standard terms; nonetheless, its varied forms are relatively easy to understand after a few trials.[1]

Also like Facebook, Twitter is an efficient tool for sharing information about oneself and one's community. From the very beginning, both Twitter and Facebook were available as networks or platforms for applications, rather than as an application alone. Both regard the status update as an essential feature, and sharing information among users as a vital mission. Both are global in nature, with multiple language settings. Despite these similarities, Twitter is fundamentally different from Facebook in other respects. For instance, it provides only one-way connections. Instead of becoming "friends" with other people, Twitter users "follow" the tweets of others. Unlike the identity-based Facebook, twitterers may not even be human. They can be a product or a brand name. These differences aside, searching for updates is far easier in Twitter than in Facebook.

Twitter at SCPL and BA

SCPL joined Twitter as @SantaCruzPL (*https://twitter.com/SantaCruzPL*) on 3 February 2010. At the time of writing it has sent 729 tweets, is following 81 other users, and has 403 followers. The Twitter account provides a glimpse of SCPL and its community. OPL also has presence on Twitter, while BA has an official Twitter account for broadcasting news and distributing information about events. At the time of writing, BA has sent 767 tweets and has 1597 followers.

Weibo at Shanghai Library

Sina Weibo is China's biggest Twitter-like application. To help its owners to make a profit, it has introduced a membership charge for premium features. For a monthly fee of 10 yuan, its 300 million users can add personalized pages, voice posts, and better security, among other features.[2] WoS at Shanghai Library opened a Weibo account (*http://weibo.com/windowofshanghai*) to broadcast breaking news and to encourage dialogue with librarians and readers around the world.

To summarize, Twitter is likely to be with us for a while, based on its rapidly growing popularity and its ubiquity both on the web and in print. Twitter has not only grown, but has expanded itself to other sites, such as through its connection to Facebook. Its simplicity and the ease of communication that it provides certainly make it an ideal tool for sharing one's community with the rest of the world.

> One of the interesting things about Twitter is that when you begin tweeting, people will begin following you. Tens of millions of people use Twitter, and whether you're using it for personal fun or for business, a lot of people are out there searching for tweets. People may end [up] finding you when they search for certain words on Twitter – and because there are so many users, chances are someone will find you.[3]

Notes

1. "leetspeak." *netlingo.com*. NetLingo, 2012. Web. Accessed 20 July 2012.
2. Moskvitch, Katia. "Weibo Starts Charging Chinese for Premium Features." *bbc.co.uk*. BBC News Technology, 19 June 2012. Web. Accessed 30 July 2012.
3. Kelsey, Todd. *Social Networking Spaces: from Facebook to Twitter and Everything in Between*. New York: Apress, c2010. 199. Print.

16

Using social sites: Facebook and Renren

Abstract: This chapter discusses Facebook. Facebook is one of the current social media favored by libraries for sharing information with their local communities for at least three reasons: technological capability, innovative durability, and a great number of users. In essence, it is a social utility that connects people with friends, people with their communities, and public institutions with their constituencies.

Key words: classmates.com, six degrees of separation, Friendster, MySpace, Mark Zuckerberg, tagging, News Feed, privacy, gift economy, Open Source Initiative, transparency, personal account, Facebook Page, Renren.

Facebook usage[1]

Among the chief social media technologies utilized in the context of library services, we will inevitably find that Facebook (*http://www.facebook.com*), along with Twitter, is one of the favorites, for at least three reasons: technological capability, innovative strength, and a great number of users, as indicated in Table 16.1. According to a 2012 estimate by Forbes, Facebook has reached an audience of 800 million worldwide.[2] The philosophy of treating Twitter and Facebook as platforms rather than as applications explains both their durability and their future potential. For this reason, my chief focus here will be on those aspects of Facebook that are relevant to libraries' special needs in bringing our local communities to the world.

Table 16.1 Facebook subscriber growth 2011–12 according to the official number of Facebook subscribers reported in 210 individual countries and/or territories

Geographic regions, in order by size	31 March 2011	30 June 2011	30 September 2011	31 December 2011	31 March 2012
Europe	200,260,360	208,907,040	214,988,320	223,376,640	232,835,740
Asia	131,556,800	157,957,480	169,392,060	183,963,780	195,034,380
North America	173,640,240	167,999,540	172,636,960	174,586,680	173,284,940
South America	69,594,760	82,207,800	92,049,480	103,294,940	112,531,100
Central America	28,090,240	33,081,140	36,333,060	38,317,280	41,332,940
Africa	27,414,240	30,665,460	34,798,940	37,739,380	40,205,580
Middle East	15,779,440	16,125,180	17,326,520	18,241,080	20,247,900
Oceania/Australia	12,333,780	12,881,560	13,177,360	13,353,420	13,597,380
Caribbean	5,362,600	5,903,520	6,182,080	6,218,960	6,355,320
World total	664,032,460	710,728,720	756,884,780	799,092,160	835,525,280

Source: www.internetworldstats.com.

A brief history

The concept of social networking is not new. In 1995, classmates.com was launched to help people find their former school- and classmates by their real names. The next networking service based on real names belongs to SixDegrees.com (1997–2001). Based in New York and named after the concept of six degrees of separation, it allowed users to list friends, family members, and acquaintances both in and outside the site, and outside contacts were invited to join the site. It was followed later by other social networking sites such as Friendster (February 2003), LinkedIn (December 2002) and Tribe.net (May 2003), MySpace (August 2003), and Facebook (February 2004). It is interesting to note that the launches of influential social networking sites or platforms were all clustered around the period 2003–4, although such sites have coexisted with the internet almost from the beginning. They have expanded and flourished as the internet became more popular and familiar to people. Over time, many networking services have either diminished or simply disappeared, and very few stand out, chief among them LinkedIn and Facebook, which shows amazing durability and growth around the world. What is the reason for this durability?

Facebook was created by Harvard student Mark Zuckerberg as his personal rebellion against the university authorities' unwillingness to approve the establishment of an online student directory. Facebook empowers users by putting them in charge of their own profiles and interactions with their friends and the community. Whether consciously or unconsciously, the founder of Facebook transferred some of his own power to his users. David Kirkpatrick writes:

> Facebook is bringing the world together. It has become an overarching common cultural experience for people worldwide, especially young people. Despite its modest beginning as the college project of a nineteen-year-old, it has become a technological powerhouse with unprecedented influence across the modern life, both public and private. Its membership spans generations, geographies, languages, and class.[3]

Table 16.1 clearly bears out this statement.

Facebook was started exclusively for Harvard students, but was expanded to other colleges in the Boston area, the Ivy League campuses, and Stanford University, and then to other universities. On 20 September

2005, it was officially registered as a company and secured the college market, with 85 percent of American college students as its users. Soon, it conquered the high school market. By February 2006, any high school students aged 13 or over could sign up. According to Kirkpatrick's estimates, there were over a million high school students on Facebook by April 2006.

Technical features

Facebook was strengthened by a series of implementations of new technical features. These include the popular photo hosting and tagging, and the controversial News Feed, based on a set of software algorithms designed to watch and broadcast as soon as users made changes in their profiles or performed certain actions such as "Like," "Comment," or "Share" their friends' or family members' birthdays.

Users' feedback on News Feed has been mixed ever since Facebook implemented it in 2006. It is based on the philosophy of pushing people towards consistency, or exposing inconsistency. The intrusive exposure of users' activity gave rise to outraged responses from protest groups and individuals. In less than a decade Facebook has been confronted with a series of painful moments and protests from users and families.

Facebook has stood up for its radical social ideal that the world and society will be better if they are more transparent and if everyone is sharing more by being consistent and responsible for their actions. Some users have been made to feel uncomfortable and, worse still, victimized, in the process. They complain of having to give up their privacy and being made to reveal too much of their private lives as a result of photo posting and tagging and inadvertent changes to their profiles. One of the fundamental privacy issues, as James Grimmelmann, a professor of law at New York Law School states, is that "There's a deep, probably irreconcilable tension between the desire for reliable control over one's information and the desire for unplanned social interaction."[4]

The concept of gift economy

Mark Zuckerberg, CEO of Facebook, is a firm believer in the gift economy. To enable the gift economy to work on a large scale, sufficient openness or transparency is needed. Zuckerberg believes that social networks like Facebook are key players in creating such openness or transparency. Unlike the prevailing market economy, the gift economy works on the principle that when you do good things, good things will come back to you; treat your participation as social capital and as karma, without expecting any direct return on the initial investment. In addition to Facebook, another telling example of the gift economy is the Open Source Initiative. The following is its mission statement:

> The Open Source Initiative (OSI) is a non-profit corporation with global scope formed to educate about and advocate for the benefits of open source and to build bridges among different constituencies in the open source community.
>
> Open source is a development method for software that harnesses the power of distributed peer review and transparency of process. The promise of open source is better quality, higher reliability, more flexibility, lower cost, and an end to predatory vendor lock-in.
>
> One of our most important activities is as a standards body, maintaining the Open Source Definition (*http://www.opensource.org/docs/osd*) for the good of the community. The Open Source Initiative Approved License trademark and program creates a nexus of trust around which developers, users, corporations and governments can organize open source cooperation.[5]

In the above statement, we can observe the outstanding features of OSI: it is a community-based culture that fosters sharing and support, and inclusion of the original source and provider. Similarly, social media facilitates the idealistic spirit of sharing, connecting, and spreading the gift economy.

Personal account vs. Facebook Page

In Facebook there are two main types of account: personal and Facebook Page. Personal accounts are designed for individuals, whereas the Facebook Page is optimized for artists, businesses, organizations, and government agencies.

As noted above, ever since the implementation of News Feed, there has been a continuous protest against Facebook for its intrusion or lack of protection of personal privacy. The viral spread of information that

News Feed creates has threatened some users who still feel increasingly unsure about making various adjustments in Privacy Settings. In order to protect and control our personal privacy, we might wish to heed President Obama's advice to Wakefield students to "be careful what you post on Facebook. Whatever you do, it will be pulled up later in your life,"[6] and leave out private details when creating and updating our profiles, or posting on the wall, or tagging photos, thus reducing unwanted notifications to all friends.

For governments, businesses, and organizations, we may want to do just the opposite. Such a suggestion might seem ironic, in view of the wish of Facebook's creator to empower individuals by shifting the power from large organizations. But the fact of the matter is that we have seldom heard any complaints about the News Feed from businesses, governments, and organizations. Instead, the increasing realization that it is by far one of the most effective tools for communicating and sharing information with their citizens, departments, and staff members has led more and more governments and organizations to create their own Facebook Pages. In "How Governments Are Using Social Media for Better and for Worse," Zachary Sniderman points out that

> Governments are starting to take serious notice and incorporate social media into their day-to-day actions. Governments may not be early adopters but the proliferation of social in national media has ramped up its importance for governments around the world. While this initial stance kept politicians on the defensive, enough time has passed that individual politicians and even entire governments are starting to use social media to connect with their communities in new, open ways.[7]

Sniderman cites a number of governments that are active users of social media, such as the United States, Canada, Russia, and the United Kingdom. Even though the responses of different governments toward social networks have been varied, one thing seems to be clear for the time being: governments and social media have established a tentative partnership. Online communities and their social tools are something that all governments are eager to reach and understand, since social media is going to be with us for a while. On 31 August 2011, the Santa Cruz City Manager proudly announced to his employees that the City of Santa Cruz had launched Facebook (*http://www.facebook.com/cityofsantacruz*) and Twitter (*http://www.twitter.com/cityofsantacruz*)

accounts, along with several City departments, in order to connect with residents, businesses, and visitors to share with them stories, photos, and videos about the community and provide a two-way communication channel so as to receive feedback from the public. In his announcement, the manager explained to the staff how they could receive regular updates from Facebook and how to follow the City on Twitter. He was excited about the opportunity to share their story and engage directly with the community.[8] Prior to the City's launching of Facebook and Twitter accounts, several departments had already ventured into the social media world, including:

- Parks and Recreation Police
- Fire
- Library
- Public Works
- Arts
- Economic Development
- Water
- the Commission for the Prevention of Violence Against Women.

One of the latest Facebook Pages created in the Santa Cruz area is that of the County Sheriff's office, to keep the public informed about emergencies, missing people, and investigations. To fully utilize Facebook's features, Sgt. Steve Carney told a reporter from the *Santa Cruz Sentinel*, the page would include press releases and information on road closures, wildfires, "rapidly evolving criminal investigations," and other events. He encouraged the community to "like" the page.[9]

Ideal platforms for strengthening communities

Unlike some ephemeral social networking applications, Facebook has shown its strength and durability through its long-term vision. Almost from day one, the creator of Facebook envisioned it as a platform, rather than as an application. By being a platform, Facebook can accept endless applications and softwares from enthusiastic developers, and thus has freed itself to focus on what it does best: maintaining users' profiles and their networks of friends' connections. This is a win-win situation, for software and application developers welcome such a platform. For them, the more users, and the more their diversity, the better. By 2010, it was estimated that there were half a million applications operating on Facebook. Those applications had been developed in over 180 countries. This development shows the vitality of the original vision and of Facebook's growth, which will surely benefit our efforts to bring our communities to the world.

Through years of usage, Facebook has now proven itself to be an efficient medium to promote businesses, music bands, causes, and local communities, on account of its social context. Think Local First, in the County of Santa Cruz (*https://www.facebook.com/thinklocalsantacruz*), created its Facebook Page in 2007 to "promote and sustain economic vitality while preserving the unique character of Santa Cruz County." The group was initiated in the early spring by half a dozen Santa Cruz businesses to focus on a common goal: if the community rallied around locally owned businesses, everyone would benefit; locally owned businesses would prosper and circulate money within the community, which in turn would promote more local spending, benefit local infrastructure, and maintain a vibrant and healthy community. Since Think Local First's initial meeting in October 2007, there has been a successful surge of community interest in Santa Cruz County and in less than 18 months it has gained nearly 250 members in six major categories, namely, Arts, Education and Entertainment; Dining, Spirits and Hospitality; Health and Wellness; Other; Professional and Financial Services; and Retail. The six categories cover 83 professions currently operating in the county.

In the holiday season of 2011, the *Santa Cruz Sentinel*, the local newspaper, listed in its "As We See It" section six helpful tips for building a sustainable local community: (1) Support yourself; (2) Keep Santa Cruz County unique; (3) Support community groups; (4) Reduce environmental impact; (5) Create more jobs, and (6) Invest in community. From 1 to 8 December 2011, more than 500 local businesses asked residents to spend their money in the county during the second annual Shop Local Week sponsored by Think Local First. All participants had a chance to win a $500 package of gift certificates from local retailers.[10]

Among the six tips from the *Santa Cruz Sentinel*, the last one claims our particular attention, that is, investment in community: local businesses are locally owned by people who live here, are less likely to leave, and are more invested in the community. This echoes the view of Paul Theroux:

A person who is in a country for life, tends to see himself or herself as part of the community, with responsibilities. Because fleeing was not an option, the people I knew had a well-developed sense of belonging. They took the long view: they had been there forever, the land was theirs, they were part of a culture, with a long memory, deep roots, old habits and customs. Living among such people intensified my sense of exclusion, of being a stranger, and it fascinated me.[11]

The strong "Shop Local," an extension of the "Think Local First" movement, can also be interpreted as part of social capital in a global village sense of keeping one's community unique, self-sustained, and fully invested, a wholesome provincialism, which has a vital function to fulfill as an essential basis of true civilization, as Josiah Royce proposed more than 100 years ago.

The existence of social networks like Facebook adds a new meaning to our community, for "Facebook is changing our notion of community, both at the neighborhood level and the planetary one. It may help us to move back toward a kind of intimacy that the ever-quickening pace of modern life has drawn us away from."[12] It rekindles the desire for old acquaintance, relationship, and old place/community. As Facebook plans to stretch and spread around whole globe, more and more users are seeing names, faces, and places/communities long forgotten from their former lives. Facebook has benefits not only for those looking for love, but, more importantly, for those looking for their former lives, or even for ancestral roots. Facebook represents a chance to try again. The City of Oslo's Facebook Page (*https://www.facebook.com/VisitOslo?sk=info*) appeals very strongly to such a sentiment. It places an emphasis on connecting friends of Oslo, its residents, and old and new visitors with relevant news and events fed from Oslo's official website (*http://www.visitoslo.com/*). In a way, the Facebook Page has become an interactive and comprehensive virtual universe for interested friends.

Library Facebook Pages

Renren (*http://renren.com/*), a Chinese Facebook

Libraries around the world are among the early users of Facebook. Its special appeal is easy to surmise: with minimum human intervention, but maximum coverage, Facebook's status updates reflect in real time any changes happening in our community. Such a labor-saving device fits exactly the two criteria proposed by Terence Huwe at University of California Berkeley: "There are two key features in the web-squared world that are driving change: community and immediacy."[13]

For reasons beyond the coverage of this book, Shanghai Library does not use Facebook Page. However, on its Simple Chinese web page it lists the Renren (meaning: Everyone) Network, a Chinese equivalent of Facebook. Formerly known as Xiaonei (meaning: On-campus) Network, the Renren Network filed with the Securities and Exchange Commission to raise $584 million in a US Initial Public Offering in April 2011, offering Renren shares on the New York Stock Exchange. Since its name and domain change in August 2009, Renren has expanded its user base from students to all users. By April 2011, it had "a total of 31 million active monthly users."[14]

Shanghai Library provides its users with a special Renren portal to enable them to sign in or register as new users of the site, so as to share its e-library, available since December 2011. Currently e-newspapers, e-books, and e-magazines are downloadable to PCs and iPads, and e-books and e-magazines are available via mobile devices.[15] In addition to Renren, Shanghai Library has connected other Chinese equivalents of Twitter and Facebook, like Weibo (meaning: Sina Microblog), for instance, Tencent Weibo (*http://jojn.net/tag/Tencent_Weibo/*) and Sina Weibo (*http://www.weibo.com/signup/mobile.php?lang=en-us*), and social networking sites like Kaixin001 (*http://www.kaixin001.com/*) (meaning: Happy Net), and YouKu (*http://www.youku.com/*) (similar to YouTube). Launched in March 2008, Kaixin attributed its success to the unavailability in China of social media such as Facebook and Twitter, and to following the successful models of Facebook friends and Happy Farm.

Facebook at BA and SCPL

BA states its mission very clearly on its Facebook Page (*http://www. facebook.com/pages/Bibliotheca-Alexandrina/23880589645?sk=info*): "To be a center of excellence in the production and dissemination of knowledge and to be a place of dialogue, learning and understanding between cultures and peoples." At the time of writing it has 32,857 BA friends worldwide.

SCPL officially joined Facebook (*http://www.facebook.com/ santacruzpl*) as a group on 3 February 2010. The "Info" provides the general Facebook description of SCPL, its mission, programs and services, branches, and resources. The page serves as a window to connect SCPL's community to the world.

In its technology-centered service model for 2012, approved unanimously by the library board, SCPL presented a series of library service performance indicators, such as a 5 percent increase in circulation and an 85 percent rate of self-check-outs. It also specified numbers for the expansion of its presence on social networking sites: to increase the number of Twitter followers from 250 to 300, and the number of Facebook friends from 625 to 800.[16]

There is no mystery behind such meticulous planning. The 2012 special issue of *Forbes Magazine* attempts to establish a model of Facebook advertising, using the formula of people having an average of 120 Facebook friends. Once users "like" a brand, their endorsement will spread instantly via the News Feed to many of those friends, who will then spread it further to their friends, and thus, in a flash, a network of millions of friends can potentially be built. Unlike the traditional advertising model, friends' endorsement in Facebook has a personal and human touch. By using the Facebook model, we can certainly bring our local community to a much wider audience simply by means of the News Feed function. Take, for instance, the news about George R. Lawrence's six panoramic aerial photographs of Santa Cruz in 1906 finally becoming available through the LC website. We could very well update the SCPL profile on Facebook, instead of posting the news on the website, as is the prevailing practice, for the news would become dated and search phrases on Google might not retrieve it.

Notes

1. "Facebook Users in the World." *internetworldstats.com*. Internet World Stats, 2012. Web. Accessed 30 July 2012.
2. Hof, Robert D. "Facebook's New Ad Model: You." *ForbesMagazine*, 20 February 2012: 108. Print.
3. Kirkpatrick, David. *The Facebook Effect: the Inside Story of the Company that Is Connecting the World*. New York: Simon & Schuster, c2010. 15. Print.
4. Grimmelmann, James. "Saving Facebook." *Iowa Law Review*, May 2009: 1137+. *General OneFile*. Web. Accessed 27 July 2012.
5. "Mission." *opensource.org*. Open Source Initiative, n.d. Web. Accessed 30 July 2012.
6. "Obama Advises Caution in What Kids Put on Facebook." *America's Intelligence Wire*, 8 September 2009. *General OneFile*. Web. Accessed 27 July 2012.

7. Sniderman, Zachary. "How Governments Are Using Social Media for Better and for Worse." *mashable.com*. Mashable, Inc., 25 July 2011. Web. Accessed 30 July 2012.

8. Bernal, Martín. "Social Media Update." Message to City of Santa Cruz departments. 31 August 2011. E-mail.

9. "Coast Lines: Jan. 26, 2012 – Santa Cruz." *Santa Cruz Sentinel*. Web. Accessed 30 July 2012.

10. "Live Locally, Shop Locally." *Santa Cruz Sentinel*, 25 November 2011: sec. A9. Print.

11. Theroux, Paul. *Fresh Air Fiend*. New York: Houghton Mifflin Company, c2000. 8. Print.

12. Kirkpatrick, David. *The Facebook Effect: the Inside Story of the Company that Is Connecting the World*. New York: Simon & Schuster, c2010. 232. Print.

13. Huwe, Terence K. "Library 2.0, Meet the 'Web-Squared' World." *Computers in Libraries*, April 2011: 25. Print.

14. Chao, Loretta. "Renren Lowers Key User Figure before IPO." *WSJ.com*. The Wall Street Journal, 29 April 2011. Web. Accessed 30 July 2012.

15. "Introduction to eResources." *e.library.sh.cn*. Shanghai Library, n.d. Web. Accessed 30 July 2012.

16. Brown, J. M. "Santa Cruz Public Libraries Board Sets Improvement Goals to Achieve Next Year." *Santa Cruz Sentinel*, 8 November 2011: B1. Print.

Part 5
Future: Library 3.0 and Beyond

17

Local needs vs. global resources

Abstract: This chapter defines the distinction between Library 2.0 and 3.0, and the reason why we need to prepare for 3.0 while 2.0 is not fully realized. It goes on to outline a map of virtualization to enable the local community to take advantage of global resources, and the impact of virtualization on library services. The outlined virtualization consists of at least three components: virtual communities; virtual resources; and virtual locations.

Key words: equity of access, virtual library, artificial intelligence, Watson, Siri, crowdsourcing, University College London Bentham Project, New York Public Library, What's on the menu? What's the Score at the Bodleian? Bodleian Library, Victorian Music Project, GeneSoc, Local News Indexing Project.

Implications of Web/Library 3.0 for libraries

One might ask, since many implications of 2.0 have hardly been fully realized and many 2.0 tools are still in the process of being developed or discarded, especially in the library setting, where the hurry is to think about 3.0. Woody Evans is of the opinion that the reason we are building 3.0 is not for trendiness, nor to blindly follow the next "Point.0," but for the improvement of library services for users, so as to avoid the pitfall of seeking the newest technologies or gadgets just in order to be cool and hip. Some library professionals have gone for a much greater goal:

> It is not the programmers, coders, engineers, and IT administrators alone who shape Web 3.0, a burgeoning and perhaps even semi-intelligent web of natural language query, discrete and contextual meaning, and the expert systems that finally rise above their humble call-and-response origins. Librarians, perhaps even while, as Bruce Sterling suggests, their skill sets are appropriated by other

professions, are well positioned to build and to serve in Library 3.0. We must move quickly, however, and very earnestly, into fields many of us may find unfamiliar.[1]

The real reason for us to move to Web/Library 3.0 lies in the presence of social media technologies that can enable us to fully realize the vision of a future library. The future library is a portable, personal, intelligent, and behavioral web. It facilitates the meeting of local/personal needs (through its ability to analyze and observe the needs of a local community and its individual residents) by mashing them with global resources (access to global resources via interconnectivity and open standards). The prevailing virtualization through social media networks and tools has greatly enhanced human interactions and broadened the reach of both virtual and real communities and of library resources. To a great extent, physical location has become irrelevant. By the means of an optimal human–machine combination (human intelligence + machine intelligence), the library of the future will be able to play on the strengths of both, and to fully realize the potential of the Semantic Web, where the meaning of data is expressed in natural human language.

Needless to say, 2.0 will be followed by even more fundamental changes than those that have enabled people to participate and share through social networks. During their information sharing, people have given voice to their need for "semantic discretion and specificity within and between groups," as Woody Evans has underlined. What are the practical implications of this for library services?

The ALA states that:

> Equity of access means that all people have the information they need – regardless of age, education, ethnicity, language, income, physical limitations or geographic barriers. It means they are able to obtain information in a variety of formats – electronic, as well as print. It also means they are free to exercise their right to know without fear of censorship or reprisal.[2]

And that:

> Libraries are major sources of information for society and they serve as guardians of the public's access to information more generally. The advent of the digital world has revolutionized how the public obtains its information and how libraries provide it. Libraries help ensure that Americans can access the information

they need – regardless of age, education, ethnicity, language, income, physical limitations or geographic barriers – as the digital world continues to evolve. Core values of the library community such as equal access to information, intellectual freedom, and the objective stewardship and provision of information must be preserved and strengthened in the evolving digital world.[3]

The ALA's vision of the evolving digital world sees libraries continuing to be major sources of information in society and guardians of the public's access to information more generally. In the world of 3.0, the core values of the library community – "equal access to information, intellectual freedom, and the objective stewardship and provision of information" – must be preserved and strengthened; and they require library professionals to provide all people with the information they need, "regardless of age, education, ethnicity, language, income, physical limitations or geographic barriers," and regardless of a great variety of information formats.

To meet the ALA's above requirements, we will inevitably be confronted with two issues: How can we serve both local/real and global/virtual communities without discrimination and with limited local resources? Can a local community afford to service the global community? These are not issues for library administrators and board members alone. They concern all of us working in library and information services. To resolve the conflict between local and global, some people suggest that we should move the virtual service into the backroom, instead of locating it on the main floor, where locals come in to ask for services – thus reducing the likelihood of complaints about being snubbed. Others suggest that we should bring the real-life community into the virtual community by offering classes to the public in order to raise their global awareness. Yet others suggest that we should involve the local community by permitting locals to become vested in the virtual community. To a great extent, all of these viewpoints are on the right track. To library professionals, virtual users are as important as the walk-in ones, for the virtual community can consist of someone from Greenland or a homebound, elderly senior down the street. Since the distinction between virtual and real users is becoming increasingly blurred, a safer policy remains our old policy: to help any and all who seek for information. One of the viable solutions for achieving a broader reach of both local community residents and those beyond is to establish a fully functional virtual library with a variety of types of information such as e-books, e-audios, e-movies, and e-music, and access devices such as e-mail, Text-a-Librarian, tablets, PCs, mobile devices, social media tools and sites. The following are a few working scenarios for extending the reach of our limited resources.

The machine as human assistant: from Watson to Siri

On 14–16 February 2011, in New York, a great event took place on American TV. The IBM *Jeopardy!* challenge show featured IBM's Watson supercomputer, optimized to tackle a specific challenge: competing with *Jeopardy*'s two all-time champions, Brad Rutter and Ken Jennings. Through thick and thin, Watson managed to become the winner of the $1 million prize. This was the second time that computers had undergone key artificial intelligence (AI) tests since IBM's Deep Blue beat world chess champion Gary Kasparov in 1999.

The contest was interesting not just for its entertainment value, but the more so because IBM has pioneered the transformation of science fiction into reality by trying to negotiate natural language and then tapping into a dedicated database to retrieve the right answer, a unique process that only the human brain is capable of.[4] In the show, Watson revealed its weaknesses, such as bulky hardware and some algorithmic errors that caused it to miss key parameters, such that it answered "Toronto" to a question about US airports. Further, Watson was born without the ability to process audio and visual information, which not only demonstrates the limited development of today's computer technology, but also has proved to be the greatest hurdle of all for the AI community to cross in enabling computers to match human intelligence, ever since Alan Turing's 1950 paper "Computing Machinery and Intelligence." Watson's development is just like that of us human beings, from imperfect to perfect. Its occasional lack of confidence has helped to bust the myth perpetuated by science fiction that the solution to all our problems is just a computer keystroke away. The reason why IBM chose *Jeopardy!* to test its supercomputer was based on the fact that the show makes great demands on its players, and even greater demands on a computer system and the team of scientists behind it. The IBM team managed to teach a machine like Watson to understand human language in order to arrive at a precise answer to a *Jeopardy!* question. This was a great leap forward, for "A computer system that can understand natural language and deliver a single, precise answer to a question requires the right combination of hardware and software."[5] The right combination of hardware and software is as important for computers as is the acquisition of the right knowledge for humans if they want to "tab into the huge databases stored in our memory to retrieve the answer 'cobalt'" when trying to tackle the quiz question what element, atomic number 27, can precede "blue" and "green," as mathematician Professor Marcus du Sautoy points out. If they are not equipped with a basic knowledge of chemistry, humans will not be able to take advantage of their memory to produce the right answer to that question, no matter how huge the database that is stored in that memory. This is a good lesson for us library professionals in coming up with the right combination. And in our services to our communities we are actually very good at providing the right answers from the right sources.

The triumph of Watson has indicated a great advance in data analytics, and its far-reaching impact on business and industry. Since Watson, the IBM team has been using the same technology in industries such as healthcare, finance, and customer service. The IBM Power 750 Express Server is especially targeted at midsize businesses to integrate information for smarter insights and better decision making, not to mention the benefit of reducing costs in terms of energy and space. Although it is not connected to the internet, but is powered by local servers, Watson has demonstrated two remarkable capabilities: its comprehension of human language and its command of natural language in delivering its replies. Despite its lack of hearing and sight, Watson is a competent reader of keyboard-typed questions.

The success of Watson has also proved the truth of three strengths of computers, namely, their excellence in learning, organizing, and analyzing data through textual feeding. Through its comprehension of the meaning of a human-like question, Watson is able to sift through structured and unstructured data in its memory to formulate knowledge that can then be processed to answer questions. Even though there will be many hurdles before computer intelligence is comparable to the human brain, we library professionals should take advantage of what these machines can offer. If Watson can learn library books, and understand the readers' inquiries, it can become a virtual librarian or a librarian assistant to help us to more accurately answer a variety of questions.

On 4 October 2011, on the West Coast of the United States, a beta application of an intelligent personal assistant and knowledge navigator was put into production on the iPhone 4S. It is none other than Siri

(Speech Interpretation and Recognition Interface), software developed by Siri Inc. and that was acquired by Apple in April 2010. Being an intelligent personal assistant, Siri is able to hear the human voice, to send messages, schedule meetings, place phone calls, answer questions, and make recommendations. There are a number of fundamental dissimilarities between Watson and Siri. Unlike Watson, Siri utilizes both internal data on one's iPhone and external data on the web. Unlike Watson, Siri has good hearing of its owner's queries and can respond without delays. Furthermore, it operates on a mobile device. It uses the processing power of the dual-core A5 chip in iPhone 4S, with 3G and Wi-Fi networks to communicate rapidly with Apple's data centers. However, there are also many similarities between the two inventions, namely, the utilization of natural language and powerful artificial intelligence engines.

Since its debut on *Jeopardy!*, Watson has made tremendous progress. It has recruited a number of clients, such as Citibank, which signed an agreement with IBM to use Watson so as to better serve its clients, and Wellpoint Health Networks, which licensed the Watson technology. The early predictions for Watson's possible future in the medical field have gradually been realized. On 22 March 2012, AllThingsD reported that Watson had officially started its first job at the prestigious Memorial Sloan-Kettering Cancer Center (*http://www.mskcc.org/*) in New York. While not fully qualified as a medical doctor, Watson is an extremely well-read physician's assistant. It can both consult the very latest medical literature and look back through the history of previous cancer cases to help doctors figure out the best way to treat a particular cancer.[6]

Needless to say, IBM's experiment has provided us with useful evidence and insight for our Library 3.0 and Semantic Web. Like Watson, "Siri isn't like traditional voice recognition software that requires you to remember keywords and speak specific commands. Siri understands your natural speech, and it asks you questions if it needs more information to complete a task."[7] In our mission to serve real and virtual communities with limited local resources, we should enlist both existing and new technological inventions. If used appropriately, the IBM Watson- and Siri-like intelligent agents could surely help libraries to save tremendous manpower by manning library services and filtering out factual as well as informational queries when libraries are either open or closed. Being professionally polite and friendly, both Watson and Siri have the ability to supply intelligent and relevant answers to their information customers.

More flexible and scalable resource usage in meeting increasing demand for library services

In order to optimize our limited local resources, we must first of all conserve, by prolonging the lifespan of the existing infrastructure, such as the ILS, and by building a truly user-friendly virtual library residing in the cloud. We upgrade, but not because neighboring libraries are upgrading; we buy new machines and systems because there is a strong and pressing need, not because it is trendy to show off – which has got many an organization into financial trouble.

Meanwhile, we will need to advocate for both local and global collaboration. "Ask the Library" is one of OPL's 24/7 library services, in which libraries all over Norway participate. Its continuing success has demonstrated that it is possible to develop such a collaborative reference model. Libraries in California or Alexandria may not enjoy the same level of funding as libraries in Norway do. However, they can contribute to the same level of collaboration. Moreover, they have the same deep-rooted tradition of collaboration and of sharing catalog records, books, and other library materials through interlibrary services.

The model of OCLC is a telling example of local, regional, national, and international collaboration among library professionals, making it the most comprehensive bibliographical resource for library materials. Since 1999, OCLC has conducted a series of significant mergers and acquisitions, mostly notably, WLN (Western Library Network, based in Lacey, Washington) in January 1999, NetLibrary in January 2002 (sold to EBSCO in March 2010), CAPCON (a District of Columbia nonprofit corporation) in November 2003, Sisis Informationssysteme GmbH in July 2005, and RLIN (Research Libraries Information Network) in July 2006.

Stretching local resources through efficient usage of social media tools

In consideration of the time needed to man the virtual library services such as e-reference, Text-a-Librarian, tablets, PCs, mobile devices, and social media sites, we need to re-evaluate our tools and workflow. In the traditional telephone reference service, some library staff would spend a huge amount of time on one user, with the result that the phone line would be clogged and waiting lights would flash. If we are not careful, we can easily get ourselves into a similar situation, even though natural query language and technology have somewhat eased our workload. On either Facebook or Twitter, the conventional five-minutes per question rule might still apply, for we cannot afford to serve or follow one single user while ignoring/snubbing the whole online community. We need to allocate our time and staff resources democratically and equally.

One possibility is the efficient utilization of social media sites by consolidating and sharing accounts. For instance, we do not have to spend our time by separating between blogging, Facebook, and Twitter. We can feed our real and virtual communities with the latest updates on library resources and programs by using the *share* application. In the same way, we can further explore social media tools like YouTube and use them to capture and archive our training sessions or typical Q&A about our local community, so as to avoid repetition of learning sessions and typical queries.

Before adopting any new technological invention for the utilization of library resources, real or virtual, we may want to do our homework thoroughly. We will need to anticipate our users' initial anxieties when they are faced with new-fangled devices, and gather relevant resources to help them to overcome these hurdles. When many elderly residents were thrown into the world of e-books and e-audios during and after Christmas 2011, some staff members at SCPL were taken by surprise at the surge in the number of Kindle and Nook queries. If they had anticipated correctly, staff members would have been fully prepared with online tutorials for various devices and information about further tutoring sessions. It is laudable that we improve our new services as we go, but it does put certain pressures on our staff, both physically and psychologically, and could affect our future services.

Better integration with other online information sources: the Semantic Web

As mentioned earlier, the Semantic Web is not just about putting data on the web, but about making links, so that a person or machine can explore the web of data. If we look back into our card catalog and today's ILS, we will find that is it not a total stranger to Tim Berners-Lee's four rules of using URLs to link and locate the exact data and other related data. For the library catalog is nothing other than a *see also* cross-reference for name, subject, and title authorities. With data in the ILS linked by either URLs or cross-references, both the card catalog and the online catalog perform the same purpose, namely, to enable users who have some data to find other related data. The only difference between the two is that the name of the game has been changed, as has the environment.

In a post-2.0 and 3.0 world, the information has many formats, of which printed books, periodicals, and documents are just one kind. For this reason, we need to expand the concept of cross-references by providing more links so as to realize a true one-stop shopping model in which users can obtain needed information all at once, instead of gathering data or images from scratch, from everywhere. In the case of George R. Lawrence's panoramic photographs of Santa Cruz County, available at LC, it will surely do local and global users a thorough service if we supply direct URL links to the LC- and SCPL-related websites.

Better information evaluation, organization, and access

In an effort to paraphrase Robert F. Kennedy, Jr.'s keynote speech at the 2012 conference of the Public Library Association in Philadelphia, John N. Berry III, editor-at-large of *Library Journal*, reminded us yet again that we library professionals have to learn to help citizens to sort out useful information from junk, and show them how to validate the information that they find, in an age when people are inundated with information. Being inundated with information is not something new in our modern society. What is new is that today the information has undergone a fundamental transformation that is typical of our time. Not only does it exist in a myriad of formats and media, but it is also complicated by the fact that "Individuals do not always have the expertise to correct all the errors, the inadvertent and purposeful misinformation pouring from thousands of tainted sources. Information is not only distorted by extremist ideologies, excessive efforts to sell things or make profits, or narrow religious convictions. It is often simply inaccurate owing to neglect, flawed methods of gathering or creating it, or cultural bigotries so deep that they are not apparent."

Here, John N. Berry III has mentioned a number of critical issues, namely, how to better evaluate, organize, and access information. The purpose of the public library as defined by the Boston Public Library in 1852 – to inform democratic self-government – can still be valid today, so long as we have an enlightened society. But, "To contribute to the enlightened society Kennedy proposed, librarians will have to enlist in a much more militant effort to find and deliver, even broadcast, the most current, accurate, comprehensive, and understandably articulated information to help people take action to build it."[8]

To start with, Google's mission to organize the world's information should be ours too. As the world's information is infinite, we need to think out of the box by organizing library collections and conducting queries in natural language and knowledge bases. Recently, reference librarian John Cupersmith of the University of California at Berkeley has compiled and added to the system-wide e-scholarship repository a study entitled "Library Terms that Users Understand." According to its findings, "Commonly misunderstood terms include acronyms and brand names, subject categories, and the words *database*, *library catalog*, *e-journals*, *index*, *interlibrary loan*, *periodicals*, *serial*, *reference*, and *resource*. Common correctly understood terms include *find books*, *find articles*, and other combinations using natural language target words that correspond to the end product the user is seeking."[9]

Crowdsourcing projects – the power of volunteering

The Bentham Project at University College London

Among social media sites and tools, YouTube and Wikipedia are two exemplary successes in crowdsourcing projects. However, they are by no means the origin of the crowdsourcing concept. There have recently been a number of projects that have attracted our attention. Take for instance the Bentham Project at University College London (*http://www.ucl.ac.uk/*; UCL). More than 50 years ago, UCL started to transcribe the papers of the Enlightenment philosopher Jeremy Bentham, which are held in its special collections. The painstaking task of transcribing the hard-to-decipher handwritten manuscripts was compounded by a lack of funding, and the project progressed at a snail's pace: fewer than half of the projected 70 volumes were published in the span of half a century.[10] In 2010, UCL received funding from the Arts and Humanities Research

Council and launched the Bentham Project. The Project adopted a crowdsourcing method by creating a Transcription Desk. Interested volunteers can log in and transcribe the as-yet unstudied and unpublished manuscripts. After they have submitted their completed transcripts, Project staff will edit them and make them fully accessible online in UCL Library's Digital Collections (*http://digitool-b.lib.ucl.ac.uk:8881/R/?func =collections&collection_id=1867*). In 2011, the Project received an Award of Distinction in the Digital Communities category of the highly prestigious Prix Ars Electronica, an award focused specifically on crowdsourcing projects.[11]

What's on the Menu? at New York Public Library

Since late April 2011, New York Public Library (*http://www.nypl.org/*; NYPL) has embarked on a crowdsourcing project called What's on the Menu? The project is to organize and transcribe a collection of more than 40,000 historical New York City restaurant menus. The collection was originated by Miss Frank E. Buttolph (1850–1924). In 1899, she donated her existing collection to the NYPL. She then continued to add to the collection until her death in 1924. The collection has continued to grow through additional gifts of graphic, gastronomic, topical, or sociological interest, especially but not exclusively New York related.[12] The unique collection has been used heavily by historians, chefs, novelists, and everyday food enthusiasts. Historically, it has not been an easy collection to use, due to the difficulties of searching the menus for the treasures they contain and specific information on dishes, prices, the organization of meals, and the history of the food and culture of a specific era and region.

In order to access and utilize the collection fully and easily, NYPL has started a crowdsourcing project by recruiting volunteers. By now, a quarter of the 40,000 menus have been digitized and made available in the NYPL Digital Gallery (*http://digitalgallery.nypl.org/nypldigital/ explore/dgexplore.cfm?topic=culture&col_id=159*). It is interesting to note that NYPL has also resorted to transcription, rather than the prevailing OCR technology. It scans the completed transcriptions and loads them into the transcription queue. The decision to use transcription is based on a number of reasons: (1) OCR can produce decent output from some of the clearer, printed menus, but many menus are handwritten, or use fancy typography and idiosyncratic layouts that defy the capabilities of OCR; (2) NYPL and its staff and volunteers are interested in unearthing some specific types of information that are highly relevant to researchers, such as dishes and prices and, eventually, menu sections, geographical locations, and perhaps other data. They are not just scooping out text from pages, they are building a database about dishes; and (3) as a library, NYPL realizes that the more people use a collection, the more they can learn about and share it. It has invited the public to help it go through menus with careful attention, menu by menu, dish by dish, not only to let users research or trace what people were eating at a certain historical period, but also in the hope of stoking people's appetite to explore the collection further. As a result of the success of its menu project, NYPL is now looking into partnering with other libraries and archives with menu collections.[13]

What's the Score at the Bodleian? at the Bodleian Library

What's the Score at the Bodleian? is one of the most recent crowdsourcing projects initiated by the Bodleian Library (*http://www.bodleian.ox.ac. uk/bodley*), to transcribe its Victorian Music collection. The majority of the sheet music is for piano, and the collection contains dance music and other pieces designed for home entertainment, comprising 64 boxes of unbound and uncataloged sheet music dating from the mid-Victorian period. The Bodleian Library opted for the economical crowdsourcing approach, based on the conclusions from a pilot study that traditional retrospective cataloging of the music collections would be both expensive and time consuming. Partially financed by Google, and hosted by Zooniverse for its crowdsourcing interface, the initial project is being carried out by the Bodleian and consists of scanning the sheet music and capturing some metadata that will be gradually enriched by the addition of crowdsourced descriptions. The ultimate goal of the project is to make the contents of the Victorian Music collection "more accessible to the wide range of people who use them, or who would do if they knew they were there."[14] The project has enlisted the help of volunteers and is using crowdsourcing to enhance the basic metadata with additional features such as Music OCR and online performances. It does not expect the volunteers to be fully equipped with music knowledge. After a selection of piano sheet music has been digitized, the project participants are asked to submit descriptions of the scores by transcribing the information that they can see. Today, What's the Score at the Bodleian? is available to the general public. It is the hope of the project's organizers that it "may lead in future to the Libraries exploring further ways in which members of the public, who may be experts in particular fields, can be encouraged to enrich the existing catalogues and other finding aids by contributing additional information about the collections."[15]

Local News Indexing Project at Santa Cruz County Genealogical Society

If we take a closer look at the three libraries that we have just examined, we will inevitably find that they have all been empowered by the crowdsourcing spirit and have benefited from the power of volunteers. The Local News Indexing Project at SCPL is also worth mentioning. Unlike many newspapers which were equipped with indexes by subject, title, or author before the advent of newspaper databases, the *Santa Cruz Sentinel*, a local newspaper published since 1856, was handicapped by having no index by which to retrieve past or present news reports, articles, announcements of weddings, births/deaths (obituaries) prior to 1999. Under these circumstances, GeneSoc decided to take upon itself the newspaper-indexing project.

Established in August 1971, GeneSoc is a nonprofit organization with several hundred members in Santa Cruz County. In early January 1972, it began to build a collection of books that would eventually be integrated with the SCPL system. On 1 March 1974, it moved into the Branciforte Branch library. In 1986, the then library director, Anne Turner, wrote a proposal to set up a Local History Branch Library overseen by an advisory board composed of members from GeneSoc, the library joint powers board, and the branch itself. With a staff of one librarian and one clerk, the branch would house a Californiana collection, the microfilm collection, the microfilm reader/printers and GeneSoc's collection. The proposed branch was a cooperative effort between SCPL and GeneSoc. While it was approved in concept by the Library Board in April 1986, the proposal underwent some modification in the implementation: GeneSoc and its collection moved to the Central (now Downtown) Branch in August 1991, rather than operating as a separate, independent branch; and the daily operation of the Local History Library has been staffed by volunteers, rather than by regular staff members.[16] With its location now clearly designated, the collection has become part of SCPL's holdings, and cataloging and processing is managed by SCPL's Technical Services (now Collection Management Service).

GeneSoc's mission is to promote general interest in the study of genealogy, to provide instruction in genealogical research, to expand the Society's genealogical library, to maintain a working relationship with other genealogical libraries and organizations, and to support efforts to preserve pertinent local, state, and federal records. It holds a meeting on the first Thursday of each month (except July, August, and December). The month of October is celebrated as Family History Month, with displays of research by early members of GeneSoc. To encourage younger generations to become involved in genealogy, Joseph Bunnett, husband of the late Sara Telfer Bunnett, proposed that children should interview their parents and grandparents for family histories, and suggested that the interviews should be incorporated into the school curriculum and the children's reports be graded as regular writing assignments.[17]

Representing GeneSoc in 1986, the late Sara Telfer Bunnett initiated the Local News Indexing Project to make the information in local newspapers more accessible to local and remote users. The finished volumes would be made available at the Downtown Branch of SCPL and McHenry Library at UCSC. Sara Bunnett was a staunch supporter of SCPL, being a founding member of the Friends of the Santa Cruz Public Libraries and serving on three library joint powers boards between 1978 and 2004. Born in Portland, Oregon and a descendant of American president William Henry Harrison, she had great enthusiasm for genealogy, and published a number of books reflecting her interests, such as *Manila Envelopes: Oregon Volunteer Lt. George F. Telfer's Spanish-American War Letters* (1987), *Telfer, Pratt, and Platts: Some Genealogical Facts* (1990), *The People Named Bunnett: the Suffolk Line* (2003). After coming to Santa Cruz in 1966 with her husband, Joseph Bunnett, a chemistry professor recruited from Brown University by the newly founded UCSC, she became a member of GeneSoc and served two terms as its president. The Local News Indexing Project not only rekindled her life-long passion for genealogical research, but also crystallized the cause of preserving historical records. Under her guidance and supervision, "volunteers started with the *Pacific Sentinel* of 1856, reviewing each edition, page by page, column by column, jotting down entries on index cards that were later entered into computer files. The index is complete up to the daily *Santa Cruz Sentinel* of 1961."[18] During the 20 years from 1986 to 2006, Sara and her volunteers met every Thursday to work on the indexing project. Over time, the indexing project grew in breadth and depth.

In addition to the *Sentinel*, they indexed other old local newspapers, like the *Santa Cruz Surf* (1883–1919) and the *Mountain Echo* (1896–1916).

Meanwhile, the scope of the indexing greatly exceeded the original plan to only "index people and places in old newspapers." The subject coverage included areas such as:

- Affidavits, applications and/or intentions to marry
- Births and deaths
- Building permits
- Divorces
- Land grants
- Marriages
- News
- Petitions to Naturalization Service
- Santa Cruz County Court of session's minutes.

The subject of "Building permits" warrants special mention. In 2004, Sara Bunnett compiled and published *Building Permits from Early Newspapers (ca 1910–1954)*. The comprehensive indexing of permits by name, street, date, and page for the whole county was an expansion of Sara Bunnett's co-authored *Every Structure Tells a Story: How to Research the History of a Property in Santa Cruz County: with research techniques; sources of information, locations of research material, and a bibliography* (1990). It also laid the foundation for "How to Research Your Property's History," a free lecture presented by SCPL in 2007 as part of "Research Workshop: House History," an event organized by Researchers Anonymous, which is an interest group that meets monthly for lectures, tours, workshops, and roundtable discussions sponsored by MAH.[19]

Since the death of Sara Bunnett in 2006, her volunteers have been meeting as usual every Thursday and continuing her indexing project by transcribing local newspapers into their laptops for the final compilation and editing. The volunteers are very seldom absent, and they look forward to their weekly indexing gathering. By now 16 newspaper indexes have been published and made available in the Genealogical Room at the SCPL Downtown Branch, and at the UCSC McHenry Library. The ongoing project is an online index of *Santa Cruz Surf* (1883–1900) and *Pacific Sentinel* and *Santa Cruz Sentinel* (1856–84). There is also an abridged online index to the whole run of *Mountain Echo*. Excerpted from a print index that contains additional subjects, the online index includes births, deaths, and personal names.

Unlike short-lived volunteering efforts in other library operations, such as deploying volunteers to shelve books, the GeneSoc indexing volunteers have taken their indexing projects very seriously. Many of them are members of Sara Bunnett's original team. Such enduring dedication is a further confirmation of the success of the Bentham Project, What's on the Menu? and What's the Score at the Bodleian?

We can draw several points from these crowdsourcing projects.

Sense of community pride

All four projects have drawn their strength from the members of their communities. Whether in an academic setting, a metropolitan city, or a small town, participating volunteers have exhibited the same pride in their respective communities.

Sense of professional pride

The projects in question have provided interested volunteers with opportunities to participate by contributing their unique experience and knowledge. As the projects grow, so does the volunteers' professional pride and satisfaction. This is another key to success. To use volunteers in the place of paid staff to perform daily tasks such as cleaning and shelving, on the other hand, might damp their initial enthusiasm for volunteering. They may prefer to crowdsource projects that are more suitable to their expertise and interest.

Need for leadership

There is a need for coordination and administration in crowdsourcing projects, which is even true of YouTube (e.g., channels) and Wikipedia (e.g., articles). All four projects mentioned have strong leadership to guide the volunteering efforts at every stage so as to fulfill both short- and long-term goals. This is the reason why GeneSoc has been able to make such great progress in using crowdsourcing to preserve and index other historical records, in addition to the newspaper indexing. The following are some of its typical publications.

Church records

1. *First Congregational Church of Santa Cruz, CA.: records index, 1852–1975* (1990).

2. *Calvary Episcopal Church: records of early parishioners* (2004). Includes 11 ministers of Calvary Episcopal Church, who conducted christenings, marriages, and burials between 1863 and 1940.

3. *Calvary Episcopal Church of Santa Cruz, California* (2005), a four-volume parish register. Registers baptisms, marriages, and burials at the church from 1853 to 1945.

4. *Parish Records of St. Andrew's Episcopal Church, Ben Lomond, California* (2005). Contains baptisms, marriages, and burials from 1904 to 2000.

5. *Parish Records of St. John the Baptist Episcopal Church, Capitola, California* (2005). Contains baptisms marriages and burials from 1961 to 2001.

Cemeteries

1. *Felton Cemetery tombstone inscriptions, Felton, Santa Cruz County, California* (1978).

2. *Santa Cruz Mausoleum: names of all those who passed through these portals and disposition of the remains* (2000). Contains records current through April 2000.

3. *Santa Cruz Memorial Park Cemetery and the Santa Cruz Mausoleum Compiled Records* (2000). Contains burial records of the Santa Cruz Memorial Park Cemetery and Crematorium. The resulting record lists nearly 30,000 persons.

4. *San Jose Mission Cemetery* (2002).

5. *Survey of Our Lady of Mt. Carmel Cemetery* (2002).

6. *Holy Cross Cemetery and Mausoleum: compiled records* (2004). A four-volume set indexing both old and new Holy Cross interments that belonged to Santa Cruz Mission and old families, some dated from 1791.

7. *Old Holy Cross Cemetery and Mausoleum: compiled records: maps and unmapped block lists* (2004).

Government documents

1. *Record Books of the Alcaldes of Santa Cruz, California, 1847–1850 and April term 1851* (1992). Contains information on land grants in Santa Cruz County.

2. *Naturalization Service, Petition and Record. Vol. 2–6, December 9, 1909–March 9, 1927, Petition nos. 50 to 550* (1996). Contains information from Declarations of intention to become a citizen of the United States and Petitions for naturalization, Superior Court of the County of Santa Cruz, California.

3. *Great Register of the County of Santa Cruz for 1890* (2001). Contains the complete registration information regarding county electors.

Notes

1. Evans, Woody. *Building Library 3.0: Issues in Creating a Culture of Participation.* Cambridge, UK: Chandos Publishing Ltd., 2009. 136. Print.
2. "Equity of Access." *ala.org/advocacy/access.* American Library Association, 2013. Web. Accessed 7 March 2013.
3. "Access." *ala.org/advocacy/access.* American Library Association, 2012. Web. Accessed 30 October 2012.
4. "Can Computers Have True Artificial Intelligence?" *bbc.co.uk.* BBC News, Technology, 3 April 2012. Web. Accessed 30 July 2012.
5. "This Is Watson." *www-03.ibm.com.* IBM, n.d. Web. Accessed 30 July 2012. (*http://www-03.ibm.com/innovation/us/watson/what-is-watson/index.html*).
6. "IBM Computer Watson Is Now a Big-Shot Doctor, and You Still Aren't." allthingsd.com. Dow Jones & Company Inc., 22 March 2012. Web. Accessed 30 July 2012.
7. "What is Siri?" apple.com. Apple Inc., 2012. Web. Accessed 30 July 2012.
8. Berry III, J. "Library Jobs in the New Society." *Library Journal* [serial online]. 15 April 2012; 137(7): 10. Available from: MasterFILE Premier, Ipswich, MA. Accessed 27 July 2012.
9. Kelley, M. "Users Don't Know What Libraries Are Talking About." *Library Journal* [serial online]. 15 April 2012; 137(7): 17. Available from: MasterFILE Premier, Ipswich, MA. Accessed 27 July 2012.
10. Cohen, Patricia. "Scholars Recruit Public for Project." *New York Times,* 27 December 2010. Web. Accessed 30 July 2012.
11. "Transcribe Bentham." *ucl.ac.uk.* University College London, 2012. Web. Accessed 30 July 2012.
12. "Miss Frank E. Buttolph American Menu Collection, 1851–1930." *digitalgallery.nypl.org.* New York Public Library, n.d. Web. Accessed 30 July 2012.
13. "Help the New York Public Library Improve a Unique Collection!" *menus.nypl.org.* New York Public Library, n.d. Web. Accessed 30 July 2012.
14. Schuessler, Jennifer. "Bodleian Announces Crowd-sourcing Victorian Music Project." *New York Times,* 2 May 2012. Web. Accessed 30 July 2012.
15. "What's the Score at the Bodleian? goes live." *whatsthescoreatthebodleian.wordpress.com.* WordPress.com, 3 May 2012. Web. Accessed 30 July 2012.

16. Swedberg, Donna. "SCPL monthly report for August 2011."
17. White, Kimberly. "Unraveling family mysteries." *Santa Cruz Sentinel*, 10 October 2011. Web. Accessed 30 July 2012.
18. Gumz, Jondi. "Civic volunteer Sara Bunnett dead at 87." *Santa Cruz Sentinel*, 2 November 2006. Web. Accessed 30 July 2012.
19. Fairchilds, Kirsten. "History Hunters: Learn How to Research Your House's Past." *Santa Cruz Sentinel*, 11 October 2007. Web. Accessed 30 July 2012.

18

The librarian's role as information manager

Abstract: This chapter redefines the role of librarians as information managers – which is not a new concept. What separates Web 3.0 from other eras is that librarians can fulfill their full potential through the promising functionality of the Semantic Web. Specific tasks include the realization of findability, accuracy, user protection, and customizing computer programming for the management and retrieval of information.

Key words: information manager, findability, accuracy of information, evaluating information, tagging, user privacy, OCLC, MarcEdit, Terry Reese, NoveList, KDL.

In the world of 3.0, we will find our role as librarians or library professionals transformed into that of information managers, a job title that dates from the dawn of the internet but that has never realized its full potential. We will inevitably act as guides in the world of information and semantic networking.

We are all limited by the finite quantity of hours and energy in one day. Many users are now practically living on the internet, and have tried to seek for information and satisfy their needs without the intervention of library professionals. More often than not, we find ourselves receiving and answering really difficult queries from these users, who do not necessarily suffer from information illiteracy. The reasons for this can be manifold. Existing search tools may not be adequate to pinpoint what they are seeking in the sea of information. The query language and strategy may need improvement. The desired information may not exist on the internet at all. As information managers, we are equipped with the knowledge and techniques for worlds both of books (library collections) and of electronic resources (web). We are confident and competent to guide our users to filter out false hits and locate the real gem.

Findability: a priority in designing and managing well-linked information

It is always a great challenge to group, classify, and connect relevant information. Take, for instance, the Harry Potter series in most public library collections. Once the great demand is over, we are left with battle scars and used-up copies. This phenomenon occurs often with popular or classic titles. In 2012 there was some revived interest in the Potter series among the community of Santa Cruz County. Unless they have read all seven books and can reel off their titles fluently, the reference staff can find themselves ill-equipped to answer users' simple question about which book to read next. One reference librarian claims that although she has read them all, she can never remember the order of the series.[1] The reason is obvious: in our rush to serve the public when the demand was high, we neglected to provide sufficient or consistent links in the catalog. In SCPL's catalog no series fields were provided, except for a few later titles in Spanish. Let's use *Harry Potter and the Deathly Hallows* for a further analysis.

In OCLC, some libraries do not provide series fields at all, except for a 500 field to state that this is the sequel to *Harry Potter and the Half-Blood Prince*. As 5XX fields are not indexed fields, users will not be able to search them if they are trying to find something sequentially. Many libraries do use series fields, but not so consistently as LC's series authority has clearly defined,

LC Authority:

Year ... at Hogwarts. (LC)

see Rowling, J. K. Year ... at Hogwarts. (0)

Harry Potter series (LC)

see Rowling, J. K. Harry Potter series. (0)

Some OCLC libraries use one or all 8XX fields, with just one 490 field, even though two 800 fields are cross-referenced to different entries, "Harry Potter series," "Year ... at Hogwarts," while the third one, "Harry Potter" in 830, is not even a valid record.

491 1 The Harry Potter series; $v bk. 7

=> 800 1 Rowling, J. K. $t Harry Potter series ; $v bk. 7

=> 800 1 Rowling, J. K. $t Year ... at Hogwarts ; $v bk. 7

=> 830 0 Harry Potter

The net effect of inconsistent series treatment will be hit-and-miss retrieval, for both users and staff. Of course we can always rely on popular tools like NoveList and KDL (*http://ww2.kdl.org/libcat/whatsnext.asp*), or even Amazon. But repetitive tool usage can be avoided, and resorting to reference services can be obviated, if the information is well defined and linked in the first place.

The Harry Potter problem can be propagated to 2.0 or 3.0 if we do not have any well-defined tagging or linking systems for organizing information either on or off the web. In 2.0, tagging is one of the most popular tools for organizing information in social sites and web resources. As Woody Evans points out, there is a danger in its ease of use: easy to create, easy to deploy, and hard to manage once deployed. To manage it well, he suggests a four-step strategy:

- Sketch: design the way you want to use tags.
- Test: test extensively for a wide variety of items.
- Pair: use categories with tags.
- Talk: communicate with your users and colleagues.

One may disagree with Evans's tagging strategy; however, the point here is to design with a strategy and with consistency when we organize information. Compared with computer language, human language-based organizational schemes can never be precise, but we are always striving for something more exact – dictionaries, thesaurus, and SMS language are but a few historical and current human endeavors. Language as a human communication system requires three basic but consistent parts: sign (sounds and symbols), meanings (semantics), and code (grammar). The same principle applies to our organization of information resources, otherwise users will have retrieval problems. As information managers, we need precise information, not a half-remembered or somewhat-like object or source.

Reference professionals are keenly aware that precise information can be extremely elusive. Since the advent of computer technology, information has existed in a variety of formats. We no longer work merely with books, but with information. To locate the exact and hard-to-find information for our users has been the challenge of the last hundred years. As information managers, we have the right resources, skills, and mentality to help our users to meet their information needs.

Accuracy: a priority in evaluating information

The Pode Project provides us with two valuable lessons. First, we, as information managers, need to avoid information overload when mashing up large amounts of content and internal and external data. The project's experience is that too much information will put people off. There is no point in adding more just because we can, which is another pitfall of our zealous, traditional reference services. Targeted information is definitely preferable. Second, we need to help users to distinguish between the library's data and data provided by others.[2]

One of the first steps in evaluating data is to find out whether it is free or copyrighted. If the former, we should help users to exercise critical thinking about data accuracy and authenticity by informing them when the boundary between internal and external data is crossed. The existence of information does not guarantee its legitimacy. At one time, users who had participated in Overseas Lottery Agents lotteries would visit public libraries to validate the agent's address. In a fraudulent situation such as this, our responsibility is not merely to locate an address that seems to have been provided legitimately but, more importantly, to inform users that they should report the incident to the Department of Consumer Affairs.

User protection: a dilemma and an opportunity for information managers

Libraries are known for their strenuous efforts to protect the privacy of their users' reading history and habits. When they use their library cards to access information, this adds another layer of complexity to librarians' responsibility, if concerned agencies inquire about browsing histories. To a great extent, reading history and habits are tangible in a controled environment.

When users sign up to social sites like Facebook, Twitter, or LinkedIn, libraries cannot protect their privacy after the fact. However, the cause is not completely lost. As information managers, we can exert a measure of control by providing online tutorials on how to set up discreet profiles, and even on how to adjust the privacy settings of accounts and postings. Such before-the-fact measures are especially important in order to protect the novice and inexperienced users in our community.

Demystifying computer programming: let's tweak some codes as needed

The cataloging department used to be one of the frowned-upon departments among professional librarians and prospective library school graduates. Whenever it was mentioned, a stereotyped image of an asocial, rule-stickling cataloger would appear in one's mind's eye. In other words, it was not a highly aspired-to position. "I hate cataloging," was often heard both inside and outside library schools. There are many reasons why the position of cataloger was not considered glamorous. Apart from invoking our dislike of any static work environment, it reminds us of an unconformable feeling when in the presence of inflexible individuals. Moreover, it rekindles our deep-rooted fear of unfamiliar codes and the rules behind those 900 fields. Since library automation and catalog's move to the web, this fear has spread to computer programming, even though many web applications are user friendly. For a long time, some library professionals have refused to have anything to do with changing and modifying codes, let alone learning to get their feet wet.

Since the new millennium, there has been a trend for libraries along the Pacific West Coast – which includes California, Oregon, and Washington – to outsource library materials processing. This trend has gathered pace through the availability of a contract package with vendors known as CLS (Customized Library Services). With this new practice, it is now almost expected of library professionals that they will know how to transfer and upload a remote file, and how to modify and make global changes for fixed and other fields, if needed, using tools like MarcEdit developed by Terry Reese. In addition to print materials, library professionals have to manage e-materials such as e-books, e-audios, e-journals, and websites. With the Semantic Web now imminent, we will be required to have more computer competency when library catalogs go beyond MARC format. As a first step, we need to overcome any symptoms of logizomechanophobia by learning a little about codes, and tweaking some codes as needed.

Notes

1. Harbison, Sarah. "Re: House Cleaning for Harry Potter." Message to the author. 27 March 2012. E-mail.
2. Westrum, A. "The Key to the Future of the Library Catalog Is Openness." *Computers in Libraries* [serial online]. April 2011; 31(3): 10. Available from: MasterFILE Premier, Ipswich, MA. Accessed 27 July 2012.

19

The librarian's role as teacher

Abstract: This chapter examines the redefined role of librarians as teachers. To help their local communities to keep abreast of new changes and trends, librarians need to learn to be a step or two ahead of the curve. The proposed suggestions include systematic and continuous training of staff members, and ongoing tutorial classes and lectures for the public using a combination of social media tools and traditional teaching methods.

Key words: staff training, Bi Sheng, Johannes Gutenberg, movable type, Kindle, Nook, digital literacy, user training, curriculum, 24-hour Library.

Systematic and continuous training of staff members

In the pre-internet era, we had limited technologies for using and reusing information. Take printing technology, for instance. After its invention by the Chinese inventor Bi Sheng, who made ceramic movable type circa 1045, and Johannes Gutenberg, who first made metal movable type cast in a hand mould circa 1450, book printing became less expensive and more widespread. Compared with today's constant supply of apps on our social sites, PCs and mobile devices, book technology is very limited: paper, ink, and machines. Therefore we need to provide systematic and continuous training for staff when we step into the world of Library 3.0, where a new set of technical and cultural challenges will occur.

A training team that does not have a well thought-out and flexible curriculum may not be up to the task. The training curriculum needs to seek out various seminars or webinars provided by library organizations and vendors, and whittle them down to those topics that are most immediately relevant to the staff and user community, such as how to download and transfer e-books and e-audiobooks, and how to use iPads and new apps built for social sites or use on our mobile devices.

Ongoing adult classes and other tutorials for the public as technologies advance

In the ideal world of 3.0, where natural language, not machine language, is used, the public will have a user-friendly and easy interface with which to search for and retrieve the results they desire. However, this will not mean that it is a trouble- and challenge-free universe. Recall our expectations of labor, time, and paper saving on the eve of the popularlization of the PC? Can we accurately quantify the total savings? With the advent of new technology, our users will inevitably face some learning curves and obstacles, and here is the opportunity for us to organize classes for the public.

The four libraries examined in this book have all demonstrated their initiative and sensitivity towards the public's social, technological, and cultural needs. Through RSS, Shanghai Library regularly feeds information to the community about its monthly lectures/webinars.[1] Averaging six per month, the lectures/webinars cover six main subject areas, such as political debates, arts and culture, legal issues, education in science, economics and finance, and healthy living. Among them, the series on decoding the mystery of happiness is one of the most popular topics. RSS feeds are typically fed via a variety of social tools, such as:

- 鲜果 (*http://xianguo.com/*)
- iGoogle (*http://www.google.com/ig*)
- Newsgator (*http://www.newsgator.com/*)
- QQ 邮箱 (*http://www.qqjia.com/*)
- My Yahoo (*http://add.my.yahoo.com/rss?url=http://feed.feedsky.com/jiangzuo&_bc=1*)
- Bloglines (*http://www.bloglines.com/*)
- 580k.com (*http://www.580k.com/*)
- netvibes (*http://www.netvibes.com/en*)
- 有道 (*http://www.youdao.com/about/index.html*), etc.

Users can receive reminders either by instant messaging 提醒哪吒 (*http://inezha.com/*), or by cell phone 手机阅读 (*http://wap.feedsky.com/jiangzuo*).

At BA, there are two venues for its future, current, and past lectures, namely, Bibliotheca Alexandrina Webcast (*http://webcast.bibalex.org/home/home.aspx*) and YouTube Bibliotheca Alexandrina (*http://www.youtube.com/user/BAchannel/videos*). Ask the Library (*http://biblioteksvar.no/en/*)

is one of the 24-hour Library services available at OPL in addition to regular library hours and services. It does not deal with questions related to loans, reservations, or hours of business, but is a national library online reference service where users are guaranteed an answer no later than the next working day. The service is a collaborative and cooperative effort by libraries throughout Norway. Users can choose one of three communication methods (e-mail, SMS, and chat) to send queries and receive the results. The existence of such a rapid service encourages the public to voice their information needs.

SCPL has a long tradition of helping the public to learn how to use library resources, one example being the Saturday Computer Catalog/Internet Classes held in 2002. This project was launched by three reference librarians at the Reference Department of Central (now Downtown) Branch in March 2002. Just as Daniel Goleman describes in *Primal Leadership* – "Some have no official leadership position, yet step forward to lead as needed, then fade back until another ripe moment arrives"[2] – these three librarians stepped forward to meet a need that had been growing ever since SCPL put its online resources on its website, but providing limited help to its users.

To begin with, the class had no official name and the facilitators just called it "Using the Santa Cruz Public Library Catalog" or "The Computer Catalog." The initial goal was simple: to help the public to learn how to use the library catalog. "This one-hour class will help you to: find books, videos, CDs and other library materials; place your own reserves and check your personal library account; learn about the many databases and other online resources on the library's homepage."[3] The requirements were equally simple: admission was free; registration was required. The same class was repeated at the same time two weeks later at one of the ten branches of the SCPL.

Ten years later, the teaching team is still teaching the public, even though the class has undergone content and personnel change and was even suspended for a time as a result of library management restructuring. Notably, the scope of the class has become more comprehensive and better defined. It has evolved from the "Computer Catalog Class" to "Free Internet Classes"; from just learning to use the Santa Cruz Public Library Catalog to learning how to acquire basic internet skills for searching the library catalog, reference databases, health information on the internet, and Library 2.0 tools and sites. Another change is that the class has made itself indispensable in the community. Class attendance has gone through a dramatic change: from one or two students initially, to an average of ten students per class now. Among the teaching staff,

James Tarjan is one of the most dedicated librarians. Apart from his heavy load of reference duties at both Downtown and Scotts Valley branches, he is tireless in learning and in teaching the public about the latest information resources and tools, in class or individually. As one of the three pioneering instructors, over the decade he has mentored a succession of new librarians and teaching staff.

Apart from tutorial classes, SCPL has a new program to help the public with their ongoing information needs, namely, one-on-one tutorial appointments with members of the Reference Team. This program has proven effective on multiple levels. It enables reference professionals to provide users with an extensive service that they cannot afford while working at a busy reference desk. A one-on-one tutorial session is less intimidating for novice Kindle or Nook senior users than a class environment or assistance by telephone or at reference desk that is constantly interrupted by other users. Follow-up sessions are also available. To help the community to improve its digital literacy, SCPL has regularly invited outside guests to teach classes, such as "Digital Literacy: the Path to the Common Core" at Aptos Branch (3 March 2012) and "Making Friends with Your Computer at Downtown Branch" (ongoing, since March 2011). The instructor for the latter has been especially popular with the community and has addressed a whole spectrum of software and hardware issues.

Notes

1. "上图讲座 - 最新讯息" (the Latest Updates on Shanghai Library Lectures) *library.sh.cn*. Shanghai Library. July 2012. Web. Accessed 30 July 2012. (*http://feed.feedsky.com/jiangzuo*).
2. Goleman, Daniel, Richard Boyatzis, and Annie McKee. *Primal Leadership*. Boston, MA: Harvard Business School Press, c2002. x. Print.
3. Lipoma, Deborah. "SCPL Class flyers."

20

The librarian's role as leader

Abstract: This chapter examines the role of librarians as leaders in the world of 3.0. They will provide a new leadership that is called upon to lead and coordinate projects such as providing active links to local and citizen-initiated content, to e-resources, and to resources that have never made it to the web. More often than not, it is easier to start a project than to complete it successfully. Success depends on effective leadership and coordination. Equally, leadership is needed to organize and evaluate information existing both on and off the web, so as to link people to relevant, reliable, and immediate sources. Without such leadership, the world will function "like radios without batteries."

Key words: citizen-initiated content, Anne Lamott, *Santa Cruz Magazine*, e-documents, file formats, Environmental Impact Reports (EIRs), Google Books Project, Newspaper Clipping File (NCF), Local Authors, digital projects, links to external sources, First Friday Art Tour.

YouTube has presented us with a successful paradigm for encouraging user-generated content. Since the place where we live matters the most, and local community is our emphasis, we need to cultivate the perfect environment for generating citizen-initiated information and materials from community residents. In the world of 3.0, not only will there still be libraries but also, more importantly, they will play an even more important role in our society. California writer Anne Lamott says of the basic role of our libraries, "A free library is a revolutionary notion, and when people don't have free access to books, then communities are like radios without batteries. You cut people off from essential sources of information – mythical, practical, linguistic, or political and you break them. You render them helpless in the face of political oppression. We were not going to let this happen." In the same breath, she outlines the role of librarians, "We were there to celebrate some of the rare intelligence capabilities that our country can actually be proud of – those of librarians. I see them as healers and magicians. Librarians can tease out of inarticulate individuals enough information about what they are after to lead them on the path of connection. They are trail guides through the forest of shelves and aisles – you turn a person loose who has limited skills, and he'll be walloped by the branches. But the librarians match up readers with the right books: 'Hey, is this too complicated? Then why don't you give this one a try?'"[1]

The above quotes clearly define the role of community, library, and librarians in our society. In a social media and soon-to-be semantic era, we will be information managers, teachers, and leaders in organizing and delivering information initiated by citizens of the community. It is a fact that most information exists on the web, which presents us with a huge workload of indexing and linking. It is also a fact that there is a substantial amount of information still residing off the web. Take SCPL, for instance. Since the 1950s it has been consciously collecting local content, and the materials in its collections are reflected in its catalog, on its home page and on its social media sites. However, there is still more information to be organized. As there is no visible leadership in the area of citizen-initiated content and materials, we see some information that arrives and goes unnoticed and unorganized. The following are some areas that potentially require the leadership of library professionals.

Provision of active links to new and future magazine articles with local content

At present, there are two local magazines devoted to the subject area of social life and customs, *Santa Cruz Magazine* (*http://www.santa cruzsentinel.com/scmagazine*), a quarterly publication of the Santa Cruz Sentinel since 2006, and *Santa Cruz Style* (*http://santacruzstyle.net/*), a magazine published four times a year by Santa Cruz Style Magazine, LLC since spring 2012.

According to a statement from Santa Cruz Style, it publishes because

> Santa Cruzans aren't content to just live a 9-to-5 existence, our magazine will take you on amazing surfing, sailing, golfing, kite-boarding and hiking adventures, giving you an inside look at our area's top sports. We'll sneak you into the kitchens of your favorite restaurants, take you behind-the-scenes at area vineyards and let

you into the lives of artists and travelers. And, we'll make having fun a little easier by helping you find things like the best cruiser bike rides, great morning mochas and even what beach to visit if you're single and looking for more than just a suntan.

Join us.[2]

In its pilot issue, it does appear that the magazine has set its focus on generating fun from local surfing, wine and winemaking, music, and interior decoration. However, a careful reader will inevitably find that the focus is heavily tipped toward historical coverage. In "Creating the Comfort Zone," the writer devotes most of her article to the early inventions of Jack O'Neil, the pioneer and entrepreneur for surfers' wetsuits, and the writing of his biography by Drew Kampion. The historical tendency is even more pronounced in other articles, such as "Generations: Handing Down Winemaking Traditions," which names three major wineries operating in Santa Cruz County since 1917, Bargetto Winery, Trout Gulch Vineyards, and Cooper-Garrod. There are six articles on local music and local music talent such as 1979 People Magazine's Best New Female Country Vocalist, Lacy J. Dalton, 2011 American Idol's James Durbin, and 2011 X Factor USA's top five performer Chris Rene. However, half of these articles are reminiscent of the golden days of pop music and jazz in the local scene, namely, "The Beat Goes On" covers well-known home-grown bands such as the Call, Camper van Beethoven, Corny and the Corvettes, Harpers Bizarre, Humans, Moby Grapes, and Snails; "Generations of Jazz" features Grammy Award-nominated tenor sax virtuoso Donny McCaslin and his musician father; and "The Summer of Ducks" sings exclusively about a magical moment in local music lore when Neil Young joined the Ducks, a trio of Santa Cruz rockers, more than 35 years ago in 1967.

The historical emphasis is by no means an accident for *Santa Cruz Style*'s writers, editor, and publisher, for Santa Cruz is a breeding ground for art and music, surfing, writing, and a unique lifestyle. Michael Seal Riley, the editor/creative director of the magazine, firmly believes that Santa Cruz County is a small town with big ideas. As a native Santa Cruzan, he has been observing the life and work of previous generations and collecting stories of Santa Cruz County from various angles. Seeing the local newspaper *Santa Cruz Sentinel* (now owned by MediaNews Group) not so engaged in the local scene and history, Riley resigned as an editor of *Santa Cruz Magazine* to start his new publication and devote himself full time to his lifelong passion for local history. Regrettably, the pilot issue came out with little publicity and had few distribution channels. Riley was overjoyed when an SCPL librarian invited him to enter his magazine in OCLC and in the library catalog, and to distribute future issues to all branch libraries throughout the county. A bridge has thus been built between the library and local content, by virtue of the library's asserting active leadership to encourage and foster citizen-initiated content and materials.

The example of *Santa Cruz Style* is revealing of a new trend in the newspaper industry, namely, that major metropolitan newspapers are reducing their local coverage, while community newspapers are increasing their local awareness and stories. The trend was acknowledged and confirmed during a recent SCPL webinar on America's News, an online newspaper database maintained by Newsbank.[3] In the participatory era of social media, readers prefer something more personal and intimate, such as local stories and obituaries. The database developer has therefore put a great emphasis on blogs, web-only and video content, and community newspapers, so as to create unique local content. Librarians, as community leaders, should be actively engaged in organizing, linking, and retrieving local content and stories.

The story of *Santa Cruz Style* has also revealed a weak point in citizen-initiated content publishing, that is, very little coordination, let alone communication, thus resulting in substantial information overlap even in today's social media age. One of the reasons for this paradox is that any information without an effective retrieval system is rendered invalid and useless, for there is no findability to speak of. Neither *Santa Cruz Style* nor *Santa Cruz Magazine* has built any indexes to its published articles by title, author, or content for current and back issues. The former magazine's format consists of big image files, whereas the latter simply puts the latest issue on the web (*http://www.santacruzsentinel.com/scmagazine*) with a list of distribution locations. To harvest the wealth of local content, we can assume leadership in organizing magazine articles by using the RSS tool for new issues and providing metadata in the cloud to link to past articles.

Links to e-documents

Full-text e-documents, or electronic documents, have been with us for a long time. In the early days they were produced and distributed by information providers such as DIALOG. Today, companies like EBSCOhost (*http://www.ebscohost.com/*) and Gale (*http://www.gale.cengage.com/*)

are still performing the same role. EBSCOhost is a platform of EBSCO Publishing (*http://www.ebsco.com/*), established in 1944 and now a leading database and e-book provider for libraries and schools. EBSCOhost is one of the most-used for-fee sites on the internet, averaging over 100 million daily page views. Its NoveList (*http://www.ebscohost. com/novelist*) division provides library professionals with powerful tools to engage readers and connect communities. It holds more than 375 full-text and secondary research databases and 300,000 e-books and e-audiobooks. Apart from its services for libraries and schools, it supplies corporations and medical and government agencies with Corporate Learning (*http://www.ebscohost.com/learning-resources/*), Sustainability (*http://www.ebscohost.com/sustainability*), Chemical Hazard Information (*http://www.ebscohost.com/corporate-research/expub*), Employee Wellness (*http://www.ebscohost.com/healthLibrary/*) and Pharmaceutical Resources.[4]

As part of Cengage Learning (*http://www.cengage.com/*), Gale is specialized in e-research and educational publishing for libraries, schools, and businesses. In addition, it licenses its proprietary content for integration with web-based information services. Its business distribution partners include Dow Jones and Thomson Financial. Gale creates and maintains more than 600 databases that are published online, in print, as e-books, and in microform. Its major brands include InfoTrac, Gale Virtual Reference Library, and Gale Digital Collections such as Eighteenth Century Collections Online.[5]

At the institutional level, the gradual development of computer networks has made it convenient to produce and distribute e-documents both within and outside the library. With improvements in electronic display technologies, users can now read documents on screen, rather than from hard copy. This not only solves the space problem of storing printed copies, but also enables users to feel good about saving paper and reducing the carbon footprint. However, the issue of file format compatibility, such as the incompatibility of MS-DOS plain text files with UNIX-style text files, different character encoding for non-English files, and the variety of word processors, spreadsheets, and graphics software used by senders and recipients, plagued us for a long time. One solution to this problem is to use proprietary file formats for screen display and printing. One such format is Adobe's Acrobat Reader. The other solution is to use standardized non-proprietary file formats such as HTML and OpenDocument.

Digitizing, indexing, and publishing full-text government historical documents on their websites may have been common practice in many libraries, but for SCPL it is still relatively new territory. As a tax-funded public agency, it is a city, county, and state government document depository library. Since its founding in 1868, it has cataloged and archived thousands of time-sensitive government documents. Owing to various reasons, such as shortage of staff, however, hundreds of uncataloged documents languished on the shelves for decades. They included local government documents and environmental impact reports (EIRs) dating from the 1960s to 1980s.

Before his retirement in 2004, the former reference system coordinator organized these documents into batches and sent them to the Cataloging Department of Technical Services (now Collection Management Services) for cataloging and processing. For the first time in SCPL's history, these unique documents were made available to the public through the library catalog. Before long they caught the attention and interest of users, both local and remote. Take, for instance, the complete files on Lighthouse Point Convention Center, a well-known rejected development proposal of the late 1960s and early 1970s. Not long after their appearance in OCLC's WorldCat, a user from Massachusetts expressed his explicit interest in the whole package. He not only wrote to SCPL for more details, but also came to Santa Cruz to use the documents.

The historical documents reflected the timeline of economic, political, commercial, and housing development in the County of Santa Cruz, Monterey Bay, and the greater San Francisco Bay Area. There has been a visible surge of development in California since the 1950s, especially through the dramatic but continual development of science and technology in California.

> Through engineering and technology, California invented itself as an American place. The completion of the trans-Sierra portion of the transcontinental railroad can be seen as an engineering feat of the highest order. The development of mining technology led to the Pelton turbine, a California invention, which in turn brought hydroelectricity to California, which in turn made possible an industrial infrastructure. Aviation had been a preoccupation since the 1880s, and when the airplane arrived in California it was adopted and perfected there. By the 1920s, California had taken the lead in vacuum tube technology, making possible radio and television. By the 1930s, Californians were taking the lead in smashing the atom. In the 1950s, Californians were bringing into being, through the semiconductor, the digital revolution. Then came biotechnology, in which California has always led the nation.[6]

Once California entered the digital age, progress gathered even greater pace, especially after Intel Corp. brought the microprocessor to the market in 1971 and Apple I became available in 1976.

In such an optimistic age, Santa Cruz County, with its geographical proximity to Silicon Valley and the San Francisco Bay Area, was boosted with confidence and possibilities. After the University of California decided to set up a campus in Santa Cruz, the whole county was ready for overall change. The upbeat era is vividly illustrated by the documents listed in Appendix 3.

The topics listed provide readers a picture of the community of Santa Cruz County in the decades of 1950 to 1980. Owing to the range of subject coverage, the original cataloger decided on two ways to aim for optimal retrieval: (1) assign call numbers in the Dewey Classification range 711.XXXX (Area Planning), broken down by different types; and (2) assign a uniform subject heading, further divided by specific geographic areas, for example,

Environmental impact statements $z California ($z Specific area)

The uniformity of the subject headings enables users to easily retrieve and read hundreds of document titles covering different decades and places, as long as they specify a time period prior to 1990. With call numbers clustered in 711, both staff and the public can conveniently browse the section for retrieval of the documents from storage.

Following the completion of cataloging of the historical documents in 2006, there were no plans to digitize them until recently, when the prospect of cloud storage and the affordability of a digital scanner at SCPL made this a possibility. A proposal has been put forward to train staff to scan and digitize local history materials, including the EIRs and state/county/city planning documents.

In his book *Social Networking Space*, Todd Kelsey emphasizes time and again the concept and importance of "captur[ing], preserv[ing] and shar[ing]" in personal digital archaeology. He calls on people to capture the stories of older generations before it is too late. For Kelsey, the era of social media can be very well regarded as a digital civilization. All civilizations in human history have risen and fallen in due time. So do social media and networks. Kelsey therefore advises people to learn to digitize and de-digitize. While he covers chiefly personal digital archaeology, his viewpoints have equal validity for social networks and post-social networks.

The future availability of e-documents will not only solve the sole-copy problem of many fragile historical documents but, more importantly, will provide immense convenience for remote users, who will not have to travel from Massachusetts or any other state, or even from any other country, to read and use them. In addition, the popular features provided by digital scanners, such as OCR, and standardized file formats such as Acrobat Reader, HTML, and OpenDocument, will surely make sharing more effective by providing users with better display and output of their search results.

To heed Kelsey's advice, we need to have a good archive system, either physically or online, as insurance in the event of a natural disaster or technical catastrophe, such as providers going out of business, things being no longer free, technology change, computer hacking, etc. In addition, there is the challenge of organizing e-documents. Shall we simply dump them on the website, or get them tagged for free on social networks like Facebook? Will multiple platforms such as the library catalog or an online database also be considered? In this respect, BA's digital projects have proven especially exemplary and comprehensive.

Links to historical e-directories

In addition to organizing historical government documents, libraries can also consider digitizing and sharing copyright-free city and county directories, so as to meet the needs of local, national, and international researchers.

SCPL houses *Santa Cruz Directories* (1876–1922), and *Polk's Santa Cruz (California) City Directory, Including Watsonville and Santa Cruz County ...* (1927–2004), with some gaps in the war years of the 1940s, and later from the 1980s to 2002 on account of the publisher's discontinuation of publication. These directories have been extremely popular with library users, especially with genealogical researchers and enthusiasts both within and outside the community. In consideration of their fragile physical condition, directories prior to the 1960s are in storage awaiting microfilming, which has been interrupted many times due to a lack of either funding or coordination.

The retrieval of the correct volume for specific area coverage was always problematic with the former library catalog (DRA, acquired later by SirsiDynix). The volumes could vary in their area coverage year from year, and the Cataloging Department tried in vain to use the limited

Notes field in the item record to indicate the area/places covered by each volume. This lack of essential metadata frustrated many a user who had come all the way to Santa Cruz, hoping to locate a person or business listed in the directory, but not knowing that the area/place had been omitted for that particular year. With the migration of the catalog to Evergreen, an open source ILS, in the fall of 2011, both Reference and Cataloging Departments were buoyed up by the hope that the limitations of the former DRA catalog would be overcome and each volume record would contain the much-needed metadata. Contrary to everyone's expectations, during data migration the new ILS deleted the information on publication year for every volume, as a consequence of incompatibility in the two systems' structures. Because DRA possessed only item record, without an entity called volume record, the data in the item record's Enumeration and Notes fields could not be automatically translated into Evergreen's volume record, where not only the call number but also other data such as publication year, edition, and volume reside. The net result is that users are still unable to pinpoint the exact year's coverage, even after searching the library catalog and coming to the library. In consequence, a cartful of directories covering a decade need to be wheeled out for them to browse.

Needless to say, the Google Books Project (*http://books.google.com/*) has made online browsing of Polk's directories for the area much more convenient and friendly. However, its list is far from complete, with only three or four volumes visible for 1916, 1926, and 1963. Under the circumstances, SCPL is in the planning stage of digitizing the set, once it has cleared copyright-related issues with the publisher.

Links to e-newspaper clippings

As has been already observed, local newspapers such as the *Santa Cruz Sentinel* had no index for retrieving their news reports, articles, and announcements prior to 1999. Apart from GeneSoc's efforts in indexing birth/death and wedding announcements, the SCPL Central Reference Department (now the System Reference Team) took another route by clipping and indexing articles by subject. Before her web career, the internet librarian started her clipping file project with a pair of scissors, compiling the information in folders under various headings of local interest and storing them in file cabinets.

Over time, the clippings file became too large to manage. Both the head of the Central Reference Department and a senior library assistant were kept busy trying to keep track of the articles in the most popular files because they kept disappearing. To begin with, the senior library assistant recorded the dates of the articles in each file on the file folder itself – until the entire file on limestone caves disappeared and she had to recreate the file without her list. At that point they decided to keep the list as a word processing file, and later transferred it to a Microsoft Access database. When the database began to get too large, they asked the new webmaster to create a database in MySQL, and thus the NCF (*http://www2.santacruzpl.org/history/clippingfile/*), an electronic index to SCPL's Newspaper Clipping File (NCF), came into being.[7]

The NCF is one of SCPL's heavily used local databases, maintained and updated continuously. It serves as a reference tool to the articles available both in the clipping files and on microfilm at the Downtown Branch. It is a large collection of articles of local interest that have been gathered from a variety of local newspapers dating from the early 1900s to the present. More than 50,000 articles in the clippings file have been indexed and entered into the database, and new articles are indexed and added regularly.[8] However, there is no plan as yet to scan the clippings into a database. The physical clippings are prone to tearing, loss, or even theft, particularly those popular in subject areas such as Murders in Santa Cruz. Sometimes a whole folder has been stolen and replaced, time and again. An electronic clippings file and index would not only prevent damage and thefts, but also make the clippings available online to multiple users.

Links to e-directories for more local organizations

The County of Santa Cruz is characterized not only by its art scene and artists' community, but also by its tolerance towards religion and spiritual organizations. According to the categorization of Santa Cruz Chamber of Commerce,[9] there are at least 8 major religions, or 19 religions according to Santa Cruz Wiki, in a county of fewer than 260,000 residents.[10]

It is true that SCPL has created and continuously updated its CID, as is described in Chapter 5. However, this does not cover some organizations, such as churches or temples. Since the CID lacks categories on both Churches and Religion, it could be enhanced with links to additional resources such as Religion and Spirituality in Santa Cruz County (*http:// www.santacruzchamber.org/cwt/external/wcpages/facts/religion.aspx*) by Santa Cruz Chamber of Commerce, or Santa Cruz Spirituality (*http:// www.santacruzspirituality.net/contents.htm*) by Paul Tutwiler, or Spiritual Organizations (*https://scruzwiki.org/Spiritual_Organizations*) by Santa Cruz Wiki. In addition, SCPL could consider capturing, compiling, and organizing in one place the related information, such as the unique founding history of churches and other religious organizations, thus creating a rich resource for the local community.

Links to promote local authors and publications

Because of the high concentration of local talent in the area, Santa Cruz County boasts a large number of world-renowned names, such as Laurie R. King, Jonathan Franzen, Frans Lanting, and Linda Christensen. To respond to and foster local authors and artists, SCPL has systematically included and cataloged their known publications in the library collections from the very beginning.

In the late 1990s, when the pool of local authors grew too large to maintain and search, the head of the Cataloging Department set up a Microsoft Word file entitled "Local Authors" to include authors, artists, and musicians who had lived and worked in the County of Santa Cruz. Using appropriate descriptors to describe local authors' major and minor contributions, her staff updated the file continuously during the course of their work. The works of local authors were searchable by call number, an additional local call number field being added for the purpose.

In 2008, with the help of a volunteer, the webmaster created a MySQL database with data migrated from the original Microsoft Word file. The Local Authors (*http://www.santacruzpl.org/readers/resources/scauthors/*) database is searchable alphabetically and by designation on the SCPL website and at the time of writing contains a total of 1118 local authors. The following is a list of the categories of local authors:

Actor	Musician
Artist	Narrator
Author	Performer
Conductor	Photographer
Director	Poet
Editor	Producer
Illustrator	Publisher
Instructor	Singer
Master of Ceremonies	Vocalist

The Local Authors database establishes a close bond between SCPL and the community, especially those budding authors who are inspired not only by the prospect of publishing, but also by the idea that their works will become part of the library's permanent collection. In this respect, social media sites like Facebook or Twitter will surely enhance their experience by capturing, connecting, and sharing with local and wider communities.

As for well-known authors and artists, SCPL is constantly inviting them for book talks and art shows. Take Laurie R. King, for instance. Over the years she has been invited to speak by several branches, such as Aptos, Downtown, and Scotts Valley. For some reason, no recordings have ever been made of these events, which could have been videotaped before the era of social media. Now, staff could very easily make use of the video features on mobile devices to record her talks and upload and archive them on a social site like YouTube, so as to enable an audience both within and outside the community to share in her experience of writing various works.

Leadership in local history, local value, and involvement

There is an untapped local history resource in the County of Santa Cruz, namely, the collection on the histories of local families, California families, and United States families maintained by the GeneSoc. As part of ongoing historical preservation projects, SCPL has been helping GeneSoc to organize, catalog, and inventory the collection, most of which are unique titles about local families. Digitizing the collection and creating a highly hyperlinked data set to interact with the digitized copy on the web would be an ideal solution for preserving the collection and making it accessible while avoiding the risk of physical deterioration through use. SCPL and GeneSoc could collaborate as they did when GeneSoc's holdings were cataloged in the SCPL catalog (see Chapter 17). SCPL could provide technical skills, including design, organization, and quality control, while GeneSoc could supply the time and expertise of its enthusiastic volunteers.

Another possibility for local involvement is with First Friday Art Tour Santa Cruz (*http://www.firstfridaysantacruz.com/*) venues. First Friday was started by Kirby Scudder, an artist who came to Santa Cruz from New York City (by way of San Jose, California) in the fall of 2003. He was puzzled to find that in such a mecca for artists as Santa Cruz County, places to exhibit their art were surprisingly limited. MAH offered very few exhibiting opportunities for budding or not so well-known artists, before its Museum 2.0 transformed the museum into a thriving central gathering place for the community around art, history, ideas, and culture.[11] Santa Cruz Art League also served as an art gallery, but on a membership basis, and had very few slots for nonmembers. The Cultural Council of Santa Cruz County's Open Studio Art Tours took place only in the month of October. There were some private galleries, such as Felix Kulpa, Artisan, or Annieglass, but they were restricted either by space or by specialized medium.

Scudder embarked on a tireless campaign for artists. He began by persuading the city redevelopment agency to let him showcase his art in a temporarily empty storefront, thus taking advantage of the busy street's foot traffic. His experiment was a success: he quickly sold 35 landscape paintings of Santa Cruz. It also astonished the whole community: "This guy comes into town from wherever, and he's doing these paintings with an incredible sense of place – he doesn't know the community – and he's capturing Santa Cruz better than anyone and selling it? Who the hell is this guy?" With support from the city mayor, Scudder experimented further with the idea of opening new galleries, until he decided to lead a walking art tour for art enthusiasts. At that time, there was a First Friday program, a self-guided art tour of the emerging downtown art scene, but it had a disappointing turnout: very few people knew about it. Scudder's guided tour idea really took off when he acquired a bus and driver to shuttle visitors around the downtown tour, starting from the old Salz Tannery and ending at the south end of downtown, close to the ocean, about three miles away. His first guided tour had a very humble beginning: only ten people showed up. But the number quickly doubled, and it quintupled in less than two years. Before long, "First Friday became a social event, an excuse for friends to get together and engage in a mini-adventure."[12]

First Friday has also become a cultural phenomenon in Santa Cruz. Eight years on, First Friday Art Tour has outgrown Kirby Scudder, who is no longer leading art tours. Since 2010, when the Downtown Association of Santa Cruz took over the event, executive director Chip has expanded the program dramatically, to areas outside downtown and to other cities, like Capitola and Watsonville. As a result the First Friday experience has exploded, reflecting the full spectrum of Santa Cruz County's creative experience. It has brought together people who are passionate about art and artists who have chosen to make Santa Cruz their home. On 6 April 2012, First Friday held its 100th event since 2004. Come rain or shine, it attracts thousands of visitors each month to downtown Santa Cruz, midtown, Westside, and other cities where the First Friday of each month is celebrated. And the story of how it all started illustrates that today's First Friday local revelers were not inevitable. The tour is publicized on its own website, First Friday Tube (*http://www.youtube.com/user/FirstFridaySantaCruz*), and in *Good Times*, a local weekly arts and entertainment paper.

SCPL did not participate in First Friday until May 2010, when the new library director decided to join its community by opening up the public meeting room of the Downtown Branch Library. It has been a consistent success, starting with Jim Bourne's photography of birds and other wildlife, landscape, musicians in concert, and a series of black and white images featuring an "urban pentimento." As First Friday Tube does not archive the art tours of all its featured artists, nor does its website maintain a list of all participants, events come and go and are soon forgotten. These circumstances provide a potential opportunity for SCPL to record and archive those art tours that take place in the library.

Notes

1. Lamott, Anne. *Grace (Eventually): Thoughts on Faith*. New York: Fivehead Books, 2007. 151–3. Print.
2. "Santa Cruz Style." *santacruzmagazine.net*. Santa Cruz Style Magazine, LLC, n.d. Web. Accessed 30 July 2012.
3. Northcutt, John B. "Online Tutorial of the Americas News Resource (Webinar to SCPL)." NewsBank Inc., 22 March 2012.
4. "About Us." *ebscohost.com*. EBSCO Industries, Inc., 2012. Web. Accessed 30 July 2012.

5. "About Gale." *gale.cengage.com*. Cengage Learning, n.d. Web. Accessed 30 July 2012.
6. Starr, Kevin. *California, a History*. New York: The Modern Library, c2005, p. [247]. Print.
7. Swedberg, Donna. "Re: Question about Newspaper Clipping File." Message to the author. 19 October 2011. E-mail.
8. "Santa Cruz Newspaper Clipping File." *santacruzpl.org*. Santa Cruz Public Libraries, n.d. Web. Accessed 30 July 2012.
9. "Religion and Spirituality in Santa Cruz County." *santacruzchamber.org*. Santa Cruz Area Chamber of Commerce, 2011. Web. Accessed 30 July 2012.
10. "Spiritual Organizations." *cruzwiki.org*. Santa Cruz Wiki, March 2012. Web. Accessed 30 July 2012.
11. "Nina Simon." *exhibitfiles.org*. ASTC – Association of Science–Technology Centers, n.d. Web. Accessed 30 July 2012.
12. Baine, Wallace. "The First Friday Art Tour Has Transformed the Santa Cruz Arts Scene – that Didn't Happen by Accident." *Santa Cruz Sentinel*, 29 March 2012. Web. Accessed 30 July 2012.

21

The librarian's role as innovator in transforming the OPAC

Abstract: This chapter discusses the history and future of open source ILS as well as commercial ILS. In addition, it examines several innovative approaches prevailing among library professionals, namely, the BISAC, bookstore, and Pode approaches. A brave new world is emerging where the validity of the Dewey Decimal Classification system has been challenged, and where the web becomes our library catalog with the implementation of such management systems as OCLC's WorldShare and Boopsie, and with the preparation for LC/PCC Phased Implementation of RDA in the United States and other major countries.

Key words: BISAC, bookstore approach, Pode approach, integrated library system (ILS), open source, mash-up, Dewey Decimal Classification, WordThink Grid, Resource Description and Access (RDA), GeoNames.

What is the OPAC?

OPAC, the Online Public Access Catalog, is an online database of library materials held by a library or a consortium of libraries. Users search the library catalog to locate those library items that are physically located within the library. According to the Wikipedia article on OPAC,[1] the first official online catalogs were developed at Ohio State University in 1975 and the Dallas Public Library in 1978, even though experiments with OPACs started in the early 1960s. In reality, the early OPACs were an electronic version of the library card catalog, with a dedicated terminal in the library through a local network, and telnet connection outside the library.

Development of the OPAC

The growth of online library catalogs did not really take off until the end of the 1980s, when the commercially developed library systems began to appear to replace locally built systems. By then, online library catalogs were not only beginning to improve their searching and retrieval capabilities but also, more importantly, adding more modules, such as circulation, acquisitions, serials, interlibrary loan, in addition to the existing OPAC and cataloging. These six main modules or applications later became known as ILS or Integrated Library Systems.

With the growth of the internet and the world wide web from the 1990s, ILS enabled users to use OPACs and web-based portals and library subscription databases through proxy authentication. This period was a golden age for the ILS market, and the industry's average annual sales rose from US$50 million in 1982 to approximately US$500 million in 2002.[2]

Since the mid to late 2000s, many library professionals became dissatisfied with the increasing prices charged by vendors and reduced flexibility offered for customizing to their special needs and to the challenges posed by Library 2.0 applications and social media tools. Even though in their early stages, open source ILS provided these professionals with some alternative. The first open source web-based ILS is Koha, which was released in January 2000. It was followed by other open source ILS in 2002 (OpenBiblio (*http://obiblio.sourceforge.net/*) and OPALS (*http://www.opals-na.org/*)) and 2007 (Evergreen).

Bookstore approach

Despite the fact that commercial ILS vendors are willing to renegotiate their prices and license fees, and to incorporate social media features into their OPACs, some library professionals have expressed their dissatisfaction with the design of the library catalog in general. To them, the library catalog is simply an old-fashioned word. To preserve the library for the future, one of the saviors would be Amazon or an Amazon-like bookstore model that retrieved search results and ranked books on popularity. Take, for example, the bookstore approach of San Jose Public Library in California, or the mash-up of Dewey/bookstore by the Darien Library in Connecticut: "'We clumped similar areas of Dewey together in eight broad categories, which we call glades,' a concept similar to the innovative 'neighborhoods' created in Hennepin County's, MN,

Brookdale Branch."[3] Some libraries, like the Topeka and Shawnee County Public Library, Kansas, Anna Porter Public Library, Tennessee, and Phoenix Public Library, Arizona, on the other hand, have not abandoned Dewey, but have split and moved Dewey numbers.

However, there is a question about the bookstore approach: will it work for academic libraries? "Academic libraries were certainly never intended to be in the popularity game. Public libraries are more than a collection of bestsellers. In scholarly research, it's as often as not the obscure book, the rarely consulted edition, which leads to the exciting breakthrough or the innovative idea. Librarians still feel profoundly (don't they?) that OPACs should bring meaning[ful] results to our patrons' searches, not the mishmash you find on sites that sell hats or hotel reservations."[4]

Another question is the dilemma of categorizing some overlapping subject areas, like True Crime. According to Molly Moyer, a librarian who had worked for the Tattered Cover bookstore in Denver but became an unofficial staff member of Rangeview Library, Colorado, "We never knew what to do with True Crime." At one time it was placed with mysteries, and at another it was filed with romance. "We finally put it next to the law books," she said. "If it's not selling and it's a popular book, we need to move it to where people can find it."[5] Even though they are not profit driven, libraries do have something in common with bookstores, namely, the need for findability. However, indecision such as that described by Moyer might be costly both staffing- and time-wise to a large library collection if we had constantly to move items around. A bookstore's inventory is different from a library collection, as far as quantity is concerned.

A further question is the flexible arrangement of titles. Bookstores like the Tattered Cover arrange their titles alphabetically, by either author or title, based on the habits of customers. If libraries were to adopt that approach, it would again be very labor intensive to move the physical library collections around – although it might give rise to some unintended consequences, such as space and shelving availability. In addition, there is a fundamental difference in numbers of items and customers between a bookstore and a library.

BISAC approach

Some library professionals have rebelled against Dewey by creating their own classification systems or adopting new approaches. Dewey Decimal

Classification has been one of the most popular classification systems in the library world since Melvil Dewey developed it in 1876. According to Barbara Fisher's estimates in 2009,[6] it is used in 138 countries by over 200,000 libraries. Up to now, it has undergone 23 major revisions and expansions. Many public librarians, however, have been increasingly vexed by the effect of its intimidating and complex classification schemes on their patrons' use of libraries. In order to attract more users back into the library by providing more browsability, the Perry Branch Library in Maricopa County, Arizona became the first library in the United States to adopt the BISAC system, in 2007.

BISAC is short for Book Industry Standards and Communications, maintained by the Book Industry Study Group, Inc., a US trade association. Used by companies like Amazon, Baker & Taylor, Barnes & Noble, Bowker, Ingram, etc., it consists of 52 broad alphabetic categories and uses a combination of subject headings and classification to organize materials and shelves. In 2007, the brand-new Perry Branch Library of MCLD in Arizona was the first public library in the United States to go BISAC.

The instigator of Perry Branch Library's adoption of BISAC was former SCPL staff member Marshall Shore, who led the dropping of Dewey and who recalls that "I was called an idiot, stupid, sacrilege ... It's interesting that conversation has really progressed beyond that. It's not really about Dropping Dewey, it's about customer service, about those hurdles we place for the public." Also seared in his memory is the Perry Branch opening day: "We bought into the hype, assigning extra staffers to guide patrons who might be confounded. They weren't."

Owing to BISAC's sensational success, the Perry Branch Library was soon joined by four more libraries in MCLD. Before long, libraries in other states were adopting the system. In 2008, the Frankfort Public Library District in Illinois planned a conversion to BISAC; in 2009, the Rangeview Library in Adams County, Colorado decided to go BISAC after five representatives returned from a visit to MCLD having decided to follow suit as soon as their plane landed in Denver. Based on the Perry Library's experience with vendors, Rangeview Library created the WordThink Grid (*http://www.docstoc.com/docs/120846772/WordThink-Grid*), which was launched in October 2009, to classify its library materials and to be used in its outsourcing, cataloging and processing services, or CLS, with Baker & Taylor. (Rangeview Collection Development Manager Rachel Fewell points out that about 90 percent of her library's materials are cataloged and processed out of house.)

Rangeview WordThink grid contains 48 BISAC subject categories. A typical BISAC category is Nature. The category and its corresponding WordThink call number are:

BISAC category	Call number
Nature	NATURE

The BISAC topic of Animals is a subcategory of Nature:

BISAC category	Call number
Nature	NATURE
Animals	ANIMALS

Other subcategories of Nature are Dinosaurs and Plants, with the following call numbers:

Call Number	Call Number
NATURE	NATURE
DINOS	PLANTS

The BISAC topic of Animals can be further divided into subtopics, such as Birds, Insects, Land, Ocean, adding a third line to the call number:

Call Number	Call Number
NATURE	NATURE
ANIMALS	ANIMALS
BIRDS	LAND

At the 2010 Public Library Association Conference held in Portland, Oregon, members of the Rangeview Library District delivered a presentation followed by a workshop session on BISAC.[7] It was estimated that more than 300 conference participants joined the workshop session to learn how the Rangeview Library had traded the Dewey Decimal Classification System for a system based on the BISAC subject headings. The session successfully recruited many initially skeptical people, who came round to the idea of change and who were willing to be more flexible, and more attentive to customers asking for books.

However, there are a number of unanswered questions concerning BISAC. There are only 52 broad categories in BISAC, and Rangeview Library has adopted 48, based on its own needs. Would those categories provide sufficient coverage for a big research library? So far, the success stories have been about smaller, popular libraries, such as Perry and Rangeview. When the content and format are clearly marked, BISAC seems to work wonders, for example, study guides, test books, and graphic novels at Rangeview are much easier to find. But at the same time, it presents a problem similar to that experienced in the bookstore approach with the categories of True Crime and of Biography and Autobiography. The rapid growth of these two categories is a clear indication that their subject matter is blurred and can be interpreted in several ways (a true crime, or a mystery, or a legal case), or as more than one category (Biography and Autobiography, or Sports and Recreation).

Some categories, like History, are extremely long. Even so, History does not have a sufficient depth of subcategories to cover all topics and has to make up for this lack by adding more call number lines. The net result is that it will take time to analyze each anomaly individually as we go along. The same is true of categories such as Science, with a scope far beyond the WordThink Grid's seven main categories, and where subcategories need to be further expanded. The improvising aspect of BISAC illustrates that it cannot perform ideally in special or research libraries. Take the example in Table 21.1, for instance.

Table 21.1 WordThink Grid call numbers based on BISAC categories

BISAC 1	History	Call number line 1	HISTORY
BISAC 2	Military	Call number line 2	MILITARY
BISAC 3	Middle East Conflicts	Call number line 3	MID EAST
		Call number line 4	IRAQ

Pode approach: making OPAC "of the web"

In Chapter 12, the Pode Project at OPL was discussed. So far it has successfully experimented in using FRBR with Semantic Web technologies to connect FRBRized records with Linked Open Data by converting the data sets to RDF and then linking the data to other sources for a semantic mash-up. Here one of the first tasks is to convert the bibliographic records from the MARC environment to web-based records with RDF.

In January 2012, LC announced that it would have fully implemented RDA (Resource Description and Access) by 31 March 2013. The partner national libraries, such as the National Agricultural Library and the National Library of Medicine, as well as the British Library, Library and Archives Canada, Deutsche Nationalbibliothek, and National Library of Australia, also targeted the first quarter of 2013 for Day One of their RDA implementations.[8] The goal is make library collections more findable and usable. It is very significant for the virtual library, because it will allow remote users to search for information. Furthermore, it is a significant move towards the realization of "the Web as context," as Karen Coyle defines it in her article "Library Data in a Modern Context,"[9] in which she raises a very important question, namely, how the library catalog can move from being "on the web" to being "of the web."

Since LC's announcement, a substantial number of RDA debates have been going on online among library professionals worldwide in order to iron out incompatibilities and other issues. But at least the die has been cast and the dialogs are happening. On 16 July 2012, an advance notice announced that the programming code for Phase 1 in preparation for the LC/PCC (Program for Cooperative Cataloging) Phased Implementation of RDA had been tested successfully. The implementation in question refers to the phased conversion of the LC/NACO (Name Authority Cooperative Program) Authority File to RDA. Many an expert has delightedly found the results for 375 – Gender (R) (*http://www.loc.gov/marc/authority/ad375.html*) eminently sensible, especially in the case of Jan Morris (1926–).[10]

There are many reasons behind the decision on such a change. Firstly, some information resources that are available on the web will never be developed by traditional publishing. In other words, the web contains many resources that can be neither captured nor recorded by printed technologies. Secondly, "Regardless of the inherent value of library owned materials, there are only twenty-four hours in a day, and the time for study, research, and recreation does not expand as more information becomes available. The famed 'information overload' is a time problem." Thirdly, in addition to the time problem, there are limits to the exertion of human energy. When the book was the sole publishing technology, we had problems catching up with all the newly printed and classic works. Today we are faced with both a dramatic increase in the rate of book publishing *and* information resources on the web. Last, but not least, because the web is where many of our community members reside virtually, and where new applications and technologies are being developed, we need to shift our focus by moving and transforming our library catalog to be part of the web.

According to Coyle, the web is flooded with bibliographic data. There is a serious issue of overlapping content because both the library catalog and websites like Amazon and collaborative projects like Wikipedia provide bibliographic data, even though the data that internet users have been accustomed to are very different from those in the library catalog. In general, users can easily locate online the basic information about an author or his/her titles, and their publication years or places of publication. With the exception of commercial databases, such as EBSCO's NoveList, that supply a direct connection between their own entries and the library catalog, there is no direct link between the library catalog and the titles that we can find in Google Books.

In this respect, the OPL experiment is laudable. It has effectively demonstrated the validity of transforming a library catalog, namely, a database of bibliographic records, into a hyperlinked data set that can interact with information resources on the web. Take the Trip Planner, for example. It provides users with a direct link between web information on country, language, place, time zone, and currency by searching GeoNames. Once the information has been retrieved, users can browse or check out relevant library materials from OPL's travel collection. Coyle argues that the lack of links between the library catalog and web information obscures the visibility of libraries and their materials. Therefore, the Linked Data technology will be a useful tool to enable sharing between these two entities. If the library catalog is linked to the web, a search on any given author will return either zero hits or a list of titles by that author in the various formats held by the library.

Despite the lack of such a link, library professionals should not lose sight of their unique advantages, experience and knowledge accumulated since the 1830s, when public libraries started to come into being in New Hampshire and Massachusetts. Firstly, the metadata or bibliographic data have already been created, even though they are fragmented. What we need to do is to turn the fragmented data into the semantic data, so as to make it sharable and linkable in the new web environment. Secondly, "Libraries are the only community with control over names, distinguishing between authors with the same or similar names and bringing together variant name forms. The addition of birth and death dates, once needed only to disambiguate similar names, is now essential information for an analysis of copyright status. Library data also facilitates the gathering of different editions around the concept of a work through the use of uniform titles."[11]

Thirdly, the library catalog, whether in the card format or the online version, was developed with sharing with other libraries in mind, and so sharing is not a strange concept to library professionals. The sharing spirit is not in conflict with the concept of social capital in social media. Take, for instance, the 2012 California Reads, a community read program organized jointly by Cal Humanities (*http://www.calhum.org/*) and the California Center for the Book (*http://www.calbook.org/*). A number of libraries in the Monterey Bay area collaborated and coordinated by placing Jeanne Wakatsuki Houston and James D. Houston's *Farewell to Manzanar* at the top of their reading list. To accompany the read, they prepared a series of reading and discussion programs, such as inviting the author to give book talks and arranging a viewing of *An American Story: World War Two Stories of the Tragedy and Triumph of Our Japanese-American Community during Wartime*, a documentary produced by Watsonville Public Library in partnership with the San Diego Media Arts Center and the Watsonville–Santa Cruz Japanese American Citizens League.

To enable readers to acquire a complete picture of the World War II Japanese-Americans' evacuation and relocation in 1942–45, it might be useful to add value to the library catalog by providing more links to related resources within and outside the library. For instance, Watsonville Public Library has produced and cataloged many unique titles on Japanese-American internment during World War II, with personal narratives, video-interviews, etc., under the following typical subject headings:

Japanese Americans – Evacuation and relocation, 1942–1945.

World War, 1939–1945 – Japanese-Americans. Japanese Americans – United States – History.

Similarly, if readers of California Reads are interested in early California history, the Bancroft Library is another great resource. In addition to its well-known Works and complete Bancroft Dictations, the library offers access to great digital resources via its web page (*http://bancroft.berkeley.edu/collections/*). This will be another reason for us to add more links from the Bancroft to the SCPL library catalog or website, for "In the Bancroft Library of the twenty-first century we shall continue to take advantage of the latest advances in information technology to make our and his collections better known and accessible from any point on the globe."[12]

Notes

1. "Online Public Access Catalog." *wikipedia.org*. Wikimedia Foundation, Inc., 27 May 2012. Web. Accessed 30 July 2012.
2. Kochtanek, Thomas R. *Library Information Systems: from Library Automation to Distributed Information Access Solutions*. Westport, CT: Libraries Unlimited, 2002. 6. Print.
3. Fister, B. "The Dewey Dilemma." *Library Journal* [serial online]. October 2009; 134(16): 22. Available from: MasterFILE Premier, Ipswich, MA. Accessed 27 July 2012.
4. McCormack, N. "User Comments and Reviews: Decline or Democratization of the Online Public Access Catalogue?" *Feliciter* [serial online]. June 2008; 54(3): 129. Available from: MasterFILE Premier, Ipswich, MA. Accessed 27 July 2012.
5. Oder, Norman. "PLA 2010 Conference: Cracking the Code: Beyond Dewey." *Library Journal*, 30 March 2010. Web. Accessed 30 July 2012.
6. Fister, B. "The Dewey Dilemma." *Library Journal* [serial online]. October 2009; 134(16): 22. Available from: MasterFILE Premier, Ipswich, MA. Accessed 27 July 2012.
7. PLA Conference Report. *Library Journal* [serial online]. May 2010; 135(8): 13. Available from: MasterFILE Premier, Ipswich, MA. Accessed 27 July 2012.
8. "Resource Description and Access (RDA). Information and Resources in Preparation for RDA." *loc.gov*. Library of Congress, 24 July 2012. Web. Accessed 30 July 2012.
9. Coyle, Karen. "Library Data in a Modern Context." *Library Technology Reports* [serial online]. January 2010; 46(1): 5. Available from: MasterFILE Premier, Ipswich, MA. Accessed 27 July 2012.
10. Brenndorfer, Thomas. "Re: Subject: [ACAT] Advance Notice: Phase 1 of the PCCAHITG Phased Implementation of RDA to begin soon." Message to listserv.syr.edu 19 July 2012. E-mail.
11. Coyle, Karen. "Library Data in a Modern Context." *Library Technology Reports* [serial online]. January 2010; 46(1): 5. Available from: MasterFILE Premier, Ipswich, MA. Accessed 27 July 2012.
12. Faulhaber, Charles, and Stephen Vincent. *Exploring the Bancroft Library: The Centennial Guide to Its Extraordinary History, Spectacular Special Collections, Research Pleasures, Its Amazing Future and How It All Works*. Salt Lake City: Signature; Bancroft Library, 2006. 12. Print.

22

Technology, staff, and community

Abstract: This chapter re-examines the role of new technology and its fascination for the library world, due to the unique function of libraries, which are concerned with the storage, representation, retrieval, and delivery of physical objects in great numbers. Also examined are its nature, functions, and impact on library staff and local communities.

Key words: technology, physical objects, Jonathan Franzen, future-proof, one-size-fits-all, local value, identity, digital civilization.

Technology

New technology never fails to exert a great fascination on libraries and library professionals. This fascination is determined by the nature of libraries, which deal with physical objects and are concerned with representations of knowledge, culture, information, facts, and beliefs "Libraries deal with texts and images – or, more strictly, with text-bearing objects and image-bearing objects, with millions of these objects on miles of shelving. It is reasonable to expect, therefore, that any significant change in the nature or characteristics of these physical objects could have profound effects for library services."[1] In as early as 1988, when information technology had made drastic inroads into a more than century-long, stable library technology based on paper and cardboard, Michael K. Buckland pointed out that different technologies would have different capabilities and limitations; any technological change would alter the constraints upon effective library services.

Twenty-five years later, information technology has made drastic changes in our life and our library services, and we still cannot produce a satisfactory answer to Buckland's six consequences, mentioned in the Preface of this book, once a record has been stored. The mythical liberating power that a new library technology promises has indeed solved some material handling and storage issues, but we have made very little progress in the matter of information retrieval. The paradoxical promise of new technology has revealed at least four innate problems of any technology.

Imperfect nature

New technology is never perfect. It may solve some old problems, but it may also carry some new ones, waiting for a solution in the next version or invention. One obvious example is the absence of searchable capabilities in Facebook when one wants to go back to refer to some feeds or comments.

Replaceable nature

We have to be aware that technology can always be replaced by newer inventions. That's part of the deal we strike with technological innovations. Any new technology is relative. The tendency now is for the replacement period to become shorter and shorter. Take, for example, the current e-readers and their new versions, in comparison to the relatively stable book technology.

Transitory nature

New technology is never permanent. Please take a look at the ILS. When we installed our first ILS two or three decades ago, did we anticipate that it would be upgraded every few years? The DRA system that SCPL used until 2011 became the laughing stock of SCPL Friends' fundraising campaign.

The same transitory nature applies to our social media. "You may take it for granted that a given company that runs a social network or web site will be around forever, but you should be skeptical in direct proportion to how precious your life media is to you ... You can reasonably make the comparison between lost civilizations and social networks. Modern social networks are like digital civilizations, but there are many reasons the digital artifacts could get lost or buried."[2] To name a few outstanding reasons, companies can go out of business, services/sites are no longer free, sites and computers are hacked, or natural disasters strike, etc. For these reasons, we need to back up and build our personal and community digital archaeology, so as to capture, preserve, and share.

Impersonal nature

The impersonal nature of technology has been under the microscope of contemporary philosophers, writers, and sociologists for over a century now. They have been questioning the effects of technology on human society and individuality, as we can observe in Aldous Huxley's *Brave New World* (1932) and Arthur C. Clarke's *2001: A Space Odyssey* (1968). Their critical voices were echoed by Jonathan Franzen in his commencement speech to the 2012 graduates of UCSC's Cowell College. In his speech, he cautioned new graduates: "Technology, at best, is a useful tool. At worst, it's a way of life." Instead of having a total obsession with technology, he advised them to make a memorable mark on the world by looking beyond modern technology, so as to bypass its impersonal nature. He was concerned that when the world has become so crowded, individual identity is becoming lost in mass identity. He was also concerned that the constant use of iPads, iPhones, and other gadgets was causing a sensation of being anesthetized with propofol (a drug used by Michael Jackson) – and waking up with no memory of the event.[3]

Franzen's "Go Easy on Technology" speech caused quite a stir among his audience. Some thought it not very inspiring as career advice. Some thought that it was because Franzen did not like people using technology, due to its impersonal nature – which is exactly where many social problems arise, when people rely on technology, to the exclusion of human interaction and intervention, and when technology is still in the stage of imperfection. As human beings, we are more or less in need of the personal touch in our life's journey. By virtue of its impersonal and imperfect nature, technology is unable to deliver such a personal service, as we can see from the limitations of Watson or Siri, or from the failed technical experiment on protagonist Alex in Anthony Burgess's *A Clockwork Orange* (1962). Storytelling has become the latest human practice to move to Facebook. According to a news report in the *Santa Cruz Sentinel*, the tenth Just Stories Storytelling Festival was to take place on Facebook for the first time from 1 to 3 August 2012. Every hour, videos of storytelling by professional artists would be uploaded to Facebook for users to view. As producer Susan O'Halloran summarized, one of the important reasons for the move was to add the human touch: "People need that human touch whether it's someone talking to them on the stage, across the kitchen table, or our online festival."[4]

Staff

By comparison, our staff can be more permanent, if you value them. Recently there has been a trend for library administrators to follow the private sector's practice of laying off staff as a first cut to remedy their ailing budgets. A notable example is Harvard University's New Organizational Design to offer buyouts to one-quarter of its full-time employees and possibly to make involuntary layoffs, throughout its 73 libraries.[5] The reasons cited inevitably include the redundancy of employing staff when everything is available online and library materials are cataloged and processed by outside vendors. If you want libraries to be open, there are eager volunteers waiting at the door.

However, there are a number of reasons why we should retain our good employees. First of all, it is decided by the changed role of computers in library services. "As labor costs rise and computing costs decline, the prospect of using electronic data processing in the massive recordkeeping inherent in library services becomes increasingly attractive. It is, however, a rather specialized field of application and unlike scientific computation or most business data process. The emphasis is on sorting, storing, and displaying rather than on computation."[6] Computer technology can assist in the provision of library services, such as search and retrieval, but cannot alter the inherent tasks of storing and handling physical objects. We are still in a hybrid of the book and digital age, whether we want to admit it or not.

The volunteer option is tempting, but not so advisable as a long-term strategy in a service-oriented organization. In early 1963, Ray E. Held concluded in his study of the California library association, a predecessor of today's public library, that "The salary of the librarian was another persistent demand upon the library. Again a distinction existed between the informal literacy club and the formal association. When the books were merely a collection shelved in store or home, the owner could act as a custodian. The formal society that had its own quarters necessarily had a librarian in order to preserve its books. A volunteer was a possibility temporarily. The Alameda association, when organizing, gladly accepted the volunteered services of an old citizen of the town, but the arrangement was shorted-lived for soon it had a paid librarian."[7]

In *Future-proof Your Library*, Rebecca Miller is of the opinion that a long-term and far-sighted plan is to assure that "Any organization that has a goal of being 'future-proof' needs to focus on its staff above all else. Plans, goals, and strategies are great – but who's going to implement those great strategies? If staff are not capable, the best-laid plans will find themselves by the wayside."[8] To future-proof our libraries, the writer suggests that we hire those people who are creative, passionate individuals, adaptable to change, and computer/social networking experts. They need to have the quality of being able to see both the trees and the forest; they need leadership, but they have already arrived.

If we value and invest in our staff, they will repay the investment with their loyalty and dedication, which goes a long way under the restraints of economic difficulty. You do not have to train them over and over again, as you would do short-term volunteers and temporary workers.

Community

Rebecca Miller presents some perspectives on strategies for adapting libraries to accommodate technological and cultural changes, suggested by a group of innovators over a period of seven years. There are two concepts that command our attention, namely, local value and involvement in the community. Why do we need to rehash these two familiar concepts here? The reason is simple: they are easy to say, but tend to be ignored, especially in our desperate efforts to catch up with the latest technologies and trends. More often than not, the "one-size-fits-all" service model just too conveniently fits our tight budget and short staffing.

Why do we need to emphasize "local value"? Mark Greek, one of the innovators, states that special collections will play a vital role in the twenty-first century. When a library is planning digitization, it is usually a local history collection or a special collection that leads the way. The items held in a special collection will continue to bring the patrons into the building, even though a twenty-first-century library may be more digital or more technological. It is the history of a community that provides its soul, its character, and its attractions. In order to enable community members to love and cherish their communities, a high level of involvement needs to be fostered. If library services such as 24-7 Safari books online at SCPL, or the 24-Hour Library at OPL are of vital importance to residents, libraries should build and maintain structures and systems that allow users to become immersed and invested time-wise, energy-wise, and emotion-wise. Lynne Cutler and Veronda J. Pitchford, two other innovators featured in Rebecca Miller's article, suggest two ways to get involved: turn libraries into an "authentic space" to engage diverse people in communities, and make these communities better places to live in; and get out of the library as much as one can. Do outreach in all languages, form a multitude of community partnerships, meet people where they live and congregate, so as to help community members to truly understand that without each other, the future would be bleak. Involve them. "Nothing for us without us!"

Here, to a great degree, involvement is related to Josiah Royce's source of local pride that is centered on a determination to give the surroundings of the community nobility, dignity, and beauty by wisely conserving our natural resources. One distinctive aspect of provincial consciousness is its constant longing and willingness to improve the community: "So learn to view your new community that every stranger who enters it shall at once feel the dignity of its past, and the unique privilege that is offered to him when he is permitted to belong to its company of citizens, that is the first rule of the people of every colonizing nation when they found a new province."[9]

To conclude, we can see that new technology is important to the library and to library professionals, for it always promises new improvements to our existing information handling, storage, and retrieval. In consideration of its imperfect, replaceable, and transient nature, we cannot afford to invest all our funding in the latest technologies. In terms of the passage of time, our staff and community are more permanent. Our staff members are the ones who fulfill goals for us, and our community is where we live and raise our children and grandchildren. We talk about generations in terms of decades, or hundreds and thousands of years. Therefore, it is the staff and the community in which we need to invest our time and money. Internally, we need to foster open communication, unity, and cohesion when we embrace the new challenge or new experiment; externally, we need to strengthen our community members' information literacy and critical thinking skills in their endeavor to seek information.

Notes

1. Buckland, Michael K. *Library Services in Theory and Context.* 2nd ed. Oxford: Pergamon Press, c1988. 208. Print.
2. Kelsey, Todd. *Social Networking Spaces: From Facebook to Twitter and Everything in Between.* New York: Apress, c2010. 4. Print.
3. McCord, Shanna. "Go Easy On Technology: Create Your Own Story, Author Jonathan Franzen Tells UCSC Grads." *Santa Cruz Sentinel,* 16 June 2012. Web. Accessed 30 July 2012.

4. Sammet, Teyva. "Local Storytelling Part of Facebook Festival." *Santa Cruz Sentinel*, 22 July 2012, sec. C3. Print.
5. Kelley, M. "Buyouts Offered through Harvard's Reorganization." *Library Journal* [serial online]. 15 March 2012; 137(5): 14. Available from: MasterFILE Premier, Ipswich, MA. Accessed 27 July 2012.
6. Buckland, Michael K. *Library Services in Theory and Context*. 2nd ed. Oxford: Pergamon Press, c1988. 9. Print.
7. Held, Ray E. *Public Libraries in California, 1849–1878*. Berkeley: University of California Press, c1963. 106. Print.
8. Miller, R. "Future-proof Your Library." *Library Journal* [serial online]. 15 August 2008; 133(13): 30. Available from: MasterFILE Premier, Ipswich, MA. Accessed 27 July 2012.
9. Royce, Josiah. *Race, Provincialism and Other American Problems*. New York: Macmillan, 1908. 72–3. Print.

Appendix 1:
Sample titles on Santa Cruz available in the SCPL and LC catalogs

I. The city of Santa Cruz

1. Coast county directory including Santa Cruz, San Diego, Ventura, Monterey, San Benito, Santa Barbara, San Luis Obispo, and Los Angeles counties [microform] : giving name, occupation, and residence of all adult persons in the cities and towns
   ...
   San Francisco, Calif. : L.M. McKenney & Co., 1884.

2. Fay, Ella E.
   Book of Santa Cruz views / Ella E. Fay.
   Santa Cruz, Calif. : Ella E. Fay, 193?

3. Forbes, Elizabeth M. C.
   Reminiscences of Seabright.
   Seabright, Cal., Elizabeth M. C. Forbes, 1915.

4. Inscriptions at Santa Cruz, California, 1891.
   [S.l.] : New England Historical and Genealogical Register, 1896.

5. Santa Cruz Venetian Water Carnival (1895 : Santa Cruz, Calif.)
   Santa Cruz Venetian Water Carnival, June 11-12-13-14, 1895.
   San Francisco CA: Traveler, [1895?]

II. The county of Santa Cruz

1. Atkinson, Fred W.
   100 years in the Pajaro Valley from 1769 to 1868 : a brief outline of the period between the discovery and naming of the River, and the

discovery and naming of the Redwoods / by the first Portola expedition to the incorporation of Watsonville; [by] Fred W. Atkinson.
Watsonville, Calif. : Register and Pajaronian Press, 1935.

2. Coast county directory including Santa Cruz, San Diego, Ventura, Monterey, San Benito, Santa Barbara, San Luis Obispo, and Los Angeles counties [microform] : giving name, occupation, and residence of all adult persons in the cities and towns ... (OVERLAPPING with section I)
San Francisco, Calif. : L.M. McKenney & Co., 1884.

3. Deleissegues, Rebecca, 1854–
Early days in Corralitos and Soquel / by Rebecca Deleissegues and Lucretia Mylar
Hollister, Cal., Evening Free Lance, [1929]

4. Harrison, Edward Sanford, 1859–
History of Santa Cruz County, California / by E.S. Harrison.
San Francisco: Printed for the author by Pacific Press Publishing Company, 1892.

5. Harrison, Edward Sanford, 1859–
Santa Cruz County / by E.S. Harrison.
Santa Cruz, Calif. : s.n., 1982, 1890.

6. Live, work and play in beautiful Santa Cruz County, California.
Santa Cruz, Calif. : Board of Supervisors [1939].

7. Resources of California.
Santa Cruz county.
San Francisco, 1870–

8. Rowland, Leon, 1884–1952.
Annals of Santa Cruz.
Santa Cruz, Calif. : Leon Rowland, c1947.

9. Rowland, Leon, 1884–1952.
Santa Cruz county; including Villa de Branciforte, The story of old Soquel; Old Santa Cruz mission, Annals of Santa Cruz.
Leon Rowland, 1940–47.

10. Rowland, Leon, 1884–1952.
Story of old Soquel
Leon Rowland, c1940.

11. Rowland, Leon, 1884–1952.
Villa de Branciforte : the village that vanished / by Leon Rowland.
[Santa Cruz, Calif.?] : Leon Rowland, c1941.

12. Santa Cruz County, California : illustrations descriptive of its scenery, fine residences, public buildings, manufactories, hotels, farm scenes, business houses, schools, churches, mines, mills, etc.; with historical sketch of the county.
San Francisco : Wallace W. Elliott & Co., 1879.

III. Titles by Margaret Koch

1. Santa Cruz: exciting early history of an era (1964)

2. Yesterday – and the day before (1964)

3. Santa Cruz County: parade of the past (1973)

4. They called it home: Santa Cruz, California (1974)

5. The walk around Santa Cruz book: a look at the city's architectural treasures (1978)

6. Going to school in Santa Cruz County: a history of the county's public school system (1978)

7. The Pasatiempo story (1990), History of US Post Office in Santa Cruz (1991)

8. Santa Cat: behind the lace curtains, 1856–1926 (2001)

IV. Titles by Sandy Lydon

1. Soquel Landing to Capitola-by-the-Sea (1978)

2. Salz Leathers: Oldest Tannery in the West, Founded 1861 (1980)

3. Chinese Gold: the Chinese in the Monterey Bay Region (1985)

4. Outline History of Agriculture in the Pajaro Valley (1989)

5. The History of the Soquel Creek Water District 1961–1988 (1989)

6. The Idea of Planning: Thoughts on the Reconstruction of Downtown... (1990)

7. The Japanese in the Monterey Bay Region: a Brief History (1997)

8. The California Agricultural Workers' History Center: Feasibility... (2000)

9. Coast Redwood: a Natural and Cultural History (2001) (*http://catalog/opac/en-US/skin/default/xml/rdetail.xml?r=132855&t=sandy%20lydon&tp=author&d=0&hc=14&rt=author*)

10. Chinatown Dreams: the Life and Photographs of George Lee (2002)

11. Bridging across the Pacific: Abalone Connections between Monterey ... (2005)

V. Titles by Stanley D. Stevens

1. F. A. Hihn Company: Agreements, Deeds, and Leases / transcribed and indexed by Jennifer Fosgate; with an introduction by Stanley D. Stevens. (2004–2011)

2. Letters (1844–1891) of Coleman Purcell Younger and His Son Charles Bruce Younger Sr. and Their Correspondents / transcribed by Kristen C. Sanders with the assistance of Sheila O'Hare; edited, indexed and produced by Stanley D. Stevens. (2008–2010)

3. Index to Biographies and Portraits in James Miller Guinn's History of the State Of California and Biographical Record Of Santa Cruz, San Benito, Monterey And San Luis Obispo Counties / comp. by Stanley D. Stevens. (2010)

4. F. A. Hihn Company Map Collection Including Maps Created by Noel Patterson Located in the UCSC Science and Engineering Library Map Room / map descriptions created by Allan Allwardt and Stanley D. Stevens; index created by Jennifer Fosgate. (2008)

5. Index to Personal Names, Portraits and Illustrations Appearing in California City, County and Regional Histories, 1867–1910 / by Stanley D. Stevens. (2005)

6. The Noel Patterson Collection: Appraisals, Correspondence and Maps / described by Donald Thomas Clark; introduction by Stanley D. Stevens; edited and indexed by Jennifer Fosgate; produced by Stanley D. Stevens. (2001)

7. A Researcher's Digest on F. A. Hihn and the Founding of California Polytechnic School at San Luis Obispo / compiled by Stanley D. Stevens. (2001)

8. Letters of F. A. Hihn & F. A. Hihn Company: December 26, 1902–May 26, 1903 / transcribed and indexed by Stanley D. Stevens. (2000)

9. Letters of F. A. Hihn & F. A. Hihn Company: November 25, 1901–March 14, 1902 / transcribed and indexed by Stanley D. Stevens. (1999)

10. A researcher's Digest on F. A. Hihn and His Santa Cruz County Pioneers / compiled by Stanley D. Stevens. (1998)

11. Hearing on petition of Charles B. Younger Jr., Esq. for Allowance of Attorney's Fees in the Matter of the Estate of F. A. Hihn, Sometimes Called Frederick A. Hihn, Deceased: Reporter's Transcript: Case No. 2569 in the Superior Court, County Of Santa Cruz, State of California, June 11th and 18th, 1917 / transcribed, edited, and indexed by Stanley D. Stevens. (1997)

12. Correspondence of Charles B. Younger Sr. and Charles B. Younger Jr., Santa Cruz, California Attorneys and Counsellors at Law / transcribed and indexed by Stanley D. Stevens. (1996)

VI. Titles on the city of Santa Cruz available at LC

1. Simpson, Lesley Byrd, 1891–
An early ghost town of California, Branciforte.
San Francisco, Priv. print. for his friends by H.W. Porte, 1935.

2. Willey, Samuel Hopkins.

A historical paper relating to Santa Cruz, California: prepared in pursuance of the resolutions of Congress for the national centennial celebration, July 4, 1876 : at the request of the Common Council of Santa Cruz / by S.H. Willey.
San Francisco: Printing department of A.L. Bancroft, 1876.

VII. Titles on the county of Santa Cruz available at LC

1. Atkinson, Fred William, 1876–
   100 years in the Pajaro Valley, from 1769 to 1868; a brief outline of the period between the discovery and naming of the river, and the discovery and naming of the redwoods, by the first Portola expedition to the incorporation of Watsonville [by] F. W. Atkinson.
   [Watsonville, Calif., Register and Pajaronian Print, 1935]

2. Harrison, E. S. (Edward Sanford), 1859–
   History of Santa Cruz County, California / by E. S. Harrison.
   San Francisco, Cal[if.] : Printed for the author by Pacific Press Pub. Co., 1892.

3. Santa Cruz County, California. Illustrations descriptive of its scenery, fine residences, public buildings, manufactories, hotels, farm scenes, business houses, schools, churches, mines, mills, etc. ... With historical sketch of the county.
   San Francisco, W. W. Elliott & Co., 1879.

Appendix 2:
Staff Picks on the Readers Link page

To enter a new review Log into the SCPL web site administration (*http://63.193.16.96:8080/admin/*). You must be on a networked computer to access this site. Your user name is your last name and first initial. Your password is your first name until you change it. After logging in for the first time, it is highly recommended that you click the "change password" link and change your password.

You will see a section called Readersblog. Click Add next to the Posts section.

In the first field, you will enter the title of your review. You do not necessarily want to enter the title of the book here, but a catchy title for your review. As you type your title, the "slug" field will automatically be filled in. This creates a unique identifier for your post. Next, you will type the title of the book you are reviewing. If the title begins with an article (a, an, or the), you will want to include it. The next step is to type your review in the body section. If you have already written your review somewhere else (a Word document, blog, or e-mail), you can copy and paste it into this section. You will want to be aware that the apostrophes and quotations may appear as "curly" or 'curly' if you copy and paste into this section. You will need to change them to "straight" or 'straight' by retyping them once you have pasted your review. If you do not do this, they will appear as error symbols once your review has been published. You will now want to enter the ISBN so that the cover art will appear with your review.

Using the catalog, search the title of the book. If more than one edition of the book is listed, click on the correct one. Check the Author and Call Number to make sure. Copy the complete ten- or 13-digit ISBN. Next, click "today" and "now" for the date and time of publication. I shall go in and change this later. Make certain the "Enable Comments" box is checked and the "Okay to Publish" box is unchecked.

Next, you will add tags for your review. Click the appropriate tag to highlight it, then click the blue arrow to move it to the "Chosen Tags" box. You can add as many of the available tags as you would like.

Save your review by clicking the Save box at the bottom of the screen. If you have another review to enter, click "Save and add another." Your reviews will be on the Readers Link page.

Appendix 3:
Historical documents at SCPL

Aquaculture

Santa Cruz County

Draft, environmental impact report: Abalone aquaculture facility proposed by Pacific Mariculture (October 1988)

Draft, environmental impact report: Silverking Oceanic Farms fish hatchery expansion (March 1987)

Business

Business parks

Aptos

Draft environmental impact report: Baird-Pierce commercial development, Aptos, California (June 1980)

Santa Cruz

Draft environmental impact report for: San Lorenzo Park Plaza commercial/retail/office building (RA-75-4), City of Santa Cruz, California (October 1975)

Old Sash Mill, Santa Cruz, California: [draft environmental impact report] (May 1974)

Shopping malls

Capitola

Draft environmental impact report: 41st Avenue Regional Shopping Center (1974)

Focused environmental impact report for the Capitola Auto Plaza (1984)

Draft environmental impact report: Baird-Pierce commercial development, Aptos, California (June 1980)

Santa Cruz

Longs Drug Store project: draft: environmental impact report (August 1991)

Draft environmental impact report: Costco wholesale-retail warehouse: general plan amendment and rezoning request (1993)

Santa Cruz County

Environmental impact report for Summit Shopping Center: the Jeske-Payne property (March 1981)

Industries

Aromas

Draft environmental impact report: Soda Lake sediment control facility for Logan Quarry, Granite Rock Company, Aromas, California (December 1975)

Davenport

Draft environmental impact report for modifications to cement plant, Lone Star Industries, Inc., Davenport, California (July 1977)

Felton

Addendum to the environmental impact report for proposed operations, Felton Quarry, Felton, California (1979)

Response to comments on the hydrologic elements of the addendum to the environmental impact report for the proposed Felton Quarry expansion (1979)

Santa Cruz

City of Santa Cruz real estate development strategy for the Sky Park Airport site. Summary report (February 1983)

Draft environmental impact report for Santa Cruz Sky Park Airport improvement projects (January 1979)

Draft environmental report on the Synertek, Inc., electronic plant and administrative offices (August 1979)

Santa Cruz County

Draft EIR: project, planned quarry (existing operation) (1976)

Draft environmental impact report on the five-year development plan for the Santa Cruz Facility, Lockheed Missile[s] and Space Company, Inc. (1977)

Scotts Valley

Borland International headquarters campus: environmental impact report (November 1991)

Borland International headquarters campus: environmental impact report: Draft (August 1991)

Watsonville

Draft EIR: project, planned quarry (existing operation) ... Cabrillo Sand and Gravel Quarry (1976)

Logging

Santa Cruz County

Draft environmental impact report on Westar 11 and 14 timber harvest and future housing development projects (December 1982)

Final environmental impact report on Westar 11 and 14 timber harvest and future housing development projects: public review comments and consultants responses (May 1983)

Cemetery

Draft environmental impact report and comments and responses Oakwood Cemetery grading permit, Santa Cruz County, California (October 1979)

Correctional institutions

Santa Cruz County

Santa Cruz County Adult Detention Facility: draft environmental impact report on a proposed new detention facility in the city of Santa Cruz (1977)

Draft environmental impact report for the medium-security detention facility, Santa Cruz County, California (July 1989)

Housing

Apartment houses

Santa Cruz

Environmental impact report: general plan amendment and redevelopment plan for Beach and Downtown Redevelopment Project area

Draft environmental impact report: Beach Hill Apartments, Santa Cruz, California, October 15, 1973 (October 1973)

Santa Cruz County

Draft environmental impact report for Shoreline Construction Apartment Complex (June 1976)

Condominiums

Aptos

Draft environmental impact report for the proposed 30-unit condominium project at 277 Aptos Beach Drive, Aptos, California (October 1979)

Draft EIR: project: Cabrillo Highlands/Cabrillo Manor/Environmental Research (April 1978)

Capitola

Draft environmental impact report for Capitola Greens (May 1977)

Draft environmental impact report for the Imperial Courts Subdivision (May 1976)

A draft focused EIR for Wharf Road Village (June 1981)

Live Oak

Draft environmental impact report for East Cliff condominiums (May 1975)

Santa Cruz

The 'Barnyard' (January 1972)

Draft environmental impact report for Brookside Glen, a 51 unit subdivision (November 1978)

Environmental impact report update for Brookside Glen, a 40 unit subdivision (August 1980)

Draft environmental impact report Laurel Glen Manor (1976)

Draft environmental impact report: prepared for 555 Western Drive, a proposed 67 unit condominium project to be developed by Far West Company (February 1973)

Draft environmental impact report: prepared for Harbour View Enterprizes, Santa Cruz, Calif. (December 1974)

Draft environmental impact report prepared for Ocean View residential project, Santa Cruz, California (November 1974)

Draft environmental impact report for Santa Cruz Villa, a 63 unit condominium development (March 1978)

Draft environmental impact report for TRACT no. 771, SUB-76-550 : a proposed 15 unit condominium project, 413 Western Drive, Santa Cruz to be developed by Moore Creek Partnership (March 1977)

Draft environmental impact report: update to Westmont Park EIR (September 1979)

Environmental assessment for a 23 unit condominium development (February 1980)

Environmental assessment on Heritage Landing, a 36-unit condominium project located on Frederick Street, City of Santa Cruz (January 1980)

Environmental impact report: Las Peñas (August 1973)

Santa Cruz County

Environmental assessment for a 23 unit condominium development (February 1980)

Mobile home parks
Live Oak

Environmental impact report: proposed 81-unit mobile home park, Capitola Road, Live Oak (1976)

Planned communities

Aptos

Draft environmental impact report for The Forest and The Meadows, a new community (1978)

Environmental impact report: final: project, Village Glen of Aptos, a planned unit development ... (April 1980)

Santa Cruz

Villa de Branciforte EIR: a 150-unit residential complex for the elderly at Frederick Gault Streets in Santa Cruz: economic/environmental analysis (September 1976)

Pajaro Valley

Draft environmental impact report on the Pajaro Headlands Agricultural and Recreational Community (October 1975)

Draft focused environmental impact report: Village Highlands subdivision (April 1989)

Santa Cruz County

Draft environmental impact report for: the proposed Fontenay Planned Unit development and Timber Harvest (May 1975)

Neary Lagoon housing projects (1987)

Soquel

Draft environmental impact report on the O'Neill Ranch specific plan, County of Santa Cruz, California (December 1979)

Watsonville

Draft focused environmental impact report for Wingspread Beach (1982)

Wingspread Beach draft environmental impact report (1985)

Row houses

Aptos

Draft environmental impact report: project : Sumner Woods Townhouses (July 1979)

Aptos Village Junction: environmental impact report: draft (November 1979)

Aptos Village Junction: environmental impact report: final (January 1980)

La Selva Beach

Draft environmental impact report: project: Punta La Selva Townhouses (1979?)

Live Oak

Draft environmental impact report on the Oak Ridge Townhouse proposal, Howe Street, Live Oak Area, Santa Cruz County (January 1980)

Santa Cruz

Draft environmental impact report for Tract no. 812, SUB-77-44 : a proposed 44 unit townhouse project at end of Kennan Street and Moon Alley, Santa Cruz to be developed by William Davidson (April 1978)

Draft environmental impact report on the Pacific Highlands Townhouses: PD-77-316 (November 1977)

Draft environmental impact report for Adobe Street project: townhouse development (SUP-75-100), City of Santa Cruz, California (December 1975)

Draft focused environmental impact report for Westlake Neighborhood Commercial Center and 34-unit townhouse project 1018 High Street, Santa Cruz, California 95060 (October 1981)

Yacht Harbor Cove initial study (August 1981)

Environmental assessment, Harbor Village Townhouses (February 1980)

Environmental assessment for Roosevelt Terrace Townhouses (February 1980)

Santa Cruz County

Environmental impact report: Cabrillo Woods in the Soquel-Aptos area (March 1981)

[Draft] Environmental impact report: Cabrillo Woods in the Soquel-Aptos area (November 1980)

Soquel

Draft environmental impact report: ... location: Soquel Drive, approximately 1250 feet east of Park Avenue, Soquel (October 1978)

Draft environmental impact report for the Willow Creek Village Townhouses (February 1978)

Watsonville

Draft environmental impact report: project: Flintridge Heights, Unit #2 (March 1978)

Convention facilities

Santa Cruz

Lighthouse Point Convention Center

1. Environmental impact report: Lighthouse Point Convention Center (1973)
2. Lighthouse Point Convention Center: [files] (1968–1974)
3. Lighthouse Point site data (1968–1974)
4. Lighthouse Point, Santa Cruz, California: [maps and plans] (1973–1974)
5. Report of the Joint Convention Center Study Committee (1968)
6. Comments on draft environmental impact statement for the City of Santa Cruz, California (Convention Center at Lighthouse Point) (1973)
7. Lighthouse Point, Santa Cruz, California (1968?)
8. Desolation row: the proposed Lighthouse Point convention center complex. Part one, History and description of the project [1972]

Santa Cruz County

Draft environmental impact report for the Christian Life Center church complex: minor land division, rezoning and use permit #76-1250 on APN 61-231-39 (1977)

Draft environmental impact report for the Christian Life Center church (July 1976)

Draft environmental impact report for the Hollins House (June 1975)

Seascape golf lodge: draft, environmental impact report (1987)

Land subdivision

Aptos

Seascape Land Use Plan, Areas A and F (1980)

Santa Cruz

Draft environmental impact report for Cardiff Court Subdivision by McBain & Gibbs, Santa Clara, California (Jun. 1974)

Draft environmental impact report on Western Heights Subdivision (1977?)

Draft environmental impact report prepared for Mission Gardens Subdivision: a project by Mission Property (September 1975)

Draft environmental impact report: proposed 40-unit subdivision near Lee Road, Santa Cruz, California (1976)

Environmental assessment for Christina Heights Subdivision (July 1978)

Environmental assessment for Oak Meadows Subdivision (August 1978)

Environmental assessment for Queen Anne Court, an 11 unit subdivision (October 1979)

Environmental assessment on River Run, a 20 unit subdivision on Pryce Street, City of Santa Cruz (February 1980)

Santa Cruz County

An addendum to an existing EIR for the Evergreen Estates Subdivision (1976)

Draft environmental impact report for a residential subdivision on Pleasant Valley Road by Mr. Bozo Gera (June 1975)

Draft environmental impact report: "Fiesta del Sol" Subdivision (October 1977)

Draft EIR: project: Maplethorpe Gardens, residential subdivision (1977)

Draft environmental impact report for the Drew Lake Subdivision (September 1975)

Environmental impact report update on the Green Valley Highlands Subdivision (June 1978)

Draft environmental impact report for the proposed Woodside Subdivision, Tract 973 (October 1979)

Soquel

Environmental impact report for Santa Cruz County applications: "Soquel Meadows" Four C's Company (May 1976)

Final environmental impact report: Soquel Meadows Four C's Company (July 1976)

Watsonville

Draft environmental impact report: Plum Hill Subdivision (September 1976)

Parks

Aptos

New Brighton State Beach: general plan, preliminary (January 1990)

Seacliff State Beach: general plan, preliminary (January 1990)

Santa Cruz

Lighthouse Field State Beach: general plan initial study (1983)

Master plan: De Laveaga Park (May 1960)

Natural Bridges State Beach: preliminary general plan (1988)

Neary Lagoon Park and Wildlife Refuge (1987)

The San Lorenzo park project: the redevelopment plan; supporting documentation (March 1957)

Santa Cruz Mission State Historic Park: preliminary general plan (January 1984)

Twin Lakes State Beach: preliminary general plan (June 1988)

Wilder Ranch State Park: preliminary general plan (March 1980)

Watsonville

Draft addendum environmental impact report: Pinto Lake Regional Park (July 1977)

Sunset State Beach general plan (April 1992)

Regional planning

Boulder Creek

Draft environmental impact report: Boulder Creek Golf and Country Club (May 1978)

Environmental impact report for water rights applications 19877, 24172, and 24804 of Big Basin Water Company, et al. (1977–1978)

Felton

Environmental study and proposed negative declaration: proposed replacement of Fall Creek Bridge 36–45 on route 9 in Felon, Santa Cruz County (January 1980)

Live Oak/Soquel

Final environmental impact report: Santa Cruz County Live Oak/Soquel Community Improvement Project: response to comments (1987)

Master plan report: 17th Avenue recreational swim center, Santa Cruz County, California (June 1991)

San Lorenzo Valley

Proposed Elementary school north of Boulder Creek (September 1986)

San Lorenzo valleywide facilities study: 201 project: draft environmental impact report (January 1983)

Santa Cruz

City of Santa Cruz real estate development strategy for the Sky Park Airport site. Summary report (February 1983)

Draft environmental impact report for the San Lorenzo River safety and beautification project: City of Santa Cruz (March 1986)

Environmental assessment for Santa Cruz Municipal Wharf design framework (1979)

Environmental impact report: expansion of the Santa Cruz Municipal Wharf (1973)

Initial study for Sky Park Airport closure (1982)

Santa Cruz, California university environs general plan (March 1963)

Santa Cruz Sky Park Airport master plan report (1979)

Santa Cruz waterfront: draft (February 1989)

Western Drive master plan (1978)

Santa Cruz County

Environmental document and proposed negative declaration: proposed modification of the Rt. 1–Soquel Dr. interchange in Santa Cruz County (September 1980)

Environmental impact report on the growth management system: final report: County of Santa Cruz, California (July 1979)

Universities and colleges

Cabrillo College

Cabrillo Community College District: master plan (December 1991)

University of California

Draft University of California, Santa Cruz long range development plan, 1988 (1988)

Environmental concerns regarding the proposed UC R&D Center: a survey of community opinion (1983)

Environmental impact assessment on the proposed Research and Development Center, University of California, Santa Cruz (May 1985)

General plan for the University environs: Santa Cruz, California (October 1963)

The economic impact of the University of California, Santa Cruz on the Santa Cruz area economy (September 1974)

Water

San Lorenzo

Draft focused supplemental environmental impact report: proposed San Lorenzo Valley Class I wastewater treatment facilities (May 1984)

Santa Cruz County

Aptos, Rio Del Mar, La Selva Beach wastewater management project : environmental impact report (March 1975)

Scotts Valley

Determination of environmental effects of the proposed Glenwood Project: courses of action and recommendations (May 1974)

Zoning

Santa Cruz

Draft EIR Pacheco property: annexation and prezoning proposal (December 1975)

Environmental impact report: general plan amendment and redevelopment plan for Beach and Downtown Redevelopment Project area (June 1973)

Environmental impact report: proposed prezoning and annexation to the City of Santa Cruz of 16 acres adjacent to Western Drive (April 1976)

Environmental impact report: Van Deren sphere of influence amendment, local coastal program amendment general plan amendment, prezoning and subdivision request at 554 Meder Street (1990)

Preliminary draft environmental impact report: density and height revisions to the zoning ordinance of the City of Santa Cruz (1973)

Watsonville

Draft environmental impact report: Westside land use plan and annexation (May 1976)

Bibliography

About Gale (n.d.), "Homepage of Cengage Learning," available at *http://www.gale.cengage.com/about/* (accessed 30 July 2012).

About the BA Libraries. Vision and Mission Statements (n.d.), Homepage of Bibliotheca Alexandrina, available at *http://www.bibalex.org/aboutus/mission_en.aspx* (accessed 30 July 2012).

About the Hihn Younger Archive (2012), Homepage of University of California Santa Cruz University of Library, available at *http://library.ucsc.edu/speccoll/hihn* (accessed 30 July 2012).

About Us (2012), Homepage of EBSCO Industries, Inc., available at *http://ebscohost.com/about-us* (accessed 30 July 2012).

Access (2012), Homepage of American Library Association, available at *http://www.ala.org/advocacy/access* (accessed 30 July 2012).

Alexander, K. (2010), "Cemex Announces It Is Shutting Its Davenport Plant," *Santa Cruz Sentinel*, 22 January.

Baine, W. (2012), "The First Friday Art Tour Has Transformed the Santa Cruz Arts Scene – that Didn't Happen by Accident," *Santa Cruz Sentinel*, 29 March.

Bancroft, H. H. (1890), *Literary Industries*, The History Co., San Francisco, CA, pp. 146, 213–14.

Bernal, M. (2011), "Social Media Update," e-mail to City of Santa Cruz departments, 31 August.

Berry III, J. (2012), "Library Jobs in the New Society," *Library Journal*, Vol. 137, No. 7, p. 10, 15 April.

Best Places to Live in Santa Cruz, California (2010), Best Places to Live and & Retire, available at *http://www.bestplaces.net/city/california/santa_cruz* (accessed 30 July 2012).

Bibliotheca Zi-Ka-Wei (The Xujiahui Library) (n.d.), Homepage of Shanghai Library, available at *http://www.library.sh.cn/Web/news/20101213/n1139775.html* (accessed 30 July 2012).

Bibliotheca Zi-Ka-Wei (The Xujiahui Library) (n.d.), shanghai-today. com, available at *http://www.shanghai-today.com/attractiondetails/print. asp?pid=12201111320* (accessed 30 July 2012).

Board Meetings: Times, Agendas, and Minutes (2011), Pacific School, available at *http://www.pacific.santacruz.k12.ca.us/pdf/Board_Minutes_ 2-17-11.pdf* (accessed 30 Jul 2012).

Borchert, D. (2007), *Free for All: Odd Balls, Geeks, and Gangstas in the Public Library*, Virgin Books, New York, NY, p. 14.

Brenndorfer, T. (2012), "Re: Subject: [ACAT] Advance Notice: Phase 1 of the PCCAHITG Phased Implentation of RDA to begin soon," e-mail to listserv.syr.edu, 19 July.

Brief History (2009), Homepage of the Bancroft Library, available at *http://bancroft.berkeley.edu/info/history.html* (accessed 30 July 2012).

Brief History1 (n.d.), Homepage of Shanghai Library, available at *http:// www.library.sh.cn/Web/news/20101213/n8761757.html* (accessed 30 July 2012).

Brooks, L. (2008), "Old School Meet School Library 2.0: Bump Your Media Program into an Innovative Model for Teaching and Learning," *Library Media Connection*, Vol. 26, No. 7, p. 14, April.

Brown, B. (n.d.), "The California Powder Works and San Lorenzo Paper Mill: Introduction," Homepage of Santa Cruz Public Libraries, available at *http://www.santacruzpl.org/history/articles/509/* (accessed 30 July 2012).

Brown, J. M. (2011), "Santa Cruz Public Libraries Board Sets Improvement Goals to Achieve Next Year," *Santa Cruz Sentinel*, 8 November.

Buckland, M. K. (1988), *Library Services in Theory and Context* (2nd ed.), Pergamon Press, Oxford, pp. 9, 208, 214.

Buckland, M. K. (1999), *Library Services in Theory and Context* (2nd ed.), University of California Berkeley, available at *http://sunsite. berkeley.edu/Literature/Library/Services/* (accessed 30 July 2012).

Building the Bancroft (2002), Homepage of the Bancroft Library, available at *http://bancroft.berkeley.edu/Exhibits/bancroft/building/ building.html* (accessed 30 July 2012).

California. Bachelor's Degree or Higher, pct of Persons Age 25+, 2006– 2010 (2012), United States Census Bureau, available at *http:// quickfacts.census.gov/qfd/states/06/06087.html* (accessed 30 July 2012).

Can Computers Have True Artificial Intelligence? (2012), BBC News Technology, 3 April, available at *http://www.bbc.co.uk/news/ technology-17547694* (accessed 30 July 2012).

Caughey, J. W. (1946), *Hubert Howe Bancroft: Historian of the West*, University of California Press, Berkeley, CA, pp. 97–8, 182.

Celius, O. (2006), "Re: Contact and Other Info Please: New Ways of Presenting and Distributing Cultural Heritage," e-mail to the author, 25 September.

Central Library System Experienced a Decade's Development (n.d.), Homepage of Shanghai Library, available at *http://www.library.sh.cn/ Web/news/201131/n62061478.html* (accessed 30 July 2012).

Chan, K. (2011), "Religion and Spirituality in Santa Cruz County," Santa Cruz Chamber of Commerce, available at *http://www.santa cruzchamber.org/cwt/external/wcpages/facts/religion.aspx* (accessed 30 July 2012).

Chao, L. (2011), "Renren Lowers Key User Figure before IPO," *Wall Street Journal*, 29 April, available at *http://online.wsj.com/article/SB1 0001424052748704729304576286903217555660.html* (accessed 30 July 2012).

Circulation of Non-book Materials 2002–2006, SCPL.

City Life and Library Service: Proceedings of the Fifth Shanghai (Hangzhou) International Library Forum (SILF) (2010), Shanghai Scientific and Technological Literature Publishing House, Shanghai, pp. 256–66.

Coast Lines: January 26, 2012 – Santa Cruz (2012), *Santa Cruz Sentinel*, 26 January, available at *http://www.santacruzsentinel.com/ci_19824571? IADID=Search-www.santacruzsentinel.com-www.santacruzsentinel. com* (accessed 30 July 2012).

Cohen, P. (2010), "Scholars Recruit Public for Project," *New York Times*, 27 December, available at *http://www.nytimes.com/2010/12/28/books/ 28transcribe.html?pagewanted=all&_r=0* (accessed 30 July 2012).

Dayton, L. (2012), "Live, Work, Create," *Good Times*, 29 May, available at *http://www.gtweekly.com/index.php/santa-cruz-arts-entertainment-lifestyles/santa-cruz-arts-entertainment-/3849-live-work-create.html* (accessed 30 July 2012).

Dempsey, B. (2012), "Voters Keep the Doors Open," *Library Journal*, Vol. 137, No. 5, pp. 64–8, 15 March.

Durrell, L. (1960), *Clea*, E. P. Dutton & Co., New York, NY, pp. 11–12.

Evans, W. (2009), *Building Library 3.0: Issues in Creating a Culture of Participation*, Chandos Publishing, Cambridge, pp. 3–12, 136.

Ever Worked a Weird Low-level Job? (2009), Homepage of Santa Cruz Public Libraries, available at *http://www.santacruzpl.org/readers/blog/ 2009/oct/04/ever-worked/* (accessed 30 July 2012).

Excerpt – Exploring the Bancroft Library (2012), Homepage of Signature Books, available at *http://signaturebooks.com/2010/12/excerpt-exploring-the-bancroft-library/* (accessed 30 July 2012).

Facebook Users in the World (2012), Internet World Stats, available at *http://www.internetworldstats.com/facebook.htm* (accessed 30 July 2012).

Fairchilds, K. (2007), "History Hunters: Learn How to Research Your House's Past," *Santa Cruz Sentinel*, 11 October.

Fairchilds, K. (2011), "Great Route to Community Resources," *Santa Cruz Sentinel*, 4 December.

FAQ – What are the Purposes of the Program? (n.d.), Homepage of Shanghai Library, available at *http://windowofshanghai.library.sh.cn/Default.aspx?tabid=67&language=en-US* (accessed 30 July 2012).

FAQ – What Obligations Should a Partner Have? (n.d.), Homepage of Shanghai Library, available at *http://windowofshanghai.library.sh.cn/Default.aspx?tabid=67&language=en-US* (accessed 30 July 2012).

Faulhaber, C., and Vincent, S. (2006), *Exploring the Bancroft Library: The Centennial Guide to Its Extraordinary History, Spectacular Special Collections, Research Pleasures, Its Amazing Future and How It All Works*, Signature, Salt Lake City, UT, pp. 10, 12.

Fialkoff, F. (2012), "Movers and Shakers 2012 (cover story)," *Library Journal*, Vol. 137, No. 5, p. 23, 15 March.

Finkleday, S. (1937), "Minutes of the Meetings of the Santa Cruz Library Board of Trustees," p. 182, 5 October.

Fister, B. (2009), "The Dewey Dilemma," *Library Journal*, Vol. 134, No. 16, p. 22, October.

Fox, B. (2011), "Design of the Times: a Field of 176 Public and Academic Building Projects Bears Fruit," *Library Journal*, Vol. 136, No. 20, p. 30, 1 Dec.

Gibbon, E. (1952), *The Decline and Fall of The Roman Empire*, Encyclopædia Britannica, Chicago, IL, Vol. 40, pp. 461–2.

Gillis, J. L. (1904), "Descriptive List of the Libraries of California: Containing the Names of All Persons Who Are Engaged in Library Work in the State," California State Library, Sacramento, CA, p. 74.

Gladwell, M. (2008), *Outliers: The Story of Success*, Little Brown and Company, New York, NY, p. 67.

Golden, L. (2012), "Putting Yourself in a Marketing Mentality (webinar to SCPL)," Cengage Learning, 12 March.

Goleman, D., Boyatzis, R., and McKee, A. (2002), *Primal Leadership*, Harvard Business School Press, Boston, MA, p. x.

Griggs, G. (2011), "Our Ocean Backyard: A 1906 View of the Santa Cruz Waterfront," *Santa Cruz Sentinel*, 17 December, available at *http://www.santacruzsentinel.com/localnews/ci_19568003* (accessed 30 July 2012).

Grimmelmann, J. (2009), "Saving Facebook," *Iowa Law Review*, Vol. 94, No. 4, p. 1137+, May.

Gumz, J. (2006), "Civic Volunteer Sara Bunnett Dead at 87," *Santa Cruz Sentinel*, 2 November.

Gumz, J. (2012), "Median Home Price in April: $479,600," *Santa Cruz Sentinel*, 6 June.

Hammond, S. (2010), "Public Library 2.0: Culture Change?" *Adriadne*, Vol. 64, 29 July, available at *http://www.ariadne.ac.uk/issue64/hammond* (accessed 30 July 2012).

Harbison, S. (2012), "Re: House Cleaning for Harry Potter," e-mail to the author, 27 March.

Held, R. E. (1963), *Public Libraries in California, 1849–1878*, University of California Press, Berkeley, CA, pp. 9, 31, 106, 129.

Held, R. E. (1973), *The Rise of the Public Libraries in California*, American Library Association, Chicago, IL, pp. 131–5, 146.

Help the New York Public Library improve a unique collection! (n.d.), Homepage of The New York Public Library, available at *http://menus.nypl.org/* (accessed 30 July 2012).

Hill, B. (2006), *Blogging for Dummies*, Wiley Publishing, New York, NY, p. 1.

History of the Monterey Public Library, Homepage of Monterey Public Library, available at *http://www.monterey.org/library/AboutUs/HistoryoftheLibrary.aspx* (accessed 30 July 2012).

Hof, R. D. (2011), "Facebook's New Ad Model: You," *Forbes*, Vol. 188, No. 10, p. 106, December.

Home (n.d.), Homepage of Bibliotheca Alexandrina, available at *http://www.bibalex.org/home/default_EN.aspx* (accessed 30 July 2012).

Housley, S. (n.d.), "Content Syndication," NotePage, Inc., available at *http://www.feedforall.com/content-syndication.htm* (accessed 30 July 2012).

Huwe, T. K. (2011), "Library 2.0, Meet the 'Web Squared' World,"*Computers in Libraries*, p. 25, April.

IBM Computer Watson Is Now a Big-Shot Doctor, and You Still Aren't (2012), Dow Jones & Company Inc., 22 March, available at *http://allthingsd.com/20120322/ibm-computer-watson-is-now-a-big-shot-doctor-and-you-still-arent/* (accessed 30 Jul 2012).

Intelligence, Innovation and Library Services: Proceedings of the Fourth Shanghai International Library Forum (2008), Shanghai Scientific and Technological Literature Publishing House, Shanghai, pp. 117–28.

Introduction to eResources (n.d.), Homepage of Shanghai Library, available at *http://www.library.sh.cn/skjs/dzts.htm* (accessed 30 July 2012).

Keep Public Libraries Public, a Checklist for Communities Considering Privatization of Public Libraries (2011), American Library Association, available at *http://www.ala.org/tools/sites/ala.org.tools/files/content/outsourcing/REVISEDSEPT2011_ALAKeepingPublicLibraries%20PublicFINAL2.pdf* (accessed 30 July 2012).

Kelley, M. (2012), "Users Don't Know What Libraries Are Talking About," *Library Journal*, Vol. 137, No. 7, p. 17, 15 April.

Kelley, M. (2012), "Buyouts Offered through Harvard's Reorganization," *Library Journal*, Vol. 137, No. 5, p. 14, 15 March.

Kelsey, T. (2010), *Social Networking Spaces: from Facebook to Twitter and Everything in Between*, Apress, New York, NY, pp. 4, 13, 199.

Khan Academy: The Future of Education (2012), CBSNewsOnline, 11 March, available at *http://www.cbsnews.com/8301-18560_162-57394905/khan-academy-the-future-of-education/* (accessed 30 July 2012).

Kirkpatrick, D. (2010), *The Facebook Effect: the Inside Story of the Company that Is Connecting the World*, Simon & Schuster, New York, NY, pp. 15, 232.

Koch, M. (1973), *Santa Cruz County: Parade of the Past*, Valley Publishers, Fresno, CA, p. 206.

Kochtanek, T. R. (2002), *Library Information Systems: From Library Automation to Distributed Information Access Solutions*, Libraries Unlimited, Westport, CT, p. 6.

Kunish, A. (2004), "Why Does the Public Library Need a Music Department, and Why Should It Continue to Be Federally Funded?" International Association of Sound and Audiovisual Archives, available at *http://2004.iasa-web.org/fontes/fontes-kunish.htm* (accessed 30 July 2012).

Kunish, A. (2005), "LåtLån: Circulating Digital Music Files via the Public Library," Archive of International Federation of Library Associations and Institutions, available at *http://archive.ifla.org/IV/ifla71/poster-pr2005.htm* (accessed 30 July 2012).

Laamann, L. (1996), "The Current State of the Beitang Collection Report from a Fact-finding Mission to the National Library of China," *BEASL*, No. 9, Available at *http://www.easl.org/beasl/be9bei.html* (accessed 30 July 2012).

Lamott, A. (2007), *Grace (Eventually): Thoughts on Faith*, Fivehead Books, New York, NY, pp. 151–3.

Leetspeak (2012), NetLingo, available at *http://www.netlingo.com/word/leetspeak.php* (accessed 30 July 2012).

Lehmann, S. (n.d.), "Industrial Development: Tanneries," Homepage of Santa Cruz Public Libraries, available at *http://www.santacruzpl.org/history/articles/22/* (accessed 30 July 2012).

Library Data in a Modern Context (2012), *Library Technology Reports*, Vol. 46, No. 1, p. 5, January.

Lipoma, Deborah (n.d.), "SCPL Class flyers."

Live Locally, Shop Locally (2011), *Santa Cruz Sentinel*, 25 November.

Local Book, Homepage of Santa Cruz Wiki, available at *https://scruzwiki. org/Local_Books* (accessed 30 July 2012).

Madensky Square – A Year in the Life (2011), Homepage of Santa Cruz Public Libraries, available at *http://www.santacruzpl.org/readers/ blog/2011/jun/09/madensky-square-year-life/* (accessed 30 July 2012).

Management Innovation and Library Services: the Proceedings of the Third Shanghai International Library Forum (2006), Shanghai Scientific and Technological Literature Publishing House, Shanghai, pp. 482–92.

McCord, S. (2012), "Community Offers Suggestions on Future of 8,500 acres Surrounding Former Cemex Property," *San Jose Mercury News*, 2 May, available at *http://www.mercurynews.com/breaking-news/ci_ 20534981/community-offers-suggestions-future-8-500-acres-surrounding* (accessed 30 July 2012).

McCord, S. (2012), "Former Leather Factory Bustling with Arts," *San Jose Mercury News*, 2 June, available at *http://www.mercurynews. com/breaking-news/ci_20770089/former-leather-factory-bustles-artists* (accessed 30 July 2012).

McCord, S. (2012), "Go Easy on Technology: Create Your Own Story, Author Jonathan Franzen Tells UCSC Grads," *Santa Cruz Sentinel*, 16 June.

McCormack, N. (2008), "User Comments and Reviews: Decline or Democratization of the Online Public Access Catalogue?" *Feliciter*, Vol. 54, No. 3, p. 29, June.

Mears, C. (2006), "RE: Pimsleur Language Greek II," e-mail to the author, 24 April.

Miller, J. (2011), "SCPL Patron Comment or Suggestion: Local Ballot Measures," e-mail to Santa Cruz Public Libraries Contact Us, 17 October.

Miller, R. (2008), "Future-proof Your Library," *Library Journal*, Vol. 133, No. 13, p. 30, 15 August.

Mills, E. (2005), "Google ETA? 300 Years to Index the World's Info," CBS Interactive, 8 October, available at *http://news.cnet.com/Google-ETA-300-years-to-index-the-worlds-info/2100-1024_3-5891779.html* (accessed 30 July 2012).

Miss Frank E. Buttolph American Menu Collection, 1851–1930 (n.d.), Homepage of The New York Public Library, available at *http:// digitalgallery.nypl.org/nypldigital/explore/dgexplore.cfm?col_id=159* (accessed 30 July 2012).

Mission (n.d.), Open Source Initiative, available at *http://opensource.org/about* (accessed 30 July 2012).

Mithassel, R. (2006), "Re: Contact and Other Info Please," e-mail to the author, 25 September.

Moseid, T. (2008), "Library 1.0 – Library 2.0 – Library 3," *Scandinavian Public Library Quarterly*, Vol. 41, No. 2, available at *http://slq.nu/?article=library-1-0-library-2-0-library-3-0* (accessed 30 July 2012).

Moskvitch, K. (2012), "Sina Weibo Starts Charging Chinese for Premium Features," BBC News Technology, 19 June, available at *http://www.bbc.co.uk/news/technology-18510214* (accessed 30 July 2012).

Nina Simon (n.d.), ExhibitFiles, available at *http://www.exhibitfiles.org/nina_simon* (accessed 30 July 2012).

Northcutt, J. B. (2012), "Online Tutorial of the Americas News Resource (webinar to SCPL)," 22 March, NewsBank Inc.

Obama Advises Caution in What Kids Put on Facebook (2009), *America's Intelligence Wire*, 8 September.

Oder, N. (2010), "PLA 2010 Conference: Cracking the Code: Beyond Dewey," 30 March, available at *http://www.libraryjournal.com/article/CA6724514.html* (accessed 30 July 2012).

Online Public Access Catalog (2012), Wikimedia Foundation, Inc., May, available at *http://en.wikipedia.org/wiki/Online_public_access_catalog* (accessed 30 July 2012).

O'Reilly, T. (2005), "What Is Web 2.0: Design Patterns and Business Models for the Next Generation of Software," O'Reilly Media, Inc., 30 September, available at *http://oreilly.com/web2/archive/what-is-web-20.html* (accessed 30 July 2012).

Ortutay, B. (2012), "Pinterest Use Is on the Rise: Here's Everything You Need to Know about the Internet's New Darling," TheHuffingtonPost.com, Inc., 12 March, available at *http://www.huffingtonpost.com/2012/03/12/pinterest-use_n_1339687.html* (accessed 30 July 2012).

Parrish, K. (2010), "Curing the Clutter Epidemic," *Saturday Evening Post*, Vol. 282, No. 4, p. 45, July–August.

Peltier-Davis, C. (2009), "Web 2.0, Library 2.0, Library User 2.0, Librarian 2.0: Innovative Services for Sustainable Libraries," *Computers in Libraries*, Vol. 29, No. 10, p. 16, November.

PLA Conference Report (2010), *Library Journal*, Vol. 135, No. 8, p. 13, May.

Profiles of State Librarians of California 1850 – Present (n.d.), Homepage of California State Library Foundation, available at *http://www.cslfdn.org/exhibits.html* (accessed 30 July 2012).

Projects. Alexandria: Old and New (n.d.), Homepage of Bibliotheca Alexandrina, available at *http://www.bibalex.org/Project/Category Projects_EN.aspx?CatID=6* (accessed 30 July 2012).

Projects. Digital Library (n.d.), Homepage of Bibliotheca Alexandrina, available at *http://www.bibalex.org/Project/CategoryProjects_EN. aspx?CatID=2* (accessed 30 July 2012).

Projects. Documentation of Heritage (n.d.), Homepage of Bibliotheca Alexandrina, available at *http://www.bibalex.org/Project/ CategoryProjects_EN.aspx?CatID=5* (accessed 30 July 2012).

Projects. Open Knowledge (n.d.), Homepage of Bibliotheca Alexandrina, available at *http://www.bibalex.org/Project/CategoryProjects_EN. aspx?CatID=14* (accessed 30 July 2012).

Projects. Science and Technology (n.d.), Homepage of Bibliotheca Alexandrina, available at *http://www.bibalex.org/Project/Category Projects_EN.aspx?CatID=9* (accessed 30 July 2012).

Provincialism, Merriam-Webster, Incorporated, available at: *http://www. merriam-webster.com/* (accessed 30 July 2012).

Reader's Link – Book Kits (n.d.), Homepage of Santa Cruz Public Libraries, available at *http://www.santacruzpl.org/readers/kits/* (accessed 30 July 2012).

Resource Description and Access (RDA). Information and Resources in Preparation for RDA, (2012), Homepage of Library of Congress, 24 July, available at *http://www.loc.gov/aba/rda/* (accessed 30 July 2012).

Royce, J. (1908), *Race, Provincialism and Other American Problems*, Macmillan, New York, NY, pp. 61–2, 72–3.

Sammet, T. (2012), "Local Storytelling Part of Facebook Festival," *Santa Cruz Sentinel*, 22 July.

Santa Cruz (Calif.) Public Libraries, Scotts Valley Library (2012), *American Libraries*, available at *http://americanlibrariesmagazine.org/ al_focus/photos/santa-cruz-calif-public-libraries-scotts-valley-library* (accessed 30 July 2012).

Santa Cruz Museum of Art and History Honoring Two Researchers, Local Historians (2012), *Santa Cruz Sentinel*, 4 January, available at *http://www.santacruzsentinel.com/localnews/ci_19675252* (accessed 30 July 2012).

Santa Cruz Newspaper Clipping File (n.d.), Homepage of Santa Cruz Public Libraries, available at *http://www2.santacruzpl.org/history/ clippingfile/* (accessed 30 July 2012).

Santa Cruz Style (n.d.), *Santa Cruz Style Magazine, LLC.*, available at *http://santacruzmagazine.net/* (accessed 30 July 2012).

Santa Cruz–Watsonville, California Unemployment (2012), Department of Numbers, available at *http://www.deptofnumbers.com/unemployment/california/santa-cruz/* (accessed 30 July 2012).

Scally, P. H. (1999), "Digital Technology Projects Already Thriving in Public Libraries," *Public Libraries*. Vol. 1, No. 1, p. 49.

Schuessler, J. (2012), "Bodleian Announces Crowd-sourcing Victorian Music Project," *New York Times*, 2 May, available at *http://artsbeat.blogs.nytimes.com/2012/05/02/bodleian-announces-crowd-sourced-victorian-music-project/* (accessed 30 July 2012).

Schultz, W. (2008), "To a Temporary Place in Time ..." *NextSpace*, No. 2, available at *http://www.oclc.org/nextspace/002/6.htm* (accessed 30 July 2012).

Shontell, A. (2012), "Chart of the Day: If You Don't Understand why Pinterest Is a Big Deal, Look at this Chart," Business Insider, Inc., 6 April, available at *http://www.businessinsider.com/pinterest-is-the-3-social-network-2012-4* (accessed 30 July 2012).

Sniderman, Z. (2011), "How Governments Are Using Social Media for Better and for Worse," Mashable, Inc., 25 July, available at *http://mashable.com/2011/07/25/government-social-media/* (accessed 30 July 2012).

Souza, M. (1970), "The History of the Santa Cruz Public Library System, a thesis presented to the Faculty of the Department of Librarianship," San Jose State College, San Jose, CA, p. 30.

Souza, M. (n.d.), "The History of the Santa Cruz Public Library System: Part 2 – 1881–1904," Homepage of Santa Cruz Public Libraries, available at *http://www.santacruzpl.org/history/articles/366/* (accessed 30 July 2012).

Spiritual Organizations (2012), Santa Cruz Wiki, available at *https://scruzwiki.org/Spiritual_Organizations* (accessed 30 July 2012).

Starr, K. (2005), *California, a History*, The Modern Library, New York, NY, pp. [247], [305].

Swedberg, D. (2011), "Re: Question about Newspaper Clipping File," e-mail to the author, 19 October.

Swedberg, D. (2011), "SCPL Monthly Report for August 2011."

Theroux, P. (2000), *Fresh Air Fiend*, Houghton Mifflin Company, New York, NY, p. 8.

This is Watson (n.d.), IBM, available at *http://www-03.ibm.com/innovation/us/watson/what-is-watson/index.html* (accessed 30 July 2012).

Thompson, J. (2008), "Don't Be Afraid to Explore Web 2.0," *Education Digest*, Vol. 74, No. 4, p. 19, December.

Titangos, H. H. (2011), "Promote Staff Publications: Library Performance Evaluation at Santa Cruz Public Libraries," *Library Management*, Vol. 32, Nos. 4–5, pp. 290–301.

Titangos, H. H., and Mason, G. L. (2009), "Learning Library 2.0: 23 Things @SCPL," *Library Management*, Vol. 30, Nos. 1–2, pp. 44–56.

Transcribe Bentham (2012), University College London, available at *http://blogs.ucl.ac.uk/transcribe-bentham/* (accessed 30 July 2012).

Van House, N. A. (1983), "Time Allocation Theory of Public Library Use," *Library and Information Science Research*, Vol. 5, No. 4, pp. 365–84, Winter.

Watson, B. (2002), "Rising Sun," *Smithsonian*, Vol. 33, No. 1, p. 78, April.

Westrum, A. (2011), "The Key to the Future of the Library Catalog Is Openness," *Computers in Libraries*, Vol. 31, No. 3, 11+, April.

What Books Are Unfit for Our Public Library Serious Problem before Local Trustees in Offering Questionable Literature for Public Perusal (1910), *Santa Cruz Morning Sentinel*, 11 September.

What Is Siri (2012)? Apple Inc., available at *http://www.apple.com/ios/siri/siri-faq/* (accessed 30 July 2012).

What Is Social Media? (n.d.) Homepage of University College London, available at *http://www.ucl.ac.uk/social-media/what-is-social-media* (accessed 30 July 2012).

What's the Score at the Bodleian? goes live (2012), 3 May, available at *http://whatsthescoreatthebodleian.wordpress.com./* (accessed 30 July 2012).

White, K. (2011), "County's Genealogical Society Marks Family History Month with Library Display," *Santa Cruz Sentinel*, 10 October.

Worster, D. (2008), *A Passion for Nature: the Life of John Muir*, Oxford University Press, Oxford, pp. 260–61, 305–6.

Young, A. (2009), "RE: Cover Art for Lime Kilns Legacies," e-mail to the author, 25 June.

Young, A. (2012), "Reply: Three Questions," e-mail to the author, 6 June.

Zandt, D. (2010), *Share This! How You Will Change the World with Social Networking*, BK, San Francisco, CA, p. 12.

上图讲座 - 最新讯息 (the Latest Updates on Shanghai Library Lectures) (2012), Homepage of Shanghai Library, available at *http://feed.feedsky.com/jiangzuo* (accessed 30 July 2012).

Index

100,000 Manuscripts Project, 124
1906 earthquake, 25, 41
1989 Loma Prieta Earthquake, 57, 68, 72
23 Things @SCPL, 105, 109–16, 118, 138

Access to Knowledge (A2K), 125
accuracy, 76, 197, 200
Acrobat Reader, 211, 214
Adams, Ansel, 53–4
aerial photographs, xxi, 173
aggregator, 151
Al-Hilal Digital Archive, 124
Alex Cinema, 123
Alexandria and Mediterranean Research Center (Alex Med), 121–3
Amazon, 102, 131, 150, 158, 199, 224, 226, 230
American Library Association, 31, 100, 105, 178–9, 194
Anderson, C. L., 15
API (Application Program Interface), 127, 129
Apple, xxi, 96, 182, 194, 213
Application Program Interface (API), 127, 129
Arabic Papyri Collections at the National Library of Egypt, 124

artificial intelligence, 180, 182, 194
artificial language, 126
Ask the Library, 183, 204
Avram, Henriette, 132

BA Supercomputer, 125
BAChannel, 149, 204
ballot measures, 7, 77–9
Bancroft, H. H., 9, 20–8, 32, 46, 81
Bancroft Dictations, 21, 231
Bancroft index, 25
Bancroft Library, 8, 23, 25–7, 32, 100, 231–2
Bathhouses of Alexandria in the 19th and 20th centuries, 123
Battle of the Bands, 150
Bay Area Rapid Transit, 42
Beacon for Freedom of Expression Database, 125
Beck, Tom, 14–15
Bentham, Jeremy, 186
Bentham Project, 186–7, 192, 194
Bergen Public Library (Bergen Offentlige Bibliotek), 98
bibliographic data, 129, 131–3, 230
Bibliotheca Alexandrina (BA), 7, 119–28, 147, 149, 152–3, 160, 172, 204
Bibliotheca Alexandrina webcast, 127, 204

Bibliotheca Zi-Ka-Wei – *See* Xujiahui Library
Bill and Melinda Gates Foundation, 148
BISAC, 223, 225–8
blog, 5–6, 102, 110–12, 114, 118, 137, 141–2, 144, 149, 153, 156, 184, 210, 247
Bodleian Library, 8, 188–9, 192
book discussion kits, 137, 143
book reviews, 137–9, 142
bookstore approach, 224–5, 228
Boone, William Jones, 82
Branciforte Branch Library, 40, 189
Bunnett, Sara Telfer, 190–2, 195
Buttolph, Frank E., 187, 194

calendar of events, SCPL, 152
California Library Association, 105
California Powder Works, 52–3, 78
California Reads, 231
California State Library, 31, 33, 37
Canton Public Library, Michigan, 8, 153, 157
CAPCON (a District of Columbia nonprofit corporation), 183
Capitola, 35–6, 56, 71, 193, 220, 243, 249, 252–3
Carnegie, Andrew, 11–12, 19
cassettes, 107–8
CDs, 107–9, 205
cement, 39–44, 46–7, 64, 250
cement industry, 44
Cemex, 47
Century, The, 28, 30–1
Cerruti, Enrique, 22
Chahine, Youssef, 123
circulation, 72, 88, 99–100, 106–8, 117, 131, 140, 143, 173, 224
citizen-initiated content, 207–8, 210

City of Oslo, 98, 171
classmates.com, 165
Community Information Database (CID), 74–6, 216–17
connecting people, 156–7
conservation, 27–30, 47, 60
County Free Library Law (1909), 34
County Library Law (1911), 34
cover art, 130, 141, 144, 247
Cowell, Henry, 44, 64
Cowell College (UCSC), 235
Cowell Ranch, 45, 64, 66
critical thinking, 200, 238
crowdsourcing, 5, 147, 186–9, 192
Cuartel, El, 9–10
Cultural Council of Santa Cruz County, 56, 219
curriculum, 110–11, 114–15, 190, 203
Customized Library Services (CLS), 201, 226

Dallas Public Library, 223
Data Research Associates, Inc. (DRA), 74, 76, 140, 214–15, 234
Davenport, California, 36, 38–44, 46–7, 272
Davenport Cement Plant, 41–2
Davenport Resource Service Center, 40, 46
Deichman, Carl, 95
Deichman Digital Workshop (Deichmans Digitale Verksted), 96
Deichman Library – *See* Oslo Public Library (OPL, Deichmanske bibliotek)
Description de l'Egypte, 123
Dewey Decimal Classification, 129–30, 153, 223, 225, 227

DIALOG, 210
digital archaeology, 213, 234
Digital Assets Repository (DAR), 127
digital civilization, 213, 234
digital library, 90, 119, 123, 128
Digital Manuscript Library, 124
digital projects, xix, 51, 58, 70, 74, 95, 119, 122, 214
DIY, 157
Documentation of the Ministry of Awqaf Drawings, 123
downloadable e-audio, 108–9, 114, 116–17
downloadable e-text, 172
Downtown Association of Santa Cruz, 55, 220
Dr. Phil, 157
Durrell, Lawrence, 119–20, 128

e-audiobooks, 108–9, 150, 203, 211
e-books, 109, 116, 132, 150, 172, 179, 184, 201, 203, 211
e-directories, 214, 216
e-documents, 210–11, 214
e-newspapers, 172
e-reader, 109, 117, 150, 234
EBSCO Publishing, 183, 211, 220, 230
EBSCOhost, 210–11, 220
Egypt, 119, 121, 123–4
elite, 159
Encyclopedia of Life (EOL), 125
Environmental Impact Report(s) (EIRs), 212–13, 249–60
equity of access, 178, 194
Eternal Egypt, 123
exhibitions, 86–7, 122, 151

Facebook Page, 116, 167–72
file formats, 211, 214

findability, 197–8, 210, 225
First Friday Art Tour, 55–6, 219–21
First Friday Tube, 220
Franzen, Jonathan, 217, 235, 238
FRBR (Functional Requirements for Bibliographic Records), 130–1, 228
Friends of the Santa Cruz Public Libraries, 106, 113, 190, 234
Friendster, 165
future-proof, 236–7, 239

Gale, 158, 210–11, 221
Genealogical Society of Santa Cruz County (GeneSoc), 69, 189–90, 192, 215, 218–19
GeoNames, 130, 132, 230
gift economy, 166–7
Gillis, James L., 31, 33–4
Gold Rush, 11, 14, 27–8, 44
Golden Gate Bridge, 42
Good Times, 220
Google, xxi, 25, 32, 102, 133, 148, 173, 186, 188
Google Books Project, 215, 230
Gotteland, Claude, 83
Great Earthquake of 1989 – See 1989 Loma Prieta Earthquake
Gutenberg, Johannes, 203

Harrison, William Henry, 190
Harvard University, 165, 206, 236, 239
Hihn, F. A., 68, 244–5
Hihn-Younger Archive, 35–6
human language, 178, 180–1, 199
Hypertrophic Cardiomyopathy (HCM) Project, 126

IBM, xxi, 123, 180–2, 194
IBM's Deep Blue, 180

identity, 119, 160, 235
illiteracy, 112, 197 – *See also* literacy
ILS (Integrated Library System, commercial), 183–5, 215, 223–4, 234 – *See also* Open Source ILS
Imperial College London, 126
individuality, 4–5, 235
information manager, 197, 199–200, 208
information network, 159, 183
information overload, 132, 157, 200, 229
instant messaging, 3, 5, 204
International School of Information Science (ISIS), 123, 127

Jennings, Ken, 180
Jeopardy! 180, 182
Just Stories Storytelling Festival, 235

Kaixin001 (meaning: Happy Net), 172
Kasparov, Gary, 180
Kennedy, Robert Francis, 185–6
Kent District Library (KDL), 199
Khan Academy, 147–8, 150
Kindle, 117, 150, 184, 206
King, Gail, 83–4
King, Laurie R., 217–18
Kinoteket (Cinematheque), 96–7
Koch, Margaret, 31, 33, 35, 69, 243
Koha, 224

L'Art Arabe, 123
Lamott, Anne, 207, 220
language learning, 105–7
Last.fm, 130, 132
LåtLån (Borrow a Tune), 98–100
Lawrence, George R., xxi, 173, 185
leadership, 33, 90, 115, 192, 205–8, 210, 218, 237

lectures, 89, 126–7, 148–9, 151–4, 191, 203–4, 206
leet, 159
leetspeak, 159–61
Library 1.0, xxii, 101–2, 132
Library 2.0, xxii, 61, 90, 101–2, 105, 109–15, 117–18, 138–9, 141, 144, 174, 177, 205, 224
Library 3.0, xxii, 25, 102, 177–8, 182, 194, 203
library associations, 9–11, 14–17, 19, 236 – *See also* subscription libraries
Library eBooks for Amazon® Kindle, 150
Library Journal, 6, 8, 72, 78, 185, 194, 232, 239
Library of Alexandria, 119–21
Library of Congress, xxi, 59–61, 100, 132, 173, 185, 198, 223, 229, 232, 241, 245–6
Library of the Society of California Pioneers, 26
lifelong learning, 117, 148
lighten-up approach, 113
lime, 43–5, 53, 64, 141, 144
lime industry, 43–4, 141
lime kiln, 43–5, 141, 144
limestone, 41, 43, 53, 66, 216
Linked Data, 129–30, 230
literacy, 97, 206, 236, 238 – *See also* illiteracy
local authors, 33, 141, 217–18
local community, xxii, 3, 5, 7, 12, 33, 39, 51, 58, 74, 76, 93, 105, 142, 152, 170, 173, 177–9, 184, 207, 217
local content, 34, 208, 210
Local History Photograph Project (LHPP), 57–70
Local News Indexing Project, 189–90

local pride, 4–5, 7, 238
local value, 218, 237
Lydon, Sandy, 33, 35, 243

MAchine-Readable Cataloging
    (MARC), 132, 201, 229
Macleish, Archibald, 100
Magdi Yacoub Research Institute
    (London), 126
mandate, SCPL, 137–8
MarcEdit, 201
mash-up, 117, 129–32, 224, 229
McHenry Library – See University of
    California Santa Cruz (UCSC)
    Library
Mechanics' Institute Library, 26
Memorial Sloan-Kettering Cancer
    Center, 182
Memory of Modern Egypt, 123
metadata, 127, 130, 141, 188, 210,
    215, 230
Millennium Excellence Award, 149
missionaries, in China, 82–4
mobile devices, 180, 183, 203, 218,
    159, 172
Monterey Bay Area, 46, 105, 231
Monterey Library Association, 9–11,
    19
Monterey Public Library, 8, 11–12, 31
Mountain Echo, 190–1
movable type, 203
Movers and Shakers, Library
    Journal, 6
Muir, John, 9, 27–32
Music Mash-up, 129–30, 132
MySpace, 165

National Geographic, 148
National Library of China, 83, 85,
    91, 93
National Library of Egypt, 124

National Library of Sweden (KB),
    124
National Park Bill (1899), 30
Native Sons of the Golden West,
    69–70
natural language, xxi, 126, 177–8,
    180–3, 186, 204
NetLibrary, 183
Netscape, 151
New Year Point, 67
New York Public Library, 8, 187,
    194
news feed, 152
News Feed, Facebook, 166–8, 173
Newsbank, Inc., 210
Newspaper Clipping File (NCF), 79,
    216, 221
nontraditional library services, 96,
    99
Nook, 184, 206
North China Herald, 84
NoveList, 199, 211, 230
NPR (National Public Radio), 148

O, the Oprah Magazine, 156
Oak, Henry Lebbeus, 23
Oakland-Alameda Coliseum, 42
Obama, Barack, 168, 173
OCLC (Online Computer Library
    Center), 103, 129, 183, 198,
    210, 212, 223
Ohio State University, 223
OneClickdigital, 109
online community/communities, 6–7,
    168, 184
O'Neil, Jack, 209
OPAC (Online Public Access
    Catalog), 74, 85, 129–31,
    223–5, 228, 232
OPALS, 224
Open Cover Letters, 6

open source software applications, 76
open source ILS, 141, 215, 223–4
Open Source Initiative (OSI), 167, 173
Open Studio Art Tour, 56, 219
OpenBiblio, 224
OpenDocument, 211, 214
Oprah Book Club, 156
Oslo Public Library (OPL, Deichmanske bibliotek), 7, 95–100, 129–31, 160, 183, 205, 228, 230, 237
Overdrive, 109, 150

Pacific Sentinel, 190–1
participation, 101–2, 141, 167
participatory consumption, 6
participatory environment, 102, 141
participatory era, 210
performance appraisals/evaluation, 91, 112–13, 138, 144–5
Perry Branch Library of Maricopa County Library District (MCLD), 8, 226, 228
personal account, 167
Phonofile, 98
physical objects, 233, 236
Pigeon Point Lighthouse, 67
pinboard, 156–8
Pinterest, xxi, 6, 155–8
Pode Project, 96, 129–33, 200, 223, 228
Polk's Santa Cruz (California) City Directory, 214
Postcard Project, 57, 70–2
Priestley, Herbert Ingram, 100
privacy, 166–8, 200
Prix Ars Electronica, 187
profiles, user, 112, 165–6, 168–9, 200
Project Gutenberg, 132

provincialism, 3–4, 8, 171, 239
Ptolemy I, of Egypt, 119
Ptolemy XII, of Egypt, 120
public librarians, 137, 139, 144, 226
Public Library Association, 105, 185, 227
Public Library of Charlotte and Mecklenburg County (PLCMC), 110, 113
Punta de Año Nuevo (New Year Point), 67

query language, 132, 184, 197

Rangeview Library, 8, 225–8
Ray, Rachael, 157
RDA (Resource Description and Access), 223, 229, 232
RDF (Resource Description Framework), 129, 131–2, 151, 228–9
RDF Rich Site Summary – See RSS
Read to Me, 150
referenda – See ballot measures
relevance, 112, 117, 142
Renren (meaning: Everyone) Network, 163, 171–2, 174
Ricci, Matteo, 83
RLIN (Research Libraries Information Network), 183
Rogers Act (aka Rogers Free Library Act), 9, 16
Roosevelt, Theodore, 30
Royce, Josiah, 3–5, 7–8, 117, 238–9
RSS (Really Simple Syndication), xxi, 5, 101, 114, 151–3, 204, 210
RSS Rich Site Summary – See RSS
Rutter, Brad, 180

Salz, Ansley Kullman, 53–4
Salz Tannery, 53–7, 219, 243

San Francisco Bay Area, 27, 53, 55, 72, 212–13

San Francisco International Airport, 42

San Francisco Public Library, 26

San Francisco War Memorial Opera House, 42

San Jose Public Library, 8, 224

San Jose State University, 32, 39, 115

San Lorenzo Paper Mill, 53, 78

Santa Cruz Art League, 55, 219

Santa Cruz Central Library – *See* Santa Cruz Downtown Branch Library

Santa Cruz County, 16, 19, 31, 34–6, 39–40, 43–7, 51–2, 55–6, 60–1, 63, 67, 69–70, 74–5, 77, 105–6, 137, 141, 170, 185, 189, 191, 193, 198, 209, 213–14, 217, 219–21

Santa Cruz Directories, 214

Santa Cruz Downtown Branch Library, 76, 113, 137, 189–91, 205–6, 216, 220

Santa Cruz History Journal, 36, 40

Santa Cruz Library Association, 9, 14–15, 17

Santa Cruz Magazine, 208–10

Santa Cruz Mountains, 34, 36, 47, 53, 63

Santa Cruz Museum of Art and History (MAH), 36, 45–7, 55, 191, 219

Santa Cruz Public Library/Libraries (SCPL), xxi, 7, 9, 14, 17, 31–2, 34, 39–40, 45, 51, 53, 57–9, 61, 64, 69–70, 74–5, 77–9, 105–18, 137–41, 143–5, 149–50, 152–3, 158, 160, 172–4, 184–5, 189–91, 195, 198, 205–6, 208, 210–21, 226, 231, 234, 237, 241, 247, 249

Santa Cruz Sentinel, xxi–ii, 35, 47, 78–9, 169, 170, 174, 189–91, 195, 208–9, 215, 221, 235, 238–9

Santa Cruz Style, 208–10, 220

Santa Cruz Surf, 69, 190–1

Schereschewsky, Samuel Isaac Joseph, 82

Science Supercourse Project, 125

Scotts Valley Branch Library, 57, 72–3, 78, 206, 218

SCPL Staff Picks, 137–44, 153, 247

semantic data, 129, 131–2, 230

Semantic Web, xxi, 131, 178, 182, 184, 197, 201, 228

seminars, 86–7, 99, 122, 152, 203

Sentinel eDialog, 24, 99

Shanghai International Library Forum (SILF), 81, 90–1, 105–6, 109–10, 117–18, 144–5

Shanghai Library, 7, 81, 83–93, 152–4, 160, 172, 174, 204, 206

Sheet Music Catalog (SMC), 74, 76–7

Shen bao, 84

Sheng, Bi, 203

Shop Local, 170–1, 174

Short Message Service (SMS), 99, 199, 205

Silicon Valley, 106, 213

Sina Weibo, 172

Siri (Speech Interpretation and Recognition Interface), xxi, 180–2, 194, 235

Sisis Informationssysteme GmbH, 183

six degrees of separation, 165

social capital, 167, 171, 231

social media sites, 7, 147, 180, 183–4, 186, 208, 218

social media technologies, xxi–xxii, 4–5, 130, 138, 163, 178 social media tools, 7, 27, 151, 178, 180, 183–4, 186, 203, 224

Sony, 96

SPARQL (Simple Protocol and RDF Query Language), 132

special collections, 32–5, 45, 186, 232, 237

SRU (Search and Retrieve URL), 130

St. Catherine's Monastery, 124

St. John's College, 82

staff training, 109

Standard Portland Cement Company, 41

Stanford Medical Center, 42

Stanford University, 165

Stewart, Martha, 157

subscribers
  Facebook, 164
  RSS, 152
  YouTube channels, 147, 149–50

subscription library/libraries, 9, 16–17, 83, 96 –See also library associations

Sutro Library, 26

syndication, 5, 101–2, 151–2, 154

tablets, 180, 183

tagging, 5, 61, 101–2, 114, 127, 166, 168, 199

Tales to Tails, 150

Tannery Arts Center, 55–6

Tencent Weibo, 172

Text-a-Librarian, 180, 183

texting abbreviations, 159

Thesaurus for Graphic Materials I (TGM I), 59–61, 63

Think Local First, 170–1

traditional media, 5–6

transparency, 166–7

Trip Planner, 129–30, 132, 230

Turing, Alan, 180

tweet, 159–61

Twitter, xxi, 6–8, 155, 158–61, 163, 168–9, 172–3, 184, 200, 218, 238

Twitter followers, 6, 160, 173

two-way communication, 137, 142, 169

UNESCO, 120, 124

Universal Networking Language (UNL) Project, 126

University College London, 5, 8, 186

University of California Berkeley, 25–7, 31–2, 34, 117, 172, 186, 239

University of California Santa Cruz (UCSC) Library, 8, 35, 37, 44–6, 56, 150, 190–1, 235, 238

University of Florence, 126

University of Pittsburgh, 125

Vallejo, Mariano Guadalupe, 22

Victorian Music Project, Bodleian Library, 194

virtual library, 6, 150, 179, 183, 229

Waterman, Minerva, 17, 19

Watson, IBM supercomputer, xxi, 180–2, 194, 235

Watsonville, 36, 79, 214, 220, 231, 242, 246, 251, 254–5, 257, 260

Watsonville Public Library, 74, 231

Web 1.0, 102

Web 2.0, 90, 101–3, 109–10, 114–16, 118, 138, 141–2, 144

Web 3.0, 177, 197

webinars, 157–8, 203–4, 210, 220

Weibo (meaning: Sina Microblog), 6, 159–61, 172

What's on the Menu? New York Public Library, 187–8, 192

What's the Score at the Bodleian?
188, 192, 194
Wheeler, Benjamin Ide, 27
wiki, 102, 110–11, 114, 120,
216–17, 221
Wikipedia, 6, 102, 111, 120, 132,
186, 192, 223, 230, 232
Willey, Samuel H., 9, 245
Window of Shanghai (WoS), 91–3, 160
Winfrey, Oprah, 156–7
WLN (Western Library Network,
based in Lacey, Washington), 183
Woodhead, H. G. W., 84
WordThink Grid, 226–8
workshop(s), 57, 96–7, 191, 227

Xiaonei (meaning: On-campus)
Network – *See* Renren
(meaning: Everyone) Network
Xu, Guangqi, 83
Xujiahui Library, 81, 83–5, 93

Yosemite, 28–9, 31
YouKu, 172
Young, Neil, 209
YouTube, xxi, 5–6, 117, 147–50,
156, 172, 184, 186, 192, 204,
207, 218, 220

Z39.50/ISO 23950, 130
Zuckerberg, Mark, 165–6

Printed and bound by CPI Group (UK) Ltd, Croydon, CR0 4YY

11/06/2025

01899296-0001